THE LANCELOT-GRAIL CYCLE

THE LANCELOT-GRAIL CYCLE

Text and Transformations

William W. Kibler, editor

 UNIVERSITY OF TEXAS PRESS   AUSTIN

Requests for permission to reproduce material from this work
should be sent to Permissions, University of Texas Press,
Box 7819, Austin, TX 78713-7819.

⊗ The paper used in this publication meets the minimum
requirements of American National Standard for Information
Sciences—Permanence of Paper for Printed Library Materials,
ANSI Z39.48-1984.

Library of Congress Cataloging-in-Publication Data

The Lancelot-Grail cycle : text and transformations / William W.
  Kibler, editor. — 1st ed.
      p.   cm.
    Includes bibliographical references and index.
    ISBN 0-292-72252-4
    1. Lancelot (Prose cycle)   2. Lancelot (Legendary character)—
Romances—History and criticism.   3. Arthurian romances—
History and criticism.   4. Grail—Romances—History and
criticism.   I. Kibler, William W., 1942–
PQ1489.L213L36   1994
843'.109351—dc20
                                                        94-2962

Contents

THE LANCELOT-GRAIL CYCLE

Introduction. The Lancelot-Grail Cycle: Text and Transformations

William W. Kibler

The essays in the present volume are the fruits of a symposium devoted to the Old French Lancelot-Grail cycle and its avatars, funded by the National Endowment for the Humanities and hosted by the University of Texas at Austin on March 3–8, 1992. Although all have been revised in light of the lively scholarly exchanges at the conference, they bear nonetheless, and unmistakably, the signs of their birth—much indeed as the Lancelot-Grail cycle itself shows not only the diversity and richness but also the occasional contradictions characteristic of a work formulated by multiple authors. The scholars who were invited to contribute to the symposium were asked only to center their study on the French Lancelot-Grail cycle or on works directly inspired by this masterpiece; no critical approaches were *de rigueur*, and no subject was considered too peripheral or too vast. The felicitous result is a volume of essays that underscore the significance of the Lancelot-Grail cycle as a seminal text in Arthurian studies. They run the gamut from lexical analyses of key terms, to a structural study of the interlace patterns in the French prose cycle, to a new historical approach to the nature of Lancelot's "sin" in Malory. A glance at the bibliography for the cycle will show that many of the scholars currently doing critical work on the Lancelot-Grail participated in the conference, either as presenters or discussants, and the resulting volume is a synthesis of their latest and best work.

The Lancelot-Grail is but one of several designations given the Old French cycle of prose romances composed between about 1220 and 1240 that was centered on the love affair between Lancelot and Guenevere. Because it was traditionally attributed to Walter Map (d. 1210), a scribe at the court of Henry II Plantagenet, it is known also as the Pseudo-Map Cycle or, since it was the standard, common ("vulgar") source for all subsequent Arthurian literature, as the Vulgate Cycle. As we have it today, it is a five-part work consisting of an immense central core, the *Lancelot Proper*, with two works to introduce it—the *Estoire del Saint Graal* and the *Estoire de Merlin*— and two to conclude the cycle—the *Queste del Saint Graal* and the *Mort Artu*. The *Estoire del Saint Graal* narrates how Joseph of Arimathea recuperated the *escuelle*, or bowl, of the Last Supper, used it to receive Christ's blood after lowering Him from the Cross, and brought it from Jerusalem to England, the new Promised Land. Whereas the *Estoire del Saint Graal* shows how God confounded the Devil's plans by offering His own Son to save humankind, the *Estoire de Merlin* begins with the Devil's attempted revenge: he begets a son, Merlin, on a pure maiden. Merlin inherits preternatural powers from his father, but because of his mother's purity, he does not have the will to use them for evil. It is Merlin who suggests to Arthur's father, Uther Pendragon, that he create the Round Table, a "third table" corresponding to the tables of the Last Supper and the Holy Grail. When the *Estoire de Merlin* was incorporated into the Lancelot-Grail cycle, a chroniclelike ending was appended to cover the early years of Arthur's life to his coronation. Thus, it forges the connection between the early Grail history and King Arthur's court. The *Lancelot Proper*, which alone accounts for half the Lancelot-Grail and is half again as long as Tolstoy's *War and Peace*, tells of Lancelot's birth, his early education by the Lady of the Lake, his love affair with Guenevere, and a multiplicity of adventures featuring King Arthur and the knights of the Round Table. Although he performs charitable acts on his numerous quests, Lancelot's chivalry is essentially secular. However, the *Queste del Saint Graal*, produced most probably under Cistercian influence, replaces the earthly loves of Lancelot and the Round Table knights with a spiritual love—a celestial chivalry—in the service of God. The chosen knight is no longer Perceval, as in Chrétien de Troyes's *Conte du Graal*, but the spotless Galahad, son of Lancelot and Amite. Finally, the *Mort Artu* relates the tragic downfall of Arthur's kingdom, linking it back to the great central theme of the entire cycle, Lancelot's love for Guenevere.

The five parts of the Lancelot-Grail, however, were not composed in the sequential order in which they narrate the events. The *Lancelot Proper* appeared first, around 1220–1225, and may or may not have originally been intended as part of a vaster whole. At any rate, other authors soon seized upon its great popularity (over 180 manuscripts and fragments still exist today, and many more are presumed to be lost) and found ways to extend its narrative in both sequels and preludes. The sequels came first. The *Queste del Saint Graal* was composed between 1225 and 1230, followed almost immediately by the *Mort Artu* (ca. 1230). In the late 1230s the final touches were added to the cycle in the form of the two preludes, the *Estoire del Saint Graal* and the *Estoire de Merlin*.

Composed about a generation before Thomas Aquinas's master-work, the Lancelot-Grail romance can be considered the *summa* of Arthurian literature. As noted above, it became the standard reference source for anyone writing Arthurian literature until Malory. It is hard to overestimate its importance. Skillfully combining and rearranging narrative threads from Geoffrey of Monmouth, Wace, Chrétien de Troyes, and Robert de Boron—to cite only the most prominent sources—the anonymous architect of the Lancelot-Grail has fashioned a tapestry of adventures unsurpassed in Western literature for their richness, complexity, and design. From Geoffrey and Wace came the tragic tale of the fall of Arthur's kingdom; Chrétien created the adulterous affair between Lancelot and Guenevere and, in a separate romance, invented the Grail and its mysteries; Robert de Boron reinterpreted the Grail in a Christian context, making it the vessel of the Last Supper. To combine all these threads, the anonymous architect drew up a complex matrix of prophecies, foreshadowings, and reminders to underscore the conjunction of sacred and secular history that animates the cycle. The vastness of his enterprise and the huge cast of characters required a new structural technique which today is generally termed "interlace." This procedure, which first appeared in several of Chrétien de Troyes's romances but was brought to perfection in the Lancelot-Grail, involves the simultaneous juxtaposition of multiple adventures, with the narrative switching from one to the next while, as it were, keeping all of them in motion at the same time. The themes, techniques, and influence of this *summa* all offered matter in abundance for the symposium, and one of the lasting results was to emphasize the vision and conscious artistic achievements of the architect of this great romance, who was able to take these disparate and originally distinct elements and combine them into a single interwoven whole.

The first two papers in the collection that follows stress the holistic overview of the Lancelot-Grail architect and the techniques he used to create and organize his text and to integrate into it an inherited cast of characters. Emmanuèle Baumgartner of Paris III (La Sorbonne Nouvelle) shows how the author of the *Lancelot Proper* went about changing the heroes of the Grail quest from Chrétien's single Perceval to a trio that, although it included Perceval, emphasized Lancelot's sinless son Galahad and, moreover, further stressed Lancelot's lineage by adding his cousin Bors to the successful triumvirate. Since the Grail hero was traditionally of the lineage of Joseph of Arimathea, the first task was to create an ancestry for Lancelot that linked him to Joseph. But this lineage was corrupted by the adultery of both Lancelot and his father Ban, so the maternal lineages became all-important as well. According to the Lancelot-Grail, Lancelot's mother, Elaine, descends from King David, to whom legend attached the Christianization of Britain; and Galahad's mother, Amite, was the daughter of the mysterious King Pellés, whose son was the guardian of the Grail. The result is the creation of an entirely "new" character, Galahad, whose lineage is linked to all the models of writing in the Lancelot-Grail: Old Testament Scriptures through his paternal grand-mother, New Testament history through his father, and Arthurian Grail fiction through his mother. Similarly, the nature of the Grail quest is altered in the Lancelot-Grail. Whereas in Chrétien's *Conte du Graal* the Grail mystery involved a series of enigmatic questions and answers of the nature "Whom does the Grail serve?" in the prose the Grail takes on a mystical nature, and the problem becomes one of meriting grace sufficient to witness it. In this new perspective, only a virgin hero—Galahad—can merit the full vision. Finally, in an argu-ment too rich for summary, Professor Baumgartner sees in the re-placement of the single Perceval by the triad Perceval-Bors-Galahad a metaphor for the principal types of medieval writers: the compiler (Perceval), the scribe (Bors), and the creator (Galahad).

Elspeth Kennedy, too, is interested in the types of writing that characterize the *Lancelot Proper* and the *Queste del Saint Graal*. She finds a telltale difference between the interlace pattern used in the early parts of the *Lancelot Proper* and the pattern found in the section leading up to the *Queste*, and is able to link these differences to the-matic developments in the work as a whole. In the earlier parts of the cycle, knights relate adventures they themselves have undertaken or witnessed, the standard for inclusion generally being the success of the adventure. In the later part, a new style of interlace subtly pre-pares the reader for a new type of adventure, the Grail quest, in which the accounts of adventures of knights who fail—notably Lan-celot—are of as much interest as those of the one knight who fully succeeds: Galahad. The inclusion of failed adventures renders the narrative more complex, and gaps appear in the interlace that were not present earlier. This more complex system of narration, combined with what appears to be an arbitrary giving or withholding of infor-mation, is characteristic of a more complex fiction in which the old certainties are being replaced by a new, magical, and visionary world, symbolized respectively by Morgan le Fay and the Grail. Both readers and characters struggle in a world of enchantments and deceits, never certain how much is hidden, how much may yet be revealed. Just as in this part of the interlace the first account cannot be regarded as final, but subject to modifications on the thematic level as the Grail theme is given more emphasis, Lancelot (and the reader) must reinterpret his earlier achievements in the light of this newest and greatest knightly adventure.

Douglas Kelly echoes this conclusion in his study of the ages of life, and of Lancelot's life in particular, in the *Lancelot Proper* and the *Queste del Saint Graal*. After showing that age is less a matter of precise chronological years than of symbolic stages, he is able to prove that Lancelot's behavior is not always appropriate to his "age." The ideal age in the *Lancelot Proper* is that of the mature *preudome* of about thirty to fifty: he has the wisdom, experience, grace, and strength to overcome both physical and moral adversity. But it is precisely during this period that Lancelot's adultery with the queen leads to a moral degeneracy that is a source of foolish excess and even madness. The earlier secular idealism of the *Lancelot Proper* is undermined by the author of the *Queste del Saint Graal* in favor of a new chivalry based on virtue and love for God. With the hindsight of the *Queste*, we are able to reread the *Lancelot Proper* and observe Lancelot as he strays from the path that would have led him to the Grail castle.

François Suard's study of Lancelot's youth places his *enfances* in the context of other narratives of youthful exploits within the *Lancelot Proper* and reaches a more positive evaluation of Lancelot's chivalric deeds. He stresses that it is Lancelot's son Galahad alone who achieves the Grail Quest and contends that even in the *Queste* Lancelot's achievements place him above the other knights of the Round Table. It was carnal love (with a little help from a magic potion!) that led to Galahad's conception. And when Amite (Malory's Elaine) comes to present her son at Arthur's court, in a moment that should be turned inexorably toward the Grail quest, carnal love is again exalted, this time when she is seduced by Lancelot. How can we understand this scene, Professor Suard asks, if we do not recognize that the author is asking us to consider the limits of the Grail quest by turning our attention once more to love as the catalyst of the entire romance and proposing a certain conciliation between the chivalric and Grail themes? It is an audacious interpretation that sets Professor Suard's study apart from those that precede and follow.

Norris Lacy's contribution serves as a sort of bridge between the more general studies that open the volume and the more focused ones that form its central section. Although concentrating on the last section of the Lancelot-Grail, the *Mort Artu*, he interprets it in light of the *Lancelot Proper* and the *Queste del Saint Graal* that preceded it.

Critics—notably the editor of the *Mort Artu*, Jean Frappier—have found fault with it for not being a fitting climax to the whole: for providing only a "flute song" rather than a bombastic orchestral finale. But Professor Lacy points out that it is more *closure* than climax. The properly Arthurian climax is in the *Lancelot Proper*, when secular knighthood knew its finest hour. The *Queste* already illustrates the moribundity of the chivalric world, and the *Mort Artu* leads inevitably to its destruction. In the *Mort*, the adventures that characterized knightly quests and that were "the lifeblood of romance" have disappeared; the marvelous and the unpredictable have given way to an inexorable course of events orchestrated by Lady Fortune that the characters are powerless to alter. The increasingly depersonalized tone and linear (rather than interlaced) style emphasize the irreversible forces at work in this understated apocalypse to the entire Lancelot-Grail cycle. We are appropriately left, in Professor Lacy's words, with "the flute song of old age, sadly recording the loss of Arthurian idealism and vigor."

With the two essays that follow, we go back from the end of the cycle to its fictional origins in the *Estoire del Saint Graal* and the *Estoire de Merlin* and to textual concerns already touched upon by Professors Baumgartner and Kennedy—the interrelationships of source, writer, and audience. Rupert Pickens studies, specifically, the emergence of pseudo-historical narrative out of autobiography in both the *Estoire del Saint Graal* and the *Estoire de Merlin*. While both begin as autobiography and sacred history, they are then transformed into purely secular and vernacular textuality. For Professor Pickens, the *Merlin* is the key text in this movement from sacred to vernacular history; it transforms by rewriting what was a story "written by Christ" into a narrative whose concerns are very much more down-to-earth. Merlin, in dictating his story to the scribe Blaise, offers a secular parallel to the divine authorship of the *Estoire del Saint Graal*, which was ostensibly given to its anonymous author by Christ Himself in the form of a book written in Pentecostal fire. As Christ and His Incarnation are central to sacred history and to the *Estoire del Saint Graal*, so Merlin's conception and story are important components of later Grail history and the matter of Britain. It is the precise function of the *Estoire de Merlin* to "translate" the history of the Grail into British history. Out of the *Merlin* emerges a secular knighthood and a secular textuality ideally suited to celebrating that knighthood and its values.

Whereas Rupert Pickens is concerned primarily with the relation of author/scribe to source, Carol Chase explores the contract between author and audience. Throughout the *Estoire del Saint Graal*, the author is unusually concerned with the reception of his account by his implied audience. Using frequent authorial interventions, he seeks to reassure his audience of the veracity of his incredible narrative, even going so far at one point as to attribute it to Christ, as Professor Pickens had pointed out. Further evidence of the narrator's concern for the proper reception of his material is found in the interventions used to organize the interlace in this section of the cycle. In studying in detail the episode of the "Turning Isle," Professor Chase shows the specular and circular nature of the proofs of authenticity: the more far-fetched the narrative, the more the author insists on its truthfulness. She concludes: "These affirmations take the form of a kind of narrative pirouette in which the story is seen to guarantee its own truth. Like the Turning Isle, the narrative thus turns, uncovering its own fictionality."

The two papers that follow and conclude those devoted specifically to the Old French cycle take up lexical problems encountered while preparing an English translation of the cycle underwritten by the National Endowment for the Humanities. Carleton Carroll is concerned with the relative status of *cité* and *vile* in references to towns, cities, and named localities. They pose an intriguing problem without a satisfactory conclusion, as is so often the case with translations, where a rigorous "one for one" mentality would seriously betray the subtlety of the original. Although some places are referred to only as one or the other, many important locales, including Camelot, are referred to as both, but not indifferently. The traditional *cité* retains a sense of prestige appropriate to the principal town of a region, whereas *vile* refers to the area enclosed by the town walls and inhabited by the bourgeois. The boundary between the two terms was not absolute, however, and *vile* was beginning to replace *cité* in the French language of the day.

E. Jane Burns offers an enlightening reflection on underwear and outerwear in medieval French literature, inspired in large measure by an amusing passage in the *Lancelot Proper* in which Lancelot is pursued into bed by an aggressive female. The key terms are *chemise* and *braies*. The former is a loose-fitting garment, usually linen, worn by both males and females next to the skin; the latter may be under- or outerwear but are worn only by men—or figuratively by women who take on male roles. Clothing is shown to denote social status and to play a role in sexual politics: a man undressed is a man without power, whereas a woman undressed is an object of sexual desire. Even elegantly robed, a woman is still powerless, still "without *braies*," both literally and figuratively. However, by metaphorically "wearing the pants," as in the episode in the *Lancelot Proper*, a woman is able to assume a degree of social dominance.

But the Lancelot-Grail was not solely a French phenomenon. It was not only reworked and rewritten in France, but it also exercised influence throughout the literatures of Western Europe. About a decade after its first appearance, the Vulgate Lancelot-Grail was reworked in what is now known as the Post-Vulgate Cycle, or *Roman du Graal*, which centered on Arthur and the Holy Grail, pushing Lancelot and Guenevere to the sidelines. Omitting the great central *Lancelot Proper*, it contained the Vulgate *Estoire del Saint Graal*, an extensively reworked *Estoire de Merlin*, and a *Queste del Saint Graal* combined with an abbreviated *Mort Artu*. The Old French *Prose Tristan* cycle, on the other hand, rewrote the traditional story of Tristan and Isolde on the model of the Lancelot-Guenevere couple and substituted Tristan for Lancelot in the Grail quest.[1] The *Livre d'Artus* and a number of other minor romances in both prose and verse show the influence of the Lancelot-Grail, but more interesting still is its influence on other European literatures. Almost immediately after its appearance in French, the whole of the cycle seems to have been translated into Dutch verse, although the *Estoire del Saint Graal* and *Merlin* sections are no longer extant, and we cannot be positive they did exist. What remains is an immense work of over 100,000 lines, divided into four books which contain, in addition to a more or less direct translation of the French cycle, a number of interspersed romances loosely based on Arthurian themes. Further north, in Scandinavia, a number of sagas evince the influence of the Matter of Britain, but it cannot be shown that the Lancelot-Grail was an immediate source. On the other hand, as we move south into Italy, Catalonia, Spain, and Portugal, the cycle was rewritten, reinterpreted, and reused in quite original ways, as the next two papers in this collection show.

Harvey Sharrer suggests that the arrival of the Lancelot-Grail cycle in the Iberian peninsula corresponds to the return in 1245 of Afonso III of Portugal, who had spent some twenty years of exile in France at precisely the time the original was being elaborated. The cycle proper exists only fragmentarily in the Hispanic languages, although other possibly complete versions are believed to have circulated in the late Middle Ages. The most important influence of the cycle on the Iberian peninsula can be found in allusions to it in songs and ballads. The popular ballads sometimes offer very original treatments of standard themes and motifs, as in the Catalan *La Faula*, which draws on the *Mort Artu*, or in Mossèn Gras's fifteenth-century sentimental reworking of that same section. A very original use of the cycle is also found in the famous *Amadís de Gaula*, although that is not elaborated here.

Elizabeth H. D. Mazzocco shows how Matteo Boiardo at the Este court in fifteenth-century Ferrara appropriated the French material, only to transform and invert it for his own political purposes. The Este court had long been one of the major centers for collecting, copying, and translating French romance, and its members were thoroughly embued with the French chivalric spirit. Professor Mazzocco argues cogently that Boiardo, a realist and a humanist, subtly employed the conventions of French romance to destroy the chivalric myth. Where superficially his work seems to celebrate the conventions and the myth, beneath the surface Boiardo undermines his characters and covertly promotes his own agenda. An obsession with chivalry blinds most knights to the realities of the new world order of the Renaissance; only those few survive who are able to break free of the chivalric code and use their own common sense and individual perception.

As important as its influence was in Spain, Portugal, Italy, or Scandinavia, there is truly nowhere that the Lancelot-Grail has had greater import than in England, and this is almost entirely due to the creative reinterpretation of the materials made by Sir Thomas Malory some two centuries after the French cycle first appeared. Malory unraveled the intricate interlace patterns that so characterize the French cycles and rearranged the materials into eight distinct books which have sufficient individual integrity that Vinaver has insisted they are separate works. James Wimsatt, after briefly tracing the development of the various Arthurian cycles in French—the Vulgate, Post-Vulgate *Roman du Graal*, and *Prose Tristan*—shows how Malory both drew upon and revised the works of his predecessors. Malory's "hoole book" is in effect a synthesis of the three great French cycles: from the Vulgate he drew the *Lancelot Proper, Queste,* and *Mort Artu;* the *Suite du Merlin* of the *Roman du Graal* provided the principal source for the opening section, "The Tale of King Arthur"; and he used the *Prose Tristan* extensively for the central part. His great originality was to center his work on King Arthur rather than on Lancelot, the Grail, or Tristan. Malory enhanced Arthur's regal status by including his continental campaign from the *Alliterative Morte Arthur* and by focusing on the deeds of "worldly" knights. Professor Wimsatt sees in Malory's new focus the influence of the popular courtesy books, which embodied the ideals of behavior for knights and lovers. In reducing the importance of Lancelot and enhancing that of several great knights from the *Prose Tristan*—Dinadan, Tristram, Lamorak, and Palamydes—Malory was able to present a broader panorama of the characteristics that could define the good knight. Although his was not a systematic manual of chivalry, it does present in almost encyclopedic fashion a range of knightly models such that its readers might, in Caxton's words, "Do after the good and leve the evyl."

In the case of Lancelot, "traitor saint," contemporary audiences found some of both. Kay Harris explores how both the thirteenth-century *Mort Artu* (the final section of the Lancelot-Grail) and Malory's fifteenth-century *Morte Darthur* treat the question of Lancelot's adultery with Guenevere within an essentially hagiographical depiction of his life. In both texts Lancelot ends his life in the odor of sanctity, and his personal holiness is stressed repeatedly. In Malory, his sanctity is a product of his own good works, whereas in the Old French romance his worthiness is more abstract and inherent. In the *Mort Artu*, Lancelot and his family share an integrated image of physical strength and spiritual holiness akin to that claimed by the contemporary Capetian monarchy through promoting its relationship to Saint Denis. By transforming Lancelot into a cult object, the *Mort Artu* effectively effaces his adultery. However, Malory's England had a different role for saints than did thirteenth-century France, and the depiction of Lancelot's sanctity in the *Morte Darthur* differs intriguingly. Whereas the cult of Saint Denis served to rally France to its monarchy, cults in England regularly fomented political agitation. And although Lancelot is raised to a measure of holiness in Malory, the scene in which he prostrates himself at Arthur's tomb can be interpreted as "a secular form of retaliation and punishment for [his] crime of treason." Once Lancelot has been accused of treason because of his adultery with the queen, the text consistently takes away his initiative and restricts his range of activities. This incapacity can be related on the historical level to the acts of attainder legislated against traitors in fifteenth-century England. All of Lancelot's ability to behave as a knight of worship is taken from him in Malory's text, which in effect, as Kay Harris writes in this volume, "subjects Lancelot to a type of punishment, a process of involuntary disablement, akin to the penalty of civil death or disablement that constituted many acts of attainder in the fifteenth century." Finally, his monasticism at the end of the *Morte Darthur* further completes his civil death by removing him from the active life of a knight. Thus, whereas the French text exalts Lancelot through his sainthood, the English work exacts a secular revenge on the ascetic knight—and traitor.

By bringing together scholars from different disciplines and with diverse areas of interest and by encouraging them all to focus on a single important text, the symposium not only opened new lines of communication between scholars in separate fields but also fostered a variety of approaches that highlighted the rich possibilities inherent in the Lancelot-Grail. New critical, structural, linguistic, new historical, comparativist, and reception theory methods combine to offer a fresh vision of this great romance. The articles in the present collection by no means exhaust the richness of the Lancelot-Grail, but they do provide an indication of some of the more fruitful ways to approach this vast text. The organizer of and participants in the symposium at Austin are grateful to Robert D. King, dean ad interim of the College of Liberal Arts; to Jon S. Whitmore, dean of the College of Fine Arts; William Livingston, vice-president and dean of the Graduate School; and especially to the National Endowment for the Humanities, an independent federal agency, for generous financial support. I would like to acknowledge special debts of gratitude to my colleague James I. Wimsatt, who kept preparations for the conference moving forward while I was on leave in France, and to Alice Hart, without whose organizational acumen it would never have run as smoothly as it did. Finally, I extend my thanks to Mr. Arthur F. Crispin for translating Emmanuèle Baumgartner's and François Suard's articles from the French.

Note

1. A more detailed description of the agglutinative process by which these various cycles grew and distinguished themselves is contained in the opening pages of James I. Wimsatt's article in the present volume.

Bibliography

Editions of the Vulgate Cycle and Related Works

Bogdanow, Fanni, ed. *La Folie Lancelot: A Hitherto Unknown Portion of the Suite du Merlin Contained in MSS. B.N. fr. 112 and 12599.* Tübingen: Niemeyer, 1965.

———, ed. *La Queste del Saint Graal et la Mort Artu Post-Vulgate, Troisième Partie du Roman du Graal.* Paris: SATF, 1991.

Boiardo, Matteo Maria. *Orlando Innamorato.* Edited by Aldo Scaglione. Turin, 1974.

*Frappier, Jean, ed. *La Mort le roi Artu: Roman du XIIIe siècle.* 3d ed., Textes littéraires français, 58. Geneva: Droz; Paris: Minard, 1964. Cited as *Mort*, followed by paragraph number, period, line number.

*Hucher, Eugène, ed. *Le Saint Graal ou le Joseph d'Arimathie, première branche des romans de la Table Ronde, publié d'après des textes et des documents inédits.* 3 vols. Le Mans: E. Monnoyer, 1875–1878. Reprint, Geneva: Slatkine, 1967.

*Editions preceded by an asterisk are used as base texts for citations in the bodies of articles in this volume.

*Kennedy, Elspeth. *Lancelot do Lac: The Non-Cyclic Old French Prose Romance.* 2 vols. Oxford: Clarendon Press, 1980. Cited as Kennedy, followed by page number.

Magen, Agusto, ed. *A Demanda do Santo Graal: Reprodução facsimilar e transcrição crítica do códice 2594 da Biblioteca Nacional de Viena.* 3 vols. Rio de Janeiro: Instituto Nacional do Livro, 1944.

*Malory, Sir Thomas. *The Works.* Edited by Eugène Vinaver. 3d ed. Revised by P. J. C. Field. 3 vols. Oxford: Clarendon, 1990. Cited as *Morte Darthur.*

*Micha, Alexandre, ed. *Lancelot: Roman en prose du XIIIe siècle.* 9 vols. Textes littéraires français, 247, 249, 262, 278, 283, 286, 288, 307, 315. Geneva: Droz, 1978–1983. Note that the narrative sequence does not follow the numbers of the volumes, but is 7, 8, 1, 2, 4, 5, 6. Volume 3 prints alternate versions of the False Guenevere and Cart episodes, and volume 9 contains indexes, glossary, notes, and errata. Cited as Micha, followed by volume number, colon, page number.

———, ed. *Merlin: Roman du XIIIe siècle.* Geneva: Droz, 1979.

*Pauphilet, Albert, ed. *La Queste del Saint Graal.* Classiques français du moyen âge, 33. Paris: Champion, 1923. Cited as *Queste,* followed by page number, period, line number.

*Sommer, H. Oskar, ed. *The Vulgate Version of the Arthurian Romances, Edited from Manuscripts in the British Museum.* 8 vols. Washington, D.C.: Carnegie Institution, 1908–1916. Reprint, New York: AMS Press, 1969. Cited as Sommer, followed by page number, period, line number.

English Translations

Cable, James, trans. *The Death of King Arthur.* Harmondsworth: Penguin, 1971.

Lacy, Norris J., et al., trans. *Lancelot-Grail: The Old French Arthurian Vulgate and Post-Vulgate in Translation.* 5 vols. New York: Garland, in press.

Matarasso, P. M., trans. *The Quest of the Holy Grail.* Harmondsworth: Penguin Books, 1969.

Critical Studies of the Lancelot-Grail

Baumgartner, Emmanuèle. *L'Arbre et le pain: Essai sur "La Queste del Saint Graal."* Paris: SEDES, 1981.

———. *Le "Tristan" en prose: Essai d'interprétation d'un roman médiéval.* Geneva: Droz, 1975.

Bogdanow, Fanni. *The Romance of the Grail: A Study of the Structure and Genesis of a Thirteenth-Century Arthurian Prose Romance.* New York: Barnes and Noble, 1966.

Burns, E. Jane. *Arthurian Fictions: Rereading the Vulgate Cycle.* Columbus: Ohio State University Press, 1985.

Crist, Larry. "Les Livres de Merlin." *Senefiance* 7 (1979): 197–210.

Dufournet, Jean, ed. *Approches du Lancelot en Prose: Etudes recueillies par Jean Dufournet.* Collection Unichamp. Paris: Champion, 1984.

Frappier, Jean. *Etude sur "La Mort le roi Artu," Roman du XIIIe siècle*. 2d ed. Publications romanes et françaises, 70. Geneva: Droz, 1968.

Kennedy, Elspeth. *Lancelot and the Grail: A Study of the Prose Lancelot*. Oxford: Clarendon Press, 1986.

Leupin, Alexandre. *Le Graal et la littérature: Etude sur la Vulgate arthurienne en prose*. Lausanne: L'Age d'Homme, 1982.

Lot, Ferdinand. *Etude sur "Le Lancelot en Prose."* Bibliothèque de l'Ecole des Hautes Etudes, 226. Paris: Champion, 1918; Reprint, 1954.

Lot-Borodine, Myrrha. *Trois Essais sur "Le Roman de Lancelot du Lac" et "La Queste del Saint Graal."* Paris: Champion, 1919.

Mela, Charles. *La Reine et le Graal: La conjointure dans les romans du Graal de Chrétien de Troyes au livre de Lancelot*. Paris: Seuil, 1984.

Micha, Alexandre. *Etude sur le "Merlin" de Robert de Boron*. Publications romanes et françaises, 151. Geneva: Droz, 1980.

———. *Essais sur le cycle du Lancelot-Graal*. Publications romanes et françaises, 179. Geneva: Droz, 1987.

Pauphilet, Albert. *Etudes sur "La Queste del Saint Graal."* Paris: Champion, 1921.

———. "Etudes sur *Le Lancelot en prose*." *Romania* 45 (1918–1919): 514–534.

Stones, M. Alison. "The Earliest Illustrated *Prose Lancelot* Manuscript?" *Reading Medieval Studies* (1977): 3–44.

Suard, François. "La Conception de l'aventure dans le *Lancelot* en prose." *Romania* 108 (1987): 230–253.

Szkilnik, Michelle. *L'Archipel du Graal: Etude de "L'Estoire del Saint Graal."* Publications romanes et françaises, 196. Geneva: Droz, 1991.

1. From Lancelot to Galahad: The Stakes of Filiation

Emmanuèle Baumgartner
Translated by Arthur F. Crispin

> *En la marche de Gaule et de la petite Bertaigne avoit .II. rois anchiene-*
> *ment qui estoient freire germain et avoient a femmes .II. serours ger-*
> *maines. Li uns des .II. rois avoit non li rois Bans de Benoïch et li autres*
> *rois avoit non li rois Bohours de Gaunes. Li rois Bans estoit viex hom et*
> *sa feme jovene et molt estoit bele et boine dame et amee de boines gens; ne*
> *onques de lui n'avoit eu enfant que .I. tout seul qui valés estoit et avoit*
> *non Lancelos en sournon, mais il avoit non en baptesme Galaaz. Et che*
> *pour coi il fu apeleis Lancelos, che devisera bien li contes cha avant, car*
> *li liex n'i est ore mie ne la raisons, anchois tient li contes sa droite voie*
> *et dist . . .*
>
> (Micha 7: 1)[1]

(In the borderland between Gaul and Brittany, there were once two kings who were brothers and whose wives were sisters. One of the two kings was named Ban of Benoic and the other, Bors of Gaunes. King Ban was an old man and his wife, young; she was a beautiful and good lady and loved by all people. She had had by him only one child, a boy whose baptismal name was Galahad but who was called Lancelot. Why he was called Lancelot the story will explain later on, for this is not the time or place. The story moves ahead, then, and tells . . .)

We may read, as we just have, the very beginning of the *Prose Lancelot* separated from the whole into which it is inserted (the method of reading suggested by modern editions, which single out each one of the components in the Lancelot-Grail cycle), or we may read it in the cyclical manuscripts, following the *Estoire de Merlin.* In either case, one is struck by the exceedingly abrupt nature of a narrative that does not burden itself with any prologue or reading protocol, which in a few lines consummates the break with the Grail tradition originating with Chrétien de Troyes and outlines, in their complexity, the major themes of its long journey. To be sure, the plot unwinds along *sa droite voie* and jumps right into the story. But right away it indicates, with the pairing of closely related lineages (the two brothers married to two sisters), the possibility of a pairing in the story, of a geographical expansion. Another question concerns the geography evoked: the kingdom of Benoic, a country located on the continent and not in Great Britain, a place that is not the traditional site of Arthurian romances[2] and that presumes that even before the story has begun there has been an uprooting, a rupture which will have to be explained and which may allow for some geographical variation.

Finally, another important milestone is the appearance of the name of Galahad, an essential name since it is presented as the baptismal name of the hero, but which is immediately pushed to the background, without any reason given, and replaced by the name of Lancelot—a surname that sends the reader back to a well-established tradition, that of Chrétien de Troyes's romance. Thus, at the beginning of the narrative, at the dawn of his destiny, the hero's duality is made clear: his two possible manifestations, his original dual nature, which he will be unable to resolve and which the text projects in the chronicled time of a filiation, Lancelot/Galahad becoming Lancelot, and then Galahad.

At this point, though, the narrator hides his game. Only in retrospect will the masterstroke be revealed: the forcible substitution of Galahad for Perceval as the chosen hero of the Grail quest—the adventure to climax and complete all the others. Undoubtedly, one may formulate many hypotheses about the reasons for this substitution, and we will come back to it. But we will first venture on less dangerous ground by considering a few of the dispositions taken by the narrator to promote Lancelot and his lineage and to make Galahad the new conqueror of the Grail.

Anchorings: The Creation of Lineages

Already with the *Roman de l'Estoire do Graal* by Robert de Boron and the *Continuations du Conte du Graal*, it was traditional to link the chosen hero of the Grail quest to Joseph of Arimathea or to one of his close relatives. In the *Prose Perceval*, Perceval thus becomes Alain le Gros's son and the grandson of Bron (or Hebron), the rich Fisher King and Joseph of Arimathea's brother-in-law. One of the first tasks of the *Prose Lancelot* was thus to give Lancelot, Galahad's future father, an ancestry that would justify the son's calling while, if necessary, rejecting the father's and that would transfer this lineage from Gaul (the starting point of the narrative) back to Great Britain. Now, the narrative's—or rather the narrator's—astuteness lies in having this done by the hero himself: it is Lancelot—the mysterious man who, at first, does not even know his name and lineage—who, like Perceval in Chrétien's *Conte du Graal*, will, from adventure to adventure, rediscover his paternal ancestry and proceed to a sort of regrouping of his *membra disjecta*. The Dolorous Guard is the first stage of this journey: there, the new knight discovers at one and the same time—a new division, a new source of stress—his association with magic (Lancelot of the Lake), his father's name (King Ban), and the name of his lost kingdom (Benoic), all engraved under the tombstone that he succeeds in lifting: CHI GERRA LANCELOS DEL LAC, LI FIEX AU ROI BAN DE BENOŸC (Micha 7: 332, "Here will lie Lancelot of the Lake, the son of King Ban of Benoic").

This first stage is followed, from cemetery to cemetery, from gravestone to gravestone, by his slow progress in retracing his hidden origins. In the episode of the *Charrette* (Micha 2: 31), Lancelot finds two graves in the Holy Cemetery and undergoes two tests. The first tomb contains the body of Galahad, "le menor fiz Joseph de Barimatie, celui qui fu engendrez en Sorelice qui puis fu apelee Gales por lui, kar il i fist la lei en non Nostre Seignor Jhesu Crist" (Micha 2: 31, "the younger son of Joseph of Arimathea. Galahad was conceived in Hoselice, which was later named Wales for him, because he established there the religion of Our Lord Jesus Christ"). After having lifted the stone covering the tomb and having discovered a knight's body fully armed with weapons as shiny as if he had just been buried, Lancelot next reads: CI GIST GALAAD, LI CONQUERRES DE SORELICE, LI PREMIERS ROIS CRESTIENS DE GALES (Micha 2: 33, "Here lies Galahad, conqueror of Hoselice, first Christian king of Wales"). The reader, if not the hero, thus understands that the original land of Lancelot's lineage is not the continental land of Benoic, but this same Wales which, until then, had been associated only with Perceval the Welshman.

Lancelot fails his second test: removing Symeu, Joseph's nephew, from his horrible grave; but at least he learns from Symeu that Galahad of Wales was the ancestor whose name he bears, although his surname comes from his grandfather, Lancelot. Symeu adds that the one who "de ci me getera et acomplira le siege perillos et les aventures de Bretaigne metra a fin" (Micha 2: 36, "will deliver me and will fulfill the adventure of the Perilous Seat and who will bring the adventures of Britain to an end") will be from the lineage of Lancelot. Finally, he reveals that Lancelot, because of the sin of his father, King Ban, who is guilty of having committed the adultery from which Hector of the Fens was born, will not be able to accomplish "the marvels" that will be performed by his "relative." Later in the story (Micha 5: 117ff), Lancelot finds the beheaded body of his grandfather

Lancelot at the Fountain of Lions. Thus, the following family tree takes shape, from tomb to tomb without a single gap: Joseph of Arimathea → Galahad → Lancelot → Ban → Lancelot → Galahad. In the center of that lineage, the name of Ban, the Fisher King, creates a break (possibly corresponding to the transplantation of the lineage from Great Britain to Gaul) in the alternation of the names Lancelot and Galahad, names which recall the two "natures," the two faces of the romance's hero, projected and displayed in chiasmus on the axis of time.

Thus, Lancelot, in the course of his adventures, has reconstructed his paternal lineage, which goes back directly to Joseph of Arimathea and is therefore superior to the lineage of the Fisher Kings as it was given in Robert de Boron.[3] This reconstruction from tomb to tomb is first of all an authentification, which in some ways reminds us of the historical discovery, in 1191, of Arthur's and Guenevere's tombs in Glastonbury abbey. Tombs are ideal sites for confirming the authenticity of paternal ancestry: they provide positive, verifiable proofs due to the presence there of always well-preserved corpses. The convincing power of the "monument" is strengthened by the "documents" produced by the narrative, such as Symeu's words from beyond the grave or the apparition of the elder Lancelot in his namesake's dream—"Je sui Lanceloz, qui fui rois de la Blanche Terre qui marchist au reaume de la Terre Foreinne, et sui tes aieux; et por amor de moi et por honor t'apela li rois Bans mes filz Lancelot; ainsi as tu non am batesme Galaad" (Micha 5: 114–115, "I am Lancelot, who was king of the White Land that borders on the Foreign Country, and I am your grandfather; for the love and honor of me, your father, my son King Ban, named you Lancelot; but your baptismal name is Galahad")—or again, the explanations of the king's death given by the hermit at the boiling fountain (Micha 5: 123–131). But we shall note how the hero's pilgrimage to his ancestors' tombs at the origins of his lineage is combined with a reconstitution of the bodies and their definitive burial in different graves: after Lancelot's intervention at the Holy Cemetery, monks carry Galahad's body back to his kingdom of Wales, where it will now rest in peace (Micha 2: 33). Later, Lancelot, after having reattached the beheaded body of his grandfather, the chaste lover of the lady of Blanche Garde, buries him next to his wife (Micha 5: 121–122).

In these two cases at least (and there are many other examples), Lancelot is a liberating hero who dispels the evil magic spells hanging over his ancestors and affords them the possibility of resting in peace; but he is also a figure of achievement, of completion. He returns to his ancestors their "integrity" and their proper place and reveals a family tree with no gaps, or nearly none, since the tomb of King Ban, over which his wife, Queen Elaine, has the abbey of Royal Minster built, is still fixed in Gaul.[4] Although we know how King Ban lost his land, we shall never learn under what circumstances he inherited the continental kingdom of Benoic, having been, in Chrétien de Troyes, the ruler of the mysterious kingdom of Gomeret.[5] Or should we assume that the geographical shift was the narrator's means of creating a break, uprooting Lancelot, tearing him away from the ready-made tradition of the Arthurian legend, and sending him, like Perceval, on a quest for his origins and the conquest of his own locale—Joyous Guard—where he will rest next to Galehaut at the end of the *Mort Artu*?

However, the parallel with Perceval ends there. In Chrétien de Troyes's story, Perceval, a "fair unknown" type, discovers his name, Perceval the Welshman, only to lose it again or hear it changed by his cousin into Perceval the *chétif*, "the wretched." In Perceval's case, it is his maternal lineage that he uncovers, a lineage whose ultimate origin, beyond the old king nourished by the Grail, will remain unknown and over which hangs an enigma, seemingly tied to the Grail, its secrets, and the questions that must be asked. In the *Lancelot Proper*, on the other hand, the call to be a Grail hero seemed at first tied to paternal lineage through the direct relationship with Joseph of Arimathea. But it was a false trail. This lineage, from which the holy name of Galahad progressively disappears and on which the tombs definitively close, has been tainted by King Ban's sin, by his death in despair, and finally by the adulterous relationship between Lancelot and Guenevere. Instead, in the first pages of the romance, everything seems to point to the importance of Lancelot's maternal lineage, entirely different from Joseph of Arimathea's: the lineage of Elaine.

According to the *Lancelot Proper*, Elaine is descended from David, a lineage established by God, as King Ban reminds us: "el regne aventureus a essauchier vostre non et la hauteche de vostre foi et a veoir vos grans repostailles, qui devant les estraignes peuples lor aviés victoire donee" (Micha 7: 24–25, "to glorify Your name and the greatness of Your faith and to witness Your great mysteries, the lineage to which You have granted victory over foreign peoples"). The maternal lineage is thus thrice exalted. It is due to it that Great Britain was Christianized, a deed elsewhere reserved only to Joseph of Arimathea and his descendants. To this lineage was granted the vision of the *grans repostailles*, an expression which in these texts means the secrets of the Holy Grail. It is also possible, as I tried to show elsewhere,[6] that Elaine, mother of Lancelot, may have descended from the Breton Saint Helen, discoverer of the True Cross. In that case, we would have to see in the last part of the quotation—"qui devant les estraignes peuples lor aviés victoire donee"—an allusion to the Miracle of the Cross and to the victory of Constantine over the barbarians.

This special calling, which associates the Holy Land with Arthurian Great Britain, proceeds moreover from a perversion of the Gospel text. According to the genealogy given by Matthew (1: 1–17), it is indeed Joseph, and not Mary, who is descended from the house of David. The lineage of Christ's "father," while prestigious, remains of an earthly nature, in contrast to the divine calling of the mother. Thus, in the *Lancelot Proper* Elaine usurps the divine lineage of David, and the text will make her a saint, a new Saint Helen, and the paternal lineage must be satisfied with a more modest ancestor, namely, Joseph of Arimathea; even his function of fathering the guardians of the Grail, traditional since Robert de Boron, seems to have been taken away from him. Indeed, it is a third lineage, entirely fictional and which apparently no longer has any ties to Joseph of Arimathea— that of the mysterious King Pellés of the Land Beyond, of his daughter, the beautiful Amite or Helizabel, and of his son Eliezer—which has the role of guarding the Holy Grail at Corbenic and welcoming there the Arthurian knights, especially Lancelot, father of Galahad, the bastard son and future Grail knight.

There are no doubt multiple reasons for this major rearrangement of lineages, and it would be difficult to list them all here. It appears, though, that one of the most important consequences, if not the main object, was to make of Galahad a new being, created in effect entirely by the new romance, in the same way that Perceval and the Grail had earlier been created by Chrétien de Troyes. But prose seeks to be more complex than poetry. Galahad is also the creation in which all the possible "sources" and all the models of writing unite, merge, and possibly end. Through Elaine, his paternal grandmother, Galahad is the "son" of the Old Testament and of Holy Scripture. Through his father Lancelot, descended from the historical figure Joseph of Arimathea, he is the son of History, as well as of the New Testament. Through his mother, Helizabel or Amite, he is the creature—magically conceived as the result of a love potion—of Arthurian fiction, which earlier had conceived the Grail. All lands converge in him, from the Holy Land, where he will return and disappear, to the land of Logres, which he will cross when leaving his enigmatic native land, "the other world" of the Land Beyond, the land of his youth, the Isle of Joy where young maidens endlessly dance around the most beautiful pine in the world (Micha 6: 234). In him, finally, are conjoined all the layers of time, from the Old Testament era of King David (but the *Queste* will go back to the time of the Fall and Exile), through the time of Arthurian adventures, to the vision of the Grail's mysteries in the final time beyond time.

If the first masterstroke of the Lancelot-Grail's conceiver, or of a first stage of the *Prose Lancelot*, is the creation of Galahad, son of Lancelot, as the hero and agent of a predicted ending, of the programmed completion of the adventures, another masterstroke is to have substituted for a single hero, Perceval, a triad made up of two "older heroes," Bors and Perceval, and a "newcomer," Galahad, and to have invented a hierarchy that relegates the traditional hero Perceval to the background while giving an unexpected role to Bors, Lancelot's cousin and "double" in the prose text.[7]

Qualifications and Hierarchies

Chrétien's *Conte du Graal* leaves several things in doubt: first a double quest, for the Grail by Perceval and for the bleeding lance by Gawain; then a motif, that of the questions one must ask in order to heal the Fisher King and bring life back to his "wasteland"; and finally, an object with an unclear function, the sword that cannot be mended. Confronted with this dispersion and lack of completion, the *Continuations* have made some adjustments, also in a dispersed manner. The Grail, the lance, and the sword have apparently been gathered together in the Grail castle, guarded by the Fisher King. During the visits of Gawain and Perceval, they are the object of questions which vary, as I tried to show elsewhere,[8] from one *Continuation* to another. For the original question, "Whom does the Grail serve?" a new one seems to have been substituted, "What is the Grail?" This question belongs on the same paradigmatic axis as the questions: Why is the lance bleeding? Why did the sword break? (No longer: Where, when and how will it break?) This readjustment leads to a strongly Christianized story, at least regarding the Grail and the lance, a story which the Fisher King progressively imparts to his visitors, Gawain and then Perceval. The broken sword, which then must be mended, has a somewhat different status. It serves as a leitmotiv leading from one *Continuation* to the other, for which it often serves as a new beginning. The fact that it cannot be perfectly repaired—a hairline crack remains in the blade until the end of the romance—no doubt represents the happy impossibility of ending the question-and-answer game, of interrupting the renewed dialogue (after Perceval's catastrophic silence) which imitates the flow and syntax of real time, whose consequences depend (chrono)logically on causes. Thus, it induces a renewal of the narrative, after each quest/failure of the heroes.

On the other hand, to ask the expected questions, to listen to the Fisher King's tale to the very end without falling asleep, to remove the last trace of fissure on the sword's blade, to repair the broken Round Table, to take one's place at the Perilous Seat and thus close the Table's circle—all this is to restore the sadly normal order of things and to risk the death of the narrative. We all know the solutions that were thought up to put this catastrophe off for a while. As the *Prose Perceval* points out through the words of Sir Kay,[9] by achieving the quest for the Grail, Perceval—who, in Chrétien's *Conte du Graal*, ushered in the period of adventures . . . *felenesses et dures*[10]—has indeed emptied the Arthurian kingdom of any enterprising spirit. Lethargy and inertia now fill the knights of the Round Table, to whom the king, seeing the emptiness of the western land, must urgently suggest new actions, new conquests, a return to the East. In the *Mort Artu*, the king more modestly decides to organize a tournament to occupy his knights, while in *Perlesvaus*, the story is explicitly built upon the renewal, the unending "variations," of adventure (the only means to hold the knights' attention) before taking the hero into the mystery of the Otherworld.

The *Manessier Continuation*, however, is the first to propose another reflex, which consists of substituting for the dangerous motif of the questions to be asked the motif of the vision, replacing the Grail *trestot descovert*, "clearly exposed" by Chrétien to Perceval's sight and questions, with a "covered" Grail which must be progressively uncovered to arrive at its transparent vision, the *veraie semblance* as it is called in the *Queste*—a new adventure in apocalyptic form which, in the Lancelot-Grail, seems to be offered to the whole of Arthurian chivalry and which sanctions, starting with the *Agravain* section, a series of (dis)qualifications and the establishment (notably while passing through Corbenic) of a new hierarchy of questors.

Within this new perspective, it is obvious that only a virgin hero, one not burdened with the weight of matter, not tainted by sin, can hope to gaze with naked eyes upon the supernatural vision. Thus, the first to be disqualified (as early as Micha 2: 373ff) is Gawain, a knight much too caught up in a literal vision of the world, much too enamored of the beauty of forms, be they of women or language. At Corbenic, he is unable to pull the lady from the vat, a feat at which Lancelot will succeed. Later, he is more dazzled by the beauty of the lady carrying the Grail than by the Grail itself, and he is therefore denied the nourishment dispensed by the Holy Vessel. Finally, Gawain is subjected to, rather than being master of, the various adventures and visions of the Perilous Palace, notably the fight between the serpent and the leopard and then between the serpent and its own offspring, two episodes foreshadowing the catastrophes of the *Mort Artu*. Although the wounds he received during the night are healed by the Grail—the narrative still needs Arthur's nephew and will for a long time to come—in the morning he is evicted *manu militari* from the castle and finds himself in the most horrible of carts (Micha 2: 385).

To disqualify Perceval and shift him from first place to second, the narrator maneuvers very subtly in the narration of the hero's youth, given in Micha 6. Without specifying the name and origin of Perceval's father (but at this stage of the story, neither King Pellés nor any other member of the Fisher King's lineage is involved), the narrator trivializes his death: the hazards of a career of chivalry are here responsible for the deaths of the father and his four sons, and no mention is made of any "dolorous blow" that would recall the wounds of the Fisher Kings. As for the mother's sin, it is to have refused a chivalrous education to her youngest son, Perceval. Agloval thus rejoices in having arrived in time, before Perceval is too old to be instructed in the use of arms, for, he says upon seeing his younger brother: "il ne puet estre, se il ert chevaliers en tel aage com il est orendroit, qu'il ne viengne a grant joie, se Diex i velt mestre conseil, a ce qu'il est de toutes parz estrez de bons chevaliers; et se il passe l'aage de jovente et il vient en l'aage de .XXX. anz, que il ne soit dedenz celui terme acoustumez de chevalerie, ja puis ne porra venir a bonté d'armes, por quoi il sera granz domages, se il demeure a estre chevalier" (Micha 6: 184, "if he were a knight at his present age, he could not fail to achieve great things, with God's help, since he was descended from good knights on all sides. But if he passed his youth and reached the age of thirty without being trained in knighthood, he could never thereafter become accomplished in arms, and so it would be great pity if he delayed in becoming a knight").

All the same, Perceval does not appear to be an ambitious man in the *Prose Lancelot*, a fact that may surprise the reader of the *Conte du Graal*. It is Agloval's arrival that makes him aware of his shortcomings and not his natural instincts or the world's *reverdie*, as at the beginning of Chrétien's narrative. It is his brother who helps him escape and introduces him to the court while his mother dies of grief, according to tradition, but without her death's having any influence on her son's destiny. At court, once dubbed by Arthur—quite expeditiously, in fact—the new knight takes his place very modestly "as plus basses tables, la ou li chevalier mains renomé de prouesce seoient" (Micha 6: 191, "at one of the lowest tables, where the knights sat who were least renowned for their prowess"). To be sure, the "maiden who had never laughed," a character inherited from the

Conte du Graal, designates him as the future second to the good knight: "et en cest siege serra li bons chevaliers et tu lez lui a destre, por ce que tu le resambleras de virginité" (Micha 6: 191, "the good knight will sit here, and you will sit beside him on his right, because you will be like him in virginity"). She also predicts, before dying, the place reserved for Bors: "et a sa senestre serra Boorz et encor savront bien li chevalier de cest ostel la senefiance de ceste chose" (Micha 6: 191, "and Bors will sit at his left, and the knights of this court will yet know the significance of this"). Even then, the young man is in no hurry to prove himself, and only Kay's taunts (an old habit of the seneschal) are needed for Perceval to decide to leave the court in search of adventures and of the temporarily insane Lancelot.

During that quest, two episodes contribute in an even more decisive way to trivialize the status of the Grail's former chosen hero: the freeing of Patrides and the battle against Hector. To rescue Patrides, seducer of a married woman whose husband has tied him to a stone pillar with a magic chain (Micha 6: 195), Perceval risks breaking his sword on the chain's iron. Despite a mighty blow, his sword does not break and is not even damaged. While Patrides fears that the sword might have been *escortee* ("shortened") by the violence of the blow, the hero raises it "contremont . . . et la trueve sainne et antiere," ("up . . . and finds it whole and entire") and, as the text explains, "si l'en est molt bel, car il l'aimme or mielz qu'il ne soloit" (Micha 6: 196, "this pleased him, for he now loved it more than he had before"). One might ask here whether, with this totally unwarranted and somewhat grotesque episode, the *Agravain* author is not eliminating, at low cost, a key motive of the *Continuations*, mainly tied to Perceval and, as we have seen, essential to the renewal of the story: the motive of the broken sword that has to be rejoined.[11] The fact that Perceval's sword does not break and does not need to be rejoined means that it is not he who will renew, prolong, and/or end the narrative.

As for the terrible fight opposing Perceval and Hector, at the end of which their wounds are healed by the Holy Grail (an episode that also appears in the *Manessier Continuation*[12]), it allows the author to give Perceval, through Hector's own words, all the necessary information regarding the Grail: "li vaissiaux ou Nostre Sires menga l'aingnel le jor de Pasques o ses deciples en la meson Symon le liepreux" ("the vessel from which Our Lord ate the lamb with his disciples, on Easter Day, in the house of Simon the Leper"); its transfer by Joseph of Arimathea to the kingdom of Logres, where it is now; and its properties—"si en a l'an puis, fait il, veu tex miracles que de la grace de lui ont esté repeu si oir et encor en est li rois Pellés repeuz chascun jor et toute sa mesnie et sera tant com il sejornera an cest païs" (Micha 6: 205, "and since then, he continued, it has been seen to produce such miracles, that by its grace his descendants have been fed, and King Pellés and all his household are still fed by it every day, and will continue to be as long as he stays in this land"). Hector's intervention thus eliminates the motif—rather banal, it is true—of the questions to be asked, and gives the young knight the desire no longer to question the relic's origin, nature, or function but, like all future questors, to see it "apertement, s'il est otroié a home mortel qu'il le voie" (Micha 6: 206, "plainly, if it is given to mortal man to see it"). We remember that, in the *Manessier Continuation*, it is Perceval who, based on his prior experience, briefly informs Hector that they were healed by the Holy Grail,[13] while in the *Prose Lancelot* it is Hector, a member of the former generation but little qualified for that role, who delivers the information.

The primary function of the brief narration of Perceval's youthful exploits as retold by the *Agravain* section's author is to introduce into the plot the man who will be the hero's second and to preserve his necessary virginity, while undercutting him by other means. Descended from a "common" lineage no longer having any connection at this point of the story to the lineage of the Fisher Kings, Perceval is narrowly rescued from his *niceté* ("naïveté") by his brother. On his own, he probably would never have left his mother. Once dubbed, he remains a rather average knight, unable, for example, to defeat Hector of the Fens, much less Lancelot, during the combat at the Isle of Joy. His first rather pathetic adventure consists of freeing a Don Juan who has been caught. He is thus deprived of the two functions which, from the *Conte du Graal* to the *Continuations*, gave substance to his quest: to ask questions about the Grail and to mend the broken sword.

That Perceval remains in the final trio of those chosen for the Quest and dies beside Galahad in the sacred city of Sarras was probably a necessary concession to the Arthurian hypotext. Or could it have been a way to eliminate, after having revived him, a hero who has become cumbersome? The presence of Bors—the chaste but not virginal hero—in the chosen trio, an invention of the Lancelot-Grail, is, on the other hand, a useful tool for the promotion of King Ban's lineage, and everything happens as if Bors were coming to fill the role forbidden his cousin Lancelot. This promotion, after all, had been in preparation as far back as King Brandegorre's tournament and the conception of Helain the White, an episode that foreshadows Galahad's conception by Lancelot in the kingdom of the Fisher King (Micha 2: 188 et seq.).

During that episode, Bors, the knight who seeks to remain pure, is confronted with a key motif of the Arthurian legend: a king, having as sole heir a beautiful daughter for whom he wants a suitable husband, organizes a tournament or some other type of qualifying contest. The winner will have the daughter and the kingdom. However, at least since Chrétien de Troyes and the *Chevalier au Lion*, the canonical form of the story is often muddled. For various reasons—because he is already married, because he wishes to remain a knight errant or a virgin—the hero turns down the proffered gift and leaves. In Bors's case, things become complicated because of the sudden love felt by the girl for the too handsome knight, which moves her governess to take pity on her and give her the magic ring that stirs the hero's passion. *Felix culpa* however, since out of this one night of love, an extraordinary knight will be born, Helain the White, who will become emperor of Constantinople. However, by limiting the ring's magical power to one night, the narrator protects Bors from the risks of amorous passion and of *recreantise* ('weakness'), while producing the necessary fault, the loss of virginity, which will later prevent the hero from being chosen for the Grail, though not completely disqualifying him: he is innocent in intent, if not in fact.

God's (i.e., the narrator's) masterstroke, which will be repeated with Galahad's birth, is clearly underscored. The Lady of the Lake knows nothing about this adventure, which she had not planned: "Et meesmement la Dame del Lac qui assés tost le sot par ses augures, si s'en merveille molt et dist c'or ne savoit ele cui croire, 'kar je cuidoie, fet ele, qu'il deust estre virges tot son aage.' Si en fu assés dolente quant ele le sot, et sans faille Boors avoit porposé a estre virges tos dis" (Micha 2: 198–199, "And even the Lady of the Lake, who soon learned of it through her sorcery, was amazed and said that now she didn't know who to believe, 'for I thought,' she said, 'that he was to remain a virgin all his life.' So she was quite saddened when she learned of it, and for a fact Bors had meant to remain a virgin all his days"). But the fairy/sorceress proposes and only the demiurgic power of the writer disposes. Thus the episode, serving as dress rehearsal for the conception of Galahad, disqualifies Bors who, having lost his virginity, may no longer be the Grail conqueror; however, it allows a knight of Ban's lineage to become a member of the chosen triad in lieu of Lancelot, who is guilty himself of lust in deed as well as in intent, since he thinks he is sleeping with the queen even as he begets Galahad. In particular, this episode permits an opening, or better, a prolongation, on the earthly level, through the birth of Helain the White and the future conquest of Constantinople, of a lineage and a narrative that Galahad closes on the heavenly level, with the conquest of the Grail and the conclusion—henceforth provisional—of the adventures.

A long analysis of Bors's adventures at Corbenic (Micha 5: 252–274) would be necessary, and they would have to be carefully compared to Gawain's. The night that Bors spends in the Adventurous Palace, in fact, foreshadows and condenses the *Queste* and its various manners of writing. After having witnessed the now classic vision of the nurturing Grail, Bors faces adventures taken from the Arthurian pre-text, which could be called qualifying adventures: the wondrous bed, associated with the flaming lance; the fight with a knight who restores his strength by entering the place where the Holy Grail is kept; followed by the fight with the lion. Then Bors, like Gawain, witnesses scenes whose meaning he has to interpret: the fight between the serpent and the leopard and then between the serpent and its own offspring. Those scenes, as we have said, foreshadow events to come in the *Mort Artu*. Finally, he is able to observe—but in an unclear, "veiled" manner—scenes that are tied to the mystery of the Grail and that will not be immediately explained: the fate and sufferings of the serpent-man who plays the "Lai de Plor," devoted to a "desputoison qui jadis avoit esté de Joseph d'Arimacie et de Orfeu l'anchanteor qui le Chastel des Anchantemenz fonda en la marche d'Escoce" (Micha 5: 266, "debate that had taken place between Joseph of Arimathea and Orpheus the Enchanter, who founded the Castle of Enchantments in the Scottish borderlands"), and in whom we should undoubtedly recognize King Pellés's father, the maimed king; the apparition of the avenging lance, whose explanation is delayed until later; and finally, the vision of the Grail placed on a silver table with four marvelous spindles, a vision that blinds Bors as later, in the *Queste*, it will paralyze Lancelot.

Through the character of Bors, the future narrator of the *Queste del Saint Graal*, and through this highly detailed episode, the constitutive elements of writing in the *Queste* are laid out. Adventures, scenes, and motifs taken for the most part from the Arthurian pre-text are used, but they are reoriented in service of a quest that has a different meaning, explained only at a later time by the coming of the ultimate representative of Arthurian knighthood: Galahad. Bors's visit to Corbenic and his partial successes qualify him, on the level of the narrative, as a future hero of the Grail; but they also display the capacity of a textual universe, which one might have thought to be exhausted, to launch a new quest—that is, to create new meaning; to seek anew why the lance is bleeding and what becomes of the drops of blood oozing from it; to see the Grail clearly; to reconstruct, from its first to its last link, the long chain of questions and answers that reveal the Grail's secret through narrative time.

Is it possible, then, to explain at least partially and in a nonmoralizing perspective the triad itself and the roles attributed to the three chosen heroes? Could the reunion of Galahad and Perceval, both buried at Sarras in the *Queste*, have a connection with the adventure of compilation, a characteristic technique of the Arthurian romance in prose? In such a case, would the purpose be to break partially with tradition by lowering Perceval's status while at the same time rehabilitating earlier texts to whose traditions he is tied? In this manner, an all-inclusive type of writing would be formulated, which would slowly encompass the whole Arthurian pre-text and whose culminating expression would be the *Prose Tristan*. One could also reconsider in this light Galahad's ancestry as established in the *Lancelot Proper*, an ancestry that incorporates all existing lineages and that would thus be perfectly representative of the notion of compilation and the search for conclusions.

On the other hand, Bors's promotion seems to be connected with the other tendency of Arthurian writing, that toward continuation, toward renewal of the narrative. As we have said, Bors's adventures and visions at Corbenic require some clarification; they call for a sequel which, at least in the case of the knight with serpents, will never be given. The birth and character of Helain the White are also loose ends, which will at least be taken up again in the *Prose Tristan*.[14] Finally, we know how Bors, returning to King Arthur's court from Sarras at the end of the *Queste*, is at the same time the actor, the authoritative witness, and the narrator of the *Queste del Saint Graal*. Thus, in the new triad substituted for the lone Perceval, several if not all the images of the medieval writer are gathered: the author (Galahad) who adds a supplement, indeed a conclusion, to earlier texts and contributes himself to the story; the compiler (Perceval) who rearranges the inherited materials and gives them new meaning; the narrator (Bors) who, fulfilling here the multiple role of knight-questor and authoritative witness, dictates to Arthur's scribes (as earlier Merlin did to Blaise) the *Queste del Saint Graal*.

In conclusion, it remains to ask what Lancelot's loss of the name Galahad might mean and what the reasons, or rather the stakes, might be. Indeed, the reasons seem obvious: the loss of the name and of the call to achieve the Grail adventure connected with that name relate first to King Ban's sin and then to Lancelot's adultery. Stained with sin, Lancelot may not accede to the pure vision of the Grail's secrets, and in the *Queste* he will meet at Corbenic with a fate identical to that of Bors in the *Lancelot Proper*: total paralysis at the sight of the Grail. But the text does not stop telling us that the "good knight," the Arthurian Messiah, can only be the son of Lancelot and must necessarily belong to King Ban's lineage, as has been determined by the established genealogy. Moreover, the text often insists on the physical resemblance between Lancelot and Galahad. Apparently, the son owes nothing to his mother. All other relationships are lost in the light of this sole filiation, in this exclusively masculine lineage, of which the *Queste* will offer the oneiric vision.[15]

The Lancelot/Galahad duality points to another split in the text, that of the adventures destined for either the father or the son. The allotment of successes and failures according to the contrast of lust/chastity seems obvious at first glance: according to the *Lancelot Proper*, Galahad will douse the boiling springs. He will free the prisoners from their torments by giving those living-dead—who may perhaps be embodiments of the souls in purgatory[16]—the right to rest. It is also stated and repeated in the *Lancelot Proper* that Galahad initiates not the era of adventures, as was the case for Perceval, but that of conclusions. Galahad, the virgin hero, carries (with)in himself the death sentence of both the adventurous kingdom and the narrative. He thus personifies one of cyclical literature's extreme cases: the quest for conclusion. Should we think then that, trapped by the cycle and the Grail, *Lancelot*'s conceiver recognized its dilemmas and invented answers? Doubling the lineages in the scope of the adventures between two brother kings, Bors and Ban and their children, and in the span of generations, between Lancelot and Galahad, allows the author at the same time to play on the infinite expansion of the story and to program or delay its conclusion. If we reexamine from this perspective Lancelot's "initiating" adventures, those in which he is competing with Galahad, their common point seems in fact to be the freeing, liberating, returning to the normal course of events and time, whether it means returning joy and light to the world (from the "Dolorous Guard" to the "Dolorous Tower"), liberating the prisoners of the "Valley of No Return," or breaking the spells of the magic carole dance. This, moreover, confirms a picture of Lancelot gleaned already from Chrétien's *Chevalier de la Charrette* and associates him with such other liberating heroes as Erec of the "Joy of the Court" and Yvain of the "Dire Adventure."

We might then wonder whether the creation of Galahad in the *Lancelot Proper*—a creation that may have occurred during the transformation of a noncyclical *Lancelot* into a cyclical text—may not have been the means to launch a cycle while delaying by one generation, by the space of a single text (but what a text!), the threat of its conclusion. This would be a different and elegant solution to the problem faced by the verse *Continuations*, which was resolved by using the themes of the broken sword, the silence or sleep of the hero, or by the simple expedient of the vendetta.

Many explanations can be found for the Lancelot-Galahad filiation: to create a new model of chivalry, or to demonstrate the power of fiction to create one from the same, accepting a tradition while marking a difference. In this regard, we should note the important number of sons "without fathers," or otherwise cut off from their origins. But the creation of the Lancelot-Galahad couple and that of the parallel couple, Bors–Helain the White, expresses more definitively the powers of Arthurian fiction and the *mise en abime* of its perilous dialectic: to program an ending, to close the circle (by seating the chosen hero on the Perilous Seat) while delaying as long as possible the conclusion. Shall we say that the genius of the cycle's architect is that, while according the mystical adventure its importance and achieving the Grail Quest with Galahad, he concluded the story on the earthly level by tying together, in the *Mort Artu*, the death of love with the death of the kingdom and the end of the narrative?

Notes

1. Alexandre Micha, ed., *Lancelot*, 9 vols. (Geneva: Droz, 1978–1983).

2. The "continent" (Gaul and Rome) is, on the contrary, very much present in the chronicle of King Arthur's reign given by Wace in the *Brut*, and also in the *Prose Perceval*, in *Lancelot*, in vol. 6 of Micha's edition, and in the *Mort Artu*.

3. We recall that, in Robert de Boron, *Le Roman de l'Estoire dou Graal*, ed. W. A. Nitze (Paris: Champion, 1927), Joseph, who does not have a son, bequeaths the Grail to Bron, the Fisher King, his brother-in-law.

4. Micha 6: 31. However, nothing is said about where Ban's brother, King Bors, is buried; his death is related in Micha 7: 32.

5. See *Erec et Enide*, edited by Mario Roques (Paris: Champion, 1955): v. 1923, "li rois Bans de Ganieret"; and *Le conte du Graal*, edited by Félix Lecoy, 2 vols. (Paris: Champion, 1972–1975): v. 467, "le Roi Ban de Gomeret" (the king into whose service one of Perceval's two brothers entered).

6. See "Sainte(s) Helene(s)" in *Femmes-Mariages-Lignages, XII–XIVe siècles: Mélanges offerts à Georges Duby* (Université De Boeck, 1992): 44–53.

7. See Elspeth Kennedy, *Lancelot and the Grail: A Study of the Prose Lancelot* (Oxford: Clarendon Press, 1986), especially pp. 283–286.

8. See "'Del Graal cui l'an an servoit': Variations sur un pronom," in *The Editor and the Text*, edited by Philip Bennett and Graham Runnalls (Edinburgh: Edinburgh University Press, 1990): 137–144.

9. William Roach, ed., *Perceval en prose* (Philadelphia: American Philosophical Society, 1941): 244–245.

10. Chrétien de Troyes, *Le conte du Graal*, vv. 1253–1254.

11. According to the story of Joseph of Arimathea and of the broken sword, as told in Micha 2: 320–340, the broken sword will be mended by the one who "les hautes aventures del Graal devra assomer" ("is to achieve the high adventures of the Grail"). It is indeed joined together by Galahad in *La Queste del Saint Graal*, edited by Alfred Pauphilet (Paris: Champion, 1923): 266–267.

12. William Roach, ed., *Les Continuations du Conte du Graal*, 5 vols. (Philadelphia: American Philosophical Society, 1949–1983) 5: 41318–41606.

13. Roach 5: 41559–41573.

14. The continuation of the story of Helain the White and his dubbing by Arthur may be read in Philippe Ménard, ed., *Le Roman de Tristan en prose* (Geneva: Droz, in press) 6: sects. 80–82.

15. See *Queste* 135–138.

16. A hypothesis suggested by Francis Dubost in *Aspects fantastiques de la littérature narrative médiévale (XII–XIIIe siècles), L'Autre, L'Ailleurs, L'Autrefois*, 2 vols. (Paris: Champion, 1991): 418–422.

2. Variations in the Patterns of Interlace in the Lancelot-Grail

Elspeth Kennedy

Most scholars have tended to treat the interlace patterns of the Lancelot-Grail as though they were the same throughout the cycle. Carol Chase has written a penetrating article[1] in which she studies in detail a part of the *Lancelot Proper*, and analyzes, among other things, the relationship between interlace and theme; but most other studies, however interesting, have until recently tended to be very general.[2] It is true that formulae of the type *"But now the tale falls silent about* so and so *and returns to* so and so *who . . . "* are to be found from the beginning of the *Marche de Gaule* section up to the end of the *Mort Artu*, but the time has surely come to make a more detailed analysis of the different branches to see whether there may not be subtle but significant variations in the technique of interlacing the different strands of narrative from one branch to another. Obviously each particular type of narrative situation may demand a different kind of interlace; for example, the recurring patterns in the account of Lancelot's childhood and the struggle with Claudas to protect the boy's young cousins, Lionel and Bors, are not the same as those to be found once the hero sets off from court in quest of adventure and other knights then set off in search of him. Similarly, after the adventures of Logres have been brought to an end by Galahad, it is not to be expected that the *Mort Artu* should contain the type of interlace characteristic of earlier branches in the cycle, for its central theme is the end of the Arthurian world: there are no more quests for adventure, and large forces are involved. I propose, therefore, at this early stage in my exploration of a vast subject,[3] to give particular attention to the variations in the intertwining of narrative threads in relation to quests for another knight and to the series of adventures encountered by a knight or knights as they journey on some mission, toward some task which has to be accomplished. I shall take as my first point of comparison those adventures that start with Lancelot's knighting and lead up to his installation as a knight of the Round Table, which I have already analyzed in some detail in my book *Lancelot and the Grail*[4] and which are to be found in the text I edited.[5] I shall compare the organization of the narrative of these adventures with that to be found in the first volume of Micha's edition,[6] particularly in relation to the adventures after the end of the cyclic version of the False Guenevere episode, those which lead up, eventually, to the death of Galehaut.[7] However, I also want to look at narrative structures in wider terms, to investigate whether some changes may be linked to thematic developments or to a differing degree of emphasis, on the one hand, on the knights' reports of the adventures or, on the other, on a literary reworking of such reports for a written book.

I shall first summarize the interlacing technique and presentation of the narrative as it is to be found in the text I edited. While a general historical introduction is provided by the tale at the beginning of the romance, there is no prologue as such, and events are normally presented as seen through the eyes of the particular character whose narrative thread is being followed in any given sequence, with extra information being introduced from time to time together with a reference to the tale such as "*ce dit li contes*" ("so says the story"). According to two passages in the text, knights will have sworn to give, on their return to court, a truthful account of their deeds (Kennedy 298.10–15; 406.9–19). Elsewhere (Kennedy 571.20–31) it is stated that these reports are set down in writing by Arthur's four learned clerks, whose names we are given. There is, therefore, a general written record of the adventures of Arthur's knights based on their own testimony, from which is drawn the material relevant to this particular tale, that of Lancelot, and there are a number of references outward to such a source in which is to be sought a complete account of the deeds of all the knights, including those that do not pertain to the story of Lancelot (Kennedy 138.33–36; 612.12–14). Thus, references to such tales are used as formulae to justify the exclusion of material rather than its inclusion.

The activities of Arthur as king cannot be confined within the tale of Lancelot. His narrative thread is not followed continuously except where he is directly involved in events that concern Lancelot, but there are from time to time allusions to his wars and to the general affairs of the kingdom which serve to place the tale being told within a wider Arthurian context. Lancelot's narrative strand is followed without unexplained gaps; the same is true of Gawain, once Lancelot comes to court and the King's nephew becomes involved in a series of quests for the young unknown hero. Once Hector is introduced into the story, when he meets Gawain on a quest for Lancelot (Kennedy 368), his narrative thread is followed without unexplained gaps.

The criterion for inclusion or exclusion of an account of a knight's adventures on a quest is that of success or failure within that quest. Thus forty knights, including Gawain, set off on a quest for Lancelot (the Red Knight). They journey for a whole year but find no news of him:

> Ce furent li quarante qui alerent en la queste. Mais onqes n'i ot si preu ne si hardi qui puis ne s'en tenist por fol, car puis en furent apelé tuit parjuré failli de la boche lo roi meesmes, car il errerent tot l'an jusque a l'asemblee, [que onques ne troverent le chevalier, ne veraies enseignes n'en aporterent (see Kennedy 361.27–32). Ne de nule aventure qui lor avenist en la qeste ne parole li contes ci, por ce que il faillirent tuit a lor qeste . . .]
>
> (Kennedy 299.12–18)

(These were the forty who went on the quest. But there was not one of them so brave and so bold that he did not afterwards consider himself a fool, for later they were all called forsworn and dishonored by the king himself, for they traveled the whole year, right up to the time fixed for the next assembly for battle, (without ever finding the knight or bringing back reliable news of him (see Kennedy 361.27–32). The tale does not relate here any of the adventures which they encountered on the quest because they all failed to achieve their quest . . .])

A second quest was started later with a certain number of the same knights who had embarked on the first quest, including Gawain:

> Si se taist d'aus toz li contes et [parole de] monseignor Gauvain por ce que il aquesta de ceste queste. Et neporqant chascuns de ces vint chevaliers a son conte tot antier, qui sont branches de monseignor Gauvain, car ce est li chiés et a cestui les covient an la fin toz ahurter, por ce que il issent de cestui.
>
> (Kennedy 365.35–366.3)

(The tale falls silent about all of them and speaks only of Sir Gawain because he achieved the quest. Nevertheless, each of these twenty knights has his own complete tale, and these are branches of the tale of Sir Gawain, for it is the source in which they must all converge, because they all stem from it.)

Great skill is used in patterning the formal moves from one strand to another in such a way as to underline the important stages in the thematic development and to highlight dramatic moments in the story. The series of adventures encountered by a knight in a particular sequence are normally narrated in the order in which they occur. However, on occasion, a reverse order is used with considerable effect, so that the reader/listener suffers the same puzzlement and suspense as the characters in the fiction when damsels or knights arrive at Arthur's court with mysterious messages before the events leading up to the sending of the message are recounted (Kennedy 401–404).[8] These occasional inversions in the order in which events are narrated are all the more effective because the narrative is normally presented in a straightforward way within the section of the strand being followed at the time, according to the natural order of events, and in the account given by the tale—it does not cheat by withholding information without warning, only to release it at a later point in the narrative.

However, this pattern changes somewhat as we move into Micha's volume 1, which gives the cyclic version of the False Guenevere episode and the death of Galehaut. At the end of the account of Lancelot's installation as a knight of the Round Table and of the celebrations which follow this, a number of variant readings suggest that we are entering a new phase of the story. Four manuscripts give variations on the following reading of the Vatican manuscript, Reg. Lat. 1439: "Ci faut la marche de Gaule et commence Galehot" ("Here ends the Marche de Gaule and the Galehaut begins").[9] If the start of the Galehaut and the opening of Micha 1 coincide according to these manuscripts, this particular volume ends with an account of the death of Galehaut, followed by the statement: "Ci finist li contes de lui et retorne a Lancelot" (Micha 1: 389, "The tale finishes with him and returns to Lancelot"), a bleak phrase which emphasizes that the end of his story and his life is contained within the story of Lancelot, the knight who is the involuntary cause of his death. This end is prepared for from the outset, for the volume begins with the statement that Galehaut has left Arthur's court, and then moves from a description of his love for Lancelot and of his anxiety lest he should lose his companionship forward into a reference to his death that would arise from this love and fear. This is then followed by a formula for the postponement of telling something of a type not to be found in the earlier branch:

Et de ceste chose ne covient pas tesmoing avoir, car bien i parut en la fin que la dolor que il en ot li toli tote joie tant que mors en fu, si com li contes meismes le devisera ça avant. Mais de sa mort ne

fet pas a parler ci endroit, kar mors a si preudome com Galehout
estoit ne fet pas a ramentevoir devant le point.

(Micha 1: 1)

(And there is no need to provide any testimony for this, for in the
end it became evident to everyone that the grief this caused him
deprived him of all joy and brought him to his death, as the tale
itself will later relate. But this is not the moment to speak of his
death, for the account of the death of a man of such great worth as
Galehaut should not be given before the appropriate time.)

This is significant because it is centered on Galehaut rather than Lancelot and leads into a moral portrait that reads rather like an obituary
published before the event. The authorities to which it refers in support of the praise given are, in the first place, "all the tales which
speak of him," which are all in agreement that he was the noblest
prince after Arthur, but in the second place (and I think that this is
important), we have a clear reference to a written source compiled by
a named, fictitious author, one of the four clerks mentioned earlier
whose duty it was to record the knights' reports of their deeds:

Et si retesmoigne li livres Tardamides de Vergials, qui plus parole
des proesces Galehout que nus des autres, que neis li rois Artus
ne fu mie de gaires plus vaillans, kar se Galehout puist vivre son
droit aage al point et al corage qu'il avoit quant il comença a guer-
roier le roi Artu, il passast tos cels qui les autres avoient passés.

(Micha 1: 1)

(And the book of Tardamides de Vergials, which says more about
the valiant deeds of Galehaut than does any other, testifies for its
part that even King Arthur was of scarcely greater worth; for if
Galehaut could have lived for his life's full span at the high level
he had reached and with the spirit he had when he began to wage
war on King Arthur, he would have surpassed all those who had
surpassed other men.)

The identification of a named redactor of a particular book as opposed
to named clerks setting down a common record, as we shall see,
seems to pave the way for a more explicitly active literary manipula-
tion of the narrative.

The passage in praise of Galehaut skillfully interweaves past and future, what has been told and what is yet to be told, presented throughout in the past tense. There is a reference to a conversation with Lancelot yet to take place; it is to be narrated later in full (Micha 2: 30–33), although there is no indication of this now, no phrase such as "the tale will tell." In this conversation Galehaut discloses his past intention, his aim to conquer the whole world; this is followed by a narratorial prediction of the age at which he would die—to be filled out later in the account of the interpretation of Galehaut's dreams—followed by an allusion to an episode recounted in the previous branch: Galehaut's surrender at the moment of victory to the king who had been defeated. This is combined with an allusion to reproaches made to him by his own men and his reply, which are not mentioned in the previous account. Then follows a narratorial comment:

> En ceste maniere torna Galehout a savoir et a gaaing ce que li autre tornoient a perte et a folie, ne nus n'osast avoir cuer de tant amer buens chevaliers com il faisoit.

> (Micha 1: 2)

> (In this way Galehaut turned into wisdom and gain what others turned into folly and loss, and no one had the spirit to love good knights as much as he did.)

This leads up to a formula switching back to the narrative present, with the decorated initial, unusually, preceding the phrase "And now the story stops speaking . . . ": "Mais or laisse li contes a parler ici endroit de ses bontés et retorne a dire ensi com il s'en vont entre lui et Lancelot et .IIII. escuier . . ." (Micha 1: 2, "And now the tale stops speaking of his good qualities and picks up the story at the point when he sets off with Lancelot and four squires"). This interweaving of additional information about events already told with a foretaste of events yet to be narrated (here without the traditional references to "as the tale will tell") seems to represent a subtle shift away from a narrative technique characterized by the presentation of events as they unfold before the eyes of the character whose thread is being followed at the time, with the occasional reference forward or backward explicitly linked to *le conte*. It is this change in attitude and in literary emphasis which I propose to examine in relation to the adventures following Gawain's abduction by Caradoc. But I want first to draw attention to a new element introduced at this stage in the evolution of the cycle, one which will have a noticeable effect on the narrative structure: the prediction that Lancelot will fail at the greatest adventure of all—that of the Grail—a prediction first revealed in the cyclic version of the interpretation of Galehaut's dreams. The leader of Arthur's clerks tells Galehaut that Lancelot will be surpassed by a knight, not yet born, who will achieve the adventure of the Perilous Seat:

> —Je sai bien de voir k'il est li mieldres chevaliers de cels qui orendroit sont. Mais il en sera uns mieldres de lui, kar ensi le dist Merlins en sa prophecie, qui par tot est voirsdisans. —Mestre, fet Galehout, savés vos comment il a non? —De son non, fet li mestres, ne sai je rien, kar je ne l'ai pas encerchié. —Comment poés vos donc savoir, fet il, que uns mieldres chevaliers sera? —Je le sai bien, fet li mestres, que cil qui achevera les aventures de Bretaigne sera li mieldres chevaliers de tot le monde et aemplira le deerain siege de la Table Reonde, et cil a en escripture la senefiance de lion.
>
> (Micha 1: 52–53)

("I know well that he is in truth the best knight of those now living. But one better than he will come, for so prophesied Merlin, who always tells the truth." "Master," said Galehaut, "do you know his name?" "I know nothing of his name," said the learned clerk, "for I have not sought for it." "Then how can you know," he said, "that he will be a better knight?" "I know," said the learned clerk, " that the man who will achieve the adventures of Britain will be the best knight in all the world and will fill the last seat at the Round Table, and this man will signify the lion in the scripture.")

Lancelot cannot recover the qualities that the man destined to achieve the Grail adventure will have, for this man will be chaste and virgin:

> Cist ne porroit recovrer les taiches que cil avra qui l'aventure del Graal achevera, kar il covient tot premierement qu'il soit de sa nativité jusqu'a sa mort virges et chastes si entierement qu'il n'ait amor n'a dame n'a damoisele. Et cist nel puet ore avoir, kar je sai greignor partie de son conseil que vos ne cuidiés.
>
> (Micha 1: 53)

(This man would not be able to recover the qualities to be found in the one who will achieve the adventure of the Grail, for he must be from his birth to his death so chaste and virgin that he loves neither lady nor damsel. And this man cannot now achieve that, for I know more of his secrets than you think.)

Up to this point, unlike the situation in the romance by Chrétien de Troyes, there had never been any question of Lancelot, the principal hero of the tale being told, failing at anything; indeed, as I have pointed out, the criterion for the inclusion of any given sequence of adventures on a quest within the tale was that they should lead to success. From this time on, as we shall see, that is no longer the case, as the reader is gradually prepared for a *Queste del Saint Graal* in which, in a way, the accounts of the adventures of the individual knights who fail are no less significant than is the account of the adventures of the only knight who fully succeeds—Galahad—and who achieves so many marvellous adventures that they cannot all be told: "si trova laienz mainte aventure qu'il mist a fin, dont li contes ne fet mie mencion, por ce que trop i eust a fere s'il vousist chascune dire par soi"[10] ("and he found there many an adventure which he brought to a successful conclusion, but these are not mentioned by the tale, for there would be too much to do if every one of these adventures were to be related").

When we turn to the adventures of Lancelot, Yvain, and the duke of Clarence as they seek to rescue Gawain from Caradoc, success is certainly not the criterion for the inclusion of adventures. When the companions separate, the adventures of the duke of Clarence and those of Yvain are related even though they are not to lead to success in the task. From the beginning of this quest, the reader and the duke are prepared for failure, although the duke does not choose to listen. The characteristic pattern for both the duke and Yvain is that success in one or two lesser tasks is followed by failure at a more significant one at which Lancelot is destined to succeed, such as Escalon li Tenebreus, the Valley of No Return, and, of course, the freeing of Gawain. Lancelot is particularly well qualified to achieve those adventures that are associated with love (the Valley of No Return, for example), and it is when he believes that Guenevere no longer loves him that, in a sequence leading up to the death of Galehaut, his side loses a tournament. He is very upset and throws down his shield, calling himself *malvés recreu* ("cowardly recreant"). Yvain and Gawain catch up with him and ask why he is so sad. He replies that he has good reason: "Or ai hui esté vaincus en un povre tornoiement" (Micha 1: 386–387, "I have today been defeated in a paltry tournament"). Significantly, there is a new criterion for giving priority to the telling of certain adventures, to be found in an inclusion formula which contains a prediction that a quest for Lancelot is doomed to failure but underlines that this is not a reason for exclusion of the knights' adventures. This occurs at the end of the first paragraph of Micha's section 30, rather than at the end of a section. The tale has just switched from Lancelot, imprisoned by Morgan, to Galehaut and three other companions—Lionel, Gawain, and Yvain—who have set out to look for Lancelot. They immediately decide to separate, and the tale explains:

> . . . mes lor queste ne puet monter a nul espleit, kar s'il fuissent mil chevalier, ne trovaissent il mie Lancelot tant com il fust en la prison Morgain, kar li enchantement dont ele savoit trop ne l'i laissoient descovrir. Et neporquant des aventures ki avindrent as .IIII. chevaliers parole li contes et premierement de Galehout ki plus est a mal aise que tuit li autre.
>
> (Micha 1: 358)

> (. . . but their quest was bound to come to nothing, for if they had been a thousand knights, they would not have found Lancelot while he was in the prison of Morgan, as the spells, of which she knew such a great number, prevented them from discovering him there. Nevertheless, the tale will relate the adventures encountered by the four knights and first those of Galehaut, whose distress was greater than that of all the others.)

It is particularly fitting that, in a branch that begins with a prediction of Galehaut's death and ends with a formula closing his story on his death, the tale should give us a reason for starting with Galehaut's adventures that his suffering over the disappearance was greater than that of any of the others. This echoes the emphasis on Galehaut's grief to be found in an earlier switching formula, when Lancelot, after killing Caradoc, leaves to return to Morgan's prison, telling only Gawain, who had to swear not to reveal his intentions:

> Ensint blasme li rois mon seignor Gauvain, mes sor tos les autres est Galehout dolens et esbahis et bien a, ce dit a soi meismes, esprové que Lancelos ne l'amoit mie, quant il a autrui dist son conseil et sans son seu s'en ala: et de la vint la grans ire dont la noire dolors le prist al cuer qui onques puis ne le laissa. Mes ci n'en fet plus a parler.
>
> (Micha 1: 347)

(Thus the king reproaches Sir Gawain. But Galehaut is more grieved and upset than anyone else and says to himself that he has discovered that Lancelot does not love him when he reveals his intentions to someone else and goes away without telling him. Whence came that great distress and the dark grief which gripped his heart and never again left him. But this is not the moment to say any more about this.)

This inclusion of failure leads to a multiplication in the number of strands followed, but, perhaps inevitably, the pattern of interweaving these is less consistent than it was in the earlier branch. Gaps of a type not to be found before occur in the accounts of a knight's adventures. For example, section 28 (Micha 1: 336) opens with Lancelot and his men traveling until they come to Felon Pas, where they find a battle going on between Arthur's army and that of Caradoc. This links up with section 18.9–11 (Micha 1: 248–249), where Arthur sets out, and with section 26.39 (Micha 1: 330), where news is brought by a squire that Caradoc has gone to fight Arthur's army, but Arthur's thread up to Felon Pas is not followed, although the king is here embarked on an adventure in which Lancelot is involved and which is, therefore, central to the story. Even more significantly, Yvain and Gawain's narrative thread, which is being followed in Micha 1: 384–385, converges with that of Lancelot when they find him at a tournament. Lancelot has been last mentioned (Micha 1: 372) when he is released by Morgan and sets off in fine armor. His thread is abandoned at that point, and there is no mention of him coming to the tournament, so there is a gap in his thread, again in sharp contrast with the situation in the earlier branch, where no unexplained gaps are ever left in the account of Lancelot's adventures.

Other instances are to be found of a more loosely organized interlace, and in particular of a greater role being given to the compiler or literary presenter of the tale as opposed to concentration on events as seen by the knight whose thread is being followed. For example, on more than one occasion there will be a sudden appearance of an eyewitness to events, not mentioned at the time, who produces extra information on what has taken place some time after the event and the narration of it. In Micha 1: 203, an account is given of Gawain's painful journey to Caradoc's castle, as he is stripped naked and beaten all the way, but in Micha 1: 217, the duke of Clarence comes across traces of a battle (much as Gawain had seen such traces in Chrétien's *Chevalier de la Charrette*, as he rode after the abducted Guenevere). The duke is then told by a squire of a battle fought by the men of the Lady of Cabrion when her party met a knight being beaten whom they identified as Gawain and tried unsuccessfully to rescue. There is no mention of battle or eyewitness in the earlier account. Similarly, after the enchantments of the Valley of No Return are brought to an end by Lancelot, a very brief account is given in section 24.47–48 (Micha 1: 303–304) of Morgan having Lancelot borne away in a litter, having first put him to sleep with a magic ring. In the next section, but not at the beginning of it (25.15–17), a damsel, eyewitness to the abduction, gives an account of how she followed the litter and talked to Morgan, who promised to release Lancelot so that he could save Gawain (Micha 1: 320). Neither the eyewitness nor Morgan's promise are mentioned in the first account. The report of the eyewitness is handled differently in the narrative of Lancelot's first adventures in *Lancelot do Lac*. After the account of his capture of the Dolorous Guard, there is an immediate switch from his narrative thread to that of a *vallet gentil home* ("noble young man"), brother of Aiglin des Vaus, who had witnessed the capture of the castle and rode at once to Arthur's court to report on what he had seen (Kennedy 195–196). Information concerning his presence is not, therefore, withheld for a time, nor does he tell Arthur anything we do not already know. Sometimes, in Micha 1, it is the tale that refers back to an event already recounted and provides additional information. For example, in Micha 1: 349 there is a reference to a magic pillow placed under Lancelot's head when he was taken from the Valley of No Return, which is missing from the earlier account (Micha 1: 303–304). An explanation concerning the damsel who helped Gawain while he was imprisoned in the Dolorous Tower is given in Micha 1: 207, then picked up again in Micha 1: 340 and extended with a reference to a magic sword not mentioned earlier. New elements are even attached through references back to events recounted in the earlier branch. For example, the queen is said to have given Lancelot a ring that uncovered enchantments "the day she gave him her love" (Micha 1: 316), when there is no mention of such a gift earlier.

This more complex system of narrating events, this apparently arbitrary giving or withholding of information on the part of the narrator, may sometimes be linked to uncertainty over the truth, over the reality of things seen. This accords well with the important role given in this part of the romance to Morgan—a lady with magic powers, but less beneficent than the Lady of the Lake. She plays with appearance and reality as she keeps Lancelot in prison, hidden by her spells from the knights looking for him who are therefore doomed to failure, as mentioned above, "since the spells, of which she knew a great number, prevented them from discovering him there" (Micha 1: 358). She juggles, too, with truth and falsehood. For example, she sends a damsel who gives an explanation of Lancelot's disappearance which repeats true information, corresponding to the account already given in the text, but supplemented with false information to stir up trouble for Guenevere (Micha 1: 350–352).

With this approach to the interlace, the reader can never be certain how much is still hidden, how much may yet be revealed; and the looser structure, the possibility of modifying the first version given of an event through references back by the tale, reflects the shifting nature of reality for the characters struggling with the enchantments and deceits so typical of this part of the cycle. It is perhaps curious, therefore, that Micha should be so uneasy with the positioning in the Corpus manuscript and its group (that is, the majority of manuscripts) of the sequence in which Lionel, in his search for the missing Lancelot, is shown him being watched by guards in a garden (Micha 1: 379–380). This is placed after section 31, at the end of which Morgan releases Lancelot, and Micha comments on "l'ordre illogique de la vulgate" (Micha 1: 367n, "the illogical order of the Vulgate"), and in the introduction (1: xiv–xv) describes it as a "faute voyante" ("obvious error"). However, there is an example near the beginning of *Lancelot do Lac* of visual contact from a certain distance made between narrative threads. It occurs in the episode in which Ban's death is recounted and makes a link with a point in the middle of an earlier narrative sequence, which then goes on to relate what happened afterward (Kennedy 12–13). We are told that Ban, on his way to seek help from Arthur, climbed a hill to take a last look at his beloved Trebe and saw it go up in flames. This makes a visual link (frequently portrayed in the historiated initials) with the account of the setting fire to the city given in the middle of the previous sequence, which then gives an account of the lengthy siege of the keep, its final surrender, and the killing of the seneschal who had betrayed the city to Claudas. The visual contact between the threads of two different characters is not so dramatic at this point in Micha 1. It recalls rather a contact made through a dream: the mother of Lionel and Bors is grieving for her lost children in her convent and is given a glimpse of them in a vision, seeing them in the company of Lancelot, Lambegue, and Pharien, safe in a garden, actually beneath the semblance of the lake, although she does not know this (Kennedy 133). Admittedly, this vision is related after we have been given an account of the taking of her children to the safety of the lake, but it is also placed after we have been told of the death of Pharien (Kennedy 131). The fact that we are told of Lancelot's release by Morgan before the recounting of the episode in which Lionel is allowed to catch a glimpse of him seems to me to reflect the disarray of the knights who seek vainly for him, as conveyed so clearly in the formula I quoted earlier: "for if they had been a thousand knights, they would not have found Lancelot while he was in the prison of Morgan, since the spells, of which she knew a great number, prevented them from discovering him there" (Micha 1: 358). Lionel may catch a glimpse of Lancelot but is allowed no contact with him. Even though he can eventually tell Galehaut that he has seen his beloved companion, Lancelot keeps on disappearing. As I have said, there are now gaps in his storyline which are never accounted for—a situation that would be unheard of in the account given of his earlier adventures. Thus the game of hide-and-seek in which the reader is involved through the pattern of the interlace reflects the helpless mystification of the characters and leads up to our one certainty, one shared with Galehaut himself, made clear from the start of the branch and reinforced by the switching formulae: that the great prince will die through his separation from Lancelot.

The pattern of references to the past, to events that took place in Arthur's kingdom or in the surrounding lands either before the beginning of the Lancelot story or before the particular events being recounted, is also a little different from the earlier branch. There are not so many "historical" explanations linking up with the end of Uther's reign or the beginning of Arthur's, whereas these are quite frequent in the account of Lancelot's childhood and early adventures. However, there is an explanation from the tale for the enmity between Morgan and Guenevere that links it to a love affair of the former. It takes us back to that time and is introduced by the characteristic formula "*Il fu voirs*" ("It was true"):

Cele haine estoit montee entre les .II. si com vos orrois. Il fu voirs que Morgue fu fille al duc de Tintajuel et a Egerne sa feme, qui puis fu roine de Bretaigne et feme Uterpandragon, et de li fu nes li rois Artus qui en li fu engendrés al vivant le duc par la traïson que Merlins fist. Quant Egerne s'en vint a Uterpandragon ki l'esposa, si amena avec li Morgain, sa fille, et un vaslés remest en la duchee de Tintajuel, qui estoit filz le duc d'une autre feme k'il avoit eue devant Egerne. Li dux estoit molt lais chevaliers et Morgue retraioit a lui, kar molt estoit laide; et quant ele vint en aage, si fu si chaude et luxuriose que plus chaude feme ne convint a querre. Lors avoit li rois Artus pris novelement la roine, si avoit en la maison le roi un chevalier ki niés la roine estoit, si avoit non Guiamors de Tarmelide et estoit molt bials chevaliers et preus. En cel termine estoit Morgue pucele la roine, si commença a amer Guia-

mor de Tarmelide de si grant amor que ne se pooit consierrer de
lui veoir.

(Micha 1: 300–301)

(That hatred arose between them in the way that you shall hear. It
was true that Morgan was the daughter of the Duke of Tintagel
and of his wife Egerne, who later became the queen of Britain and
wife of Uther Pendragon and gave birth to King Arthur who was
engendered in her while the duke was still alive, through the cun-
ning machinations of Merlin. When Egerne came to Uther Pendragon who married her, she brought with her Morgan, her
daughter, and a boy remained in the duchy of Tintagel who was
the son of the duke by another wife he had had before Egerne.
The duke was a very ugly knight, and Morgan resembled him, for
she too was very ugly; and when she grew up, she was so passionate and sensual that a more passionate woman was not to be
found. King Arthur had recently married the queen, and there
was in the king's household a knight who was nephew to the
queen; he was called Guiamor de Tarmelide and he was a handsome and valiant knight. At that time Morgan served the queen
and she began to love Guiamor de Tarmelide with such a great
love that she could not do without his company.)

Another explanation, this time of the origin of the Valley of No Return or Valley of False Lovers, also involves Morgan's problems over
love and refers back to the "time when the adventures began"—
magical time rather than historical time. The explanation is introduced by elaborate formulae denoting a switch away from the narrative line:

Ci lesserom ore de lui a parler un petit et de ses aventures tant
que li contes avra devisé quels li vals estoit et por quoi il estoit par
deus nons apelés et comment c'estoit que nus chevaliers ne pooit
issir, puis que il estoit entrez.
　　Ce dist li contes tot avant que li vals estoit apelés le Val sans
Retor et li Vals as Faus Amans. Li Vals sans Retor avoit il non por
ce que nus chevaliers n'en retornoit; et si avoit non li Vals as Faus
Amans por ce que tuit li chevalier i remanoient, s'il avoient fausé a
lor amies de quel que meffet que ce fust, neïs de pensé, et si orrois
coment ce avint. Il fu voirs que Morgue le suer al roi Artu sot
d'enchantement et de caraies sor totes femes . . .

(Micha 1: 274–275)

(At this point we will stop speaking of him and of his adventures for a little until the tale has explained what kind of valley it was and why it was known under two names, and how it came about that no knight, once he had entered it, could ever escape from it.

The tale first tells us that the valley was called the Valley of No Return and the Valley of False Lovers. It was called the Valley of No Return because no knight returned from it; and it was called the Valley of False Lovers because all the knights remained in it if they had been false to their ladies in any way, even if only in thought, and you will hear how this came about. It was true that Morgan, the sister of King Arthur, had greater knowledge of magic and spells than any other woman . . .)

The explanation closes with another formula underlining the switch back to the narrative line:

Tiels estoit li vals com vos avés oï et par tele aventure fu clos a tos cels qui i enterroient. Mes des ore est bien raisons et tens de conter coment li dux i entra et l'aventure qui li avint.

Or dist li contes, quant li dus fu partis del vaslet qu'il laissa a la chapele . . .

(Micha 1: 279)

(As you have heard, such was the valley and such were the events that led to the enclosure within it of all those knights who might enter it. But now it is the appropriate time to relate how the duke entered it and what happened to him there.

Now the tale says that when the duke had parted from the squire whom he left at the chapel . . .)

There are also a number of explanations of evil customs and the like that are introduced by formulae such as "it was true" and attributed to a character rather than to the tale. See, for example, the explanation given of the situation of the knight in the chest. It opens as follows: "Et si vos dirai coment. Il est voirs qu'en l'issue de ceste forest a un chevalier le plus felon . . . " (Micha 1: 198, "And I shall tell you how this happened. It is true that at the way out of the forest is to be found a very fierce knight . . . "). The explanation of the darkness at Escalon li Tenebreus opens with a formula typical of explanations requested by a knight and given by another character, "Jel vos dirai, . . . kar trop m'en avés conjuré" (Micha 1: 231, "I shall tell you, . . . since you have so strongly urged me to do so") and ends with a closing formula and a prediction of future events:

Or vos ai je contee la verité de cest chastel et comment ces grans
tenebres i avindrent; et bien sacheis que encore dit l'en que li chevaliers qui ceste aventure acomplira ostera les malvaises costumes
de la Dolerose Tor ou vos alés por mon seignor Gauvain rescorre.

(Micha 1: 232)

(Now I have given you a true account of this castle and of how it
became covered by such great darkness; and I tell you that it is
also still said that the knight who achieves this adventure will put
an end to the evil customs of the Dolorous Tower to which you are
going to rescue Sir Gawain.)

An explanation may be deferred by the tale, as, for example, that
concerning the damsel hanging by her hair from a tree:

Et la pucele qui au chaisne estoit pendue si estoit cele qui avoit
amené mon seignor Gauvain a la fille al roi de Norgales, si comme
li contes l'a devisé ça en arrieres, mais il n'esclaire mie comment et
por quoi li chevalier avoient si hontosement mené la damoisele et
Saigremor, kar bien vendra a tens a esclarier ça en avant.

(Micha 1: 243)

(And the damsel who was hanging from the oak was the one who
had brought Sir Gawain to the daughter of the king of Norgales,
as the tale related earlier, but it does not explain now how it had
come about and for what reason the knights had treated the damsel and Sagremor so shamefully, for the right time will come later
for light to be shed on this.)

This is picked up later (Micha 1: 252–253), when Sagremor, the damsel, and another knight give an account of the events that led up to
this and refer back to an adventure of Gawain with the king of Norgales's daughter, which occurred during his quest for the Black
Knight, Lancelot, before his identity was known at court (Kennedy
484–515).

If there are many explanations given for adventures to be achieved
by knights or strange situations to be put right, they are mainly,
therefore, of a rather different type from those to be found in the
narration of the events in Lancelot's early career as a knight. Notice-
ably absent are the references, or explanations, that involve the
knight's strand of adventures with Arthur's responsibilities as suzer-
ain by underlining feudal links, as are so often given in the earlier

branch. Nor are to be found those allusions that bring the knight whose thread is being followed into intermittent contact with other conflicts between barons, contact that often helps to provide cross-references between the various strands. In Micha 1, Lancelot becomes a member of the king's *mesnie* ("household"), as well as lover of Guenevere. Arthur's failure to fulfill his obligations toward Lancelot's father has been allowed to recede into the background, and the potentially destructive elements in Lancelot's love for Guenevere are gradually allowed to surface, while the positive aspects of this love are still given importance through the number of adventures which he as lover succeeds in achieving. The historical dimension is thus given less importance, and there is not quite the same contrast between the continuity of the main narrative threads and the deliberately fragmentary nature of the allusions to events not directly relevant to the tale of Lancelot, a contrast which, in the earlier branch, does not cast doubt on the existence of an authentic Arthurian world outside the immediate confines of the romance but, on the contrary, suggests that Lancelot's tale is part of a wider whole. The extreme rarity of this type of allusion outward in Micha 1 and the succeeding volumes tends to give a different texture to the cyclic romance.

I said earlier that in Micha 1 the interlace pattern is less tightly organized than in the earlier volume around the figure of Lancelot and around the view of events as seen by the particular knight whose adventures are being followed at the time. I also suggested that in *Lancelot do Lac* the narrative is presented as a faithful record (with some supplementary information ascribed to the tale) of what was relevant to "*le conte Lancelot*" ("the story of Lancelot") in the report made by the knight on his return to court and set down by Arthur's clerks, a relevance that is firmly linked to the idea of success in relation to the quest for Lancelot; however, the completeness of information given in the account provided by the tale is more problematic in Micha 1. In saying this, I intend to imply not that the interlace pattern in Micha 1 is, therefore, inferior but that it is a little different and reflects a change in the way the narrative is presented. This may well be connected with a change in authorship, but it is also, in my opinion, related in some degree to new thematic developments linked with a preparation for a Grail quest in which the main hero and many other worthy knights are destined to fail, failures from which much can be learned. We have more narrative strands, but also more silences, more breaks, more later additions of information that can modify what we have already been told. It is also, I believe, significant that the name of the clerk Tardamides is attached to the book that is said to include more of the deeds of Galehaut than any other. This

may perhaps be a small step away from the anonymity of the tale
toward the attribution of the romance to a named author. It is only in
the *Queste* and the *Mort Artu* that the attribution of the work to Walter
Map becomes an integral part of the text.[11] In the cycle as a whole
there is as yet no marked intervention by a named author or *transla-
teur*, as is to be found in the *Prose Tristan*. The formulae concerned
with the techniques of storytelling, the justification for inclusion or
exclusion of material, are still resolutely in the third person, although
in Micha 2 an explanation of the name "Crois Noire" ("Black Cross"),
placed within a quest for Lancelot by Gawain, is introduced by a
lengthy formula using *je* ("I"):

> Et quant il vienent a l'entree, si s'arestent a une crois que l'en
> apeloit la Crois Noire, et la raison por quoi ele fu ensi apelee vos
> deviserai je, kar se je le vos trespassoie, vos ne savriés mie le
> porquoi et por ce le vos conterai je, kar molt est bele a oïr.
> Il fu voirs que quant Joseph de Barimathie, le gentils chevaliers
> qui tant ama Jhesu Crist vint en la Grant Bretaigne o tot le pueple
> des crestiens qu'il amenoit des estranges contrees, qu'il vint
> droitement a la cité de Camaalot que li rois Agrestes tenoit . . .
>
> (Micha 2: 320–321)

> (And when they came to the way in, they halted by a cross called
> the Black Cross, and I shall tell you why it was called this, for if
> I failed to do so, you would not know the reason for the name;
> I will, therefore, give you the explanation, for it is well worth
> having.
> It was true that when Joseph of Arimathea, the noble knight
> who so loved Jesus Christ, came to Great Britain with all the band
> of Christians whom he was bringing from foreign countries, he
> came straight to the city of Camelot which was held by King
> Agrestes . . .)

This use of the first person in such formulae is unusual within this
romance, but will be developed very much further in the *Prose Tristan*, where there are many comments on methods of narration which
include first-person interventions. There is only a small beginning
here in the later branches of the *Prose Lancelot*. It is also noticeable
that it is at the point when the interlace starts to become somewhat
more relaxed that different versions begin to develop; this is in contrast with the situation in the text covering Lancelot's early adventures, culminating with his triumphant installation as knight of the

Round Table, where the variations, although often revealing, are on a small scale. In Micha 1, the tale still uses some of the familiar phrases as it leaves Lancelot to return to Gawain or moves from Galehaut back to Lancelot, but there is a subtle change as failure on a quest no longer necessarily excludes the knights' adventures from the narrative. Nor is the knights' testimony concerning events relevant to the tale of Lancelot presented in such comparatively straightforward terms. This means that the first account given by the tale of any particular episode can no longer be regarded as final and complete, but is subject to continuing modification within the narrative, and here I am not speaking of later scribal modifications. This presents an interesting parallel on the level of the interlace technique with a new requirement on the thematic level, as the Grail theme is given increasing importance: a requirement for Lancelot (and the reader) to reinterpret his earlier achievements in the light of the different demands of the greatest adventure of all and of the coming of a new Grail hero. Thus, the changing pattern of the narrative and the increasingly problematic nature of the text reflect the need, as the cycle develops, to question constantly earlier presentations of past events.

Notes

1. Carol J. Chase, "Multiple Quests and the Art of Interlacing in the 13th-century *Lancelot,*" *Kentucky Romance Quarterly* 33 (1981): 407–420; and "Sur la théorie de l'entrelacement: Ordre et désordre dans le *Lancelot en prose,*" *Modern Philology* 70 (1983): 227–241.

2. For treatment of interlace in general terms, see, for example, Ferdinand Lot, *Etude sur "Le Lancelot en prose"* (Paris: Champion, 1918), chapter 2; Eugene Vinaver, *The Rise of Romance* (Oxford: Oxford University Press, 1971), chapter 5; W. W. Ryding, *Structure in Medieval Narrative* (The Hague and Paris: Mouton, 1971); and E. Jane Burns, *Arthurian Fictions: Rereading the Vulgate Cycle* (Columbus: Ohio State University Press, 1985).

3. I propose to publish a study on interlace in medieval romance.

4. Elspeth Kennedy, *Lancelot and the Grail: A Study of the Prose Lancelot* (Oxford: Clarendon, 1986); issued as a paperback in 1990.

5. Elspeth Kennedy, ed., *Lancelot do Lac: The Non-Cyclic Old French Prose Romance* (Oxford, 1980); abbreviated as Kennedy and cited by page number.

6. Alexandre Micha, ed., *Lancelot: Roman en prose du XIIIe siècle,* 9 vols. (Paris and Geneva: Droz, 1978–1983); vols. 7 and 8 cover the same part of the text as my edition (see note 5).

7. Micha 1, sections 10 to 35.

8. I explored this subject in a paper at the Sixteenth International Arthurian Congress (Durham, 1990), "Rupture de la linéarité temporelle dans la technique narrative du cycle *Lancelot-Graal.*"

9. The reading of the Vatican manuscript relates to Kennedy 572.15, at

which point the manuscript moves from the noncyclic version to the cyclic version of the journey to Sorelois. It then goes back to the beginning of the journey to Sorelois, having already given the first few sentences of the noncyclic version. The following manuscripts give none of the noncyclic version and mark the beginning of the cyclic version in the following terms: "Et ce est la fin de la marche de gaule et recommence galehoux" ("And this is the end of the Marche de Gaule and Galehaut begins anew"), Paris, B. N. fr. 121; "si se repose li contes d'auz toz ici endroit et commence galehoult apres ici fenist la marche de gaule" ("and at this point the tale takes a break from them all and begins Galehaut after here finishing the Marche de Gaule"), Chicago, Newberry Library R 34; "si se repose li contes d'eus tous en si endroit. Explicit la marche de gaule" ("and at this point the tale takes a break from all of them. Explicit the Marche de Gaule"), Madrid, Bibl. Naz. 485; "Explicit la marche de gaule" ("Explicit the Marche de Gaule"), Paris, B. N. fr. 96. See Kennedy 2: 378–380. The use of *Galehaut* to designate the next part of the story does not, however, correspond with Dante's use of the title Galeotto in *Inferno*, canto 5, line 137, where he links it with the episode in which Lancelot and Guenevere kiss for the first time: "Galeotto fu il libro e chi lo scrisse."

10. Albert Pauphilet, ed., *La Queste del Saint Graal* (Paris: Champion, 1923): 195.22–24.

11. The colophon that precedes the opening of the *Queste del Saint Graal* and names Walter Map as the author of the *Lancelot Proper* only occurs in some manuscripts: "Si fenist ici Mestre Gautiers Map son livre et conmance le Graal" (Micha 6: 244, "Master Walter Map ends his book here and the Grail begins").

3. Age and the Ages of Life in the *Prose Lancelot*

Douglas Kelly

The *Prose Lancelot*—the *Lancelot Proper, Queste del Saint Graal*, and *Mort Artu*—uses topical narrative schemes like the *gradus amoris* and alternating meetings and quarrels between lovers in the *conservatio amoris* (as Andreas Capellanus understands it), as well as the stages in redemption in the *Queste*: contrition, confession, penance, and salvation. Other commonplace or custumal patterns follow or adapt those inherited from Chrétien and other verse romancers: hospitality, custom itself in its various kinds and varieties, combat and tournament, adventure and quest, and so on.[1] The schemes are not artificial. They do not impose rigid patterns onto recalcitrant narrative matter. Quite the contrary. Topical schemes admit diversity and, thus, striking inter- and intratextual reflection and reverberation. This is most obvious in the adaptations of the redemption scheme in the *Queste*. As Gawain, Lancelot, Bors, and Perceval undergo analogous adventures in the Grail quest, they respond differently to challenges and temptations, as, for example, when Gawain declines to do penance, but Lancelot accepts the full weight of it; or the different responses to temptation by Bors, chaste but not virginal and thus more experienced than the simple, yet naive (*nice*) Perceval. In the *Lancelot Proper*, the Corbenic experiences of the Grail ceremony establish different typologies for Gawain, too full with lust to see what passes before his eyes; Lancelot, able to see but not to comprehend; and Bors, who knows the Grail before the great quest even begins.

The diversity of topical schemes and of their narrative actualization is apparent not only for the major characters. My former student, Stacey Hahn, succeeded in showing as much in her thesis by analyzing numerous episodic loves in the *Lancelot Proper* and then studying Lancelot's and Guenevere's love in the light of that multicolored background.[2] Her work suggests that the lifelong biography of Lancelot may be illuminated through other topical schemes.

Here I have chosen to examine the scheme of the ages of life—the

so-called ages of man[3]—in Lancelot's career and that of other personages who appear and disappear in the *Prose Lancelot*. I wished to find
out first whether the careful chronology of events in the *Prose Lancelot*
was reflected in the numerical ages of Lancelot and other figures as
time passed. The careful narrative chronology uncovered by Ferdinand Lot has recently been confirmed by Alexandre Micha.[4] If it carries over to the different years of Lancelot's life and of other figures',
it would not be surprising.

However, what we discover seems at first disappointing. The chronology of Lancelot's years does not fit that of Arthurian adventures
(although it does not alter or contradict Lot's chronology either).
Rather, like the *Queste* and, to a lesser extent, the *Mort* (but for different reasons),[5] Lancelot's different ages are less numerically precise
and are occasionally even ambiguous. Age, it turns out, is not a matter of years, it is a matter of stages—stages in a scheme the Middle
Ages knew as the *cursus aetatis*, or "ages of life." As we shall see,
attributes like *petit, jeune, prodom, d'eage, vieux,* and *vieux et ancien*
("little, young, in the prime, elderly, old," and "old and aged") are
important in identifying age and in evaluating characters and the actions appropriate to those ages.

We may begin by looking at precise numerical indications of Lancelot's age in the *Prose Lancelot*. At three he is living with the Lady of
the Lake (Micha 7: 44, 70); at ten (Micha 7: 75) he is acting in an exemplary way. These are his years of "boines enfanches" (Micha 7: 75,
86, "good youthful achievements"). At eighteen (Micha 7: 243–244)
he goes to Arthur's court and becomes a knight, although later he is
said to have been fifteen at that time (Micha 1: 128).[6] Ferdinand Lot's
calculations support the age of eighteen; they also permit him to
make Lancelot twenty-eight during the *demoiselle guérisseuse* ("healing
damsel") episode (Lot 42).

The next precise date is found in the *Mort*. Lancelot has been bearing arms for twenty-five years when the tournament at Teneborc
takes place (*Mort* 46.27–28), which, if Lot is correct, would make him
forty-three years old. Later, at the judicial combat with Gawain at
Gaunes, he is fifty-five (*Mort* 158.58–62).

Two remarks: First, the three-year discrepancy regarding Lancelot's
age when he becomes a knight—eighteen or fifteen—is not significant in the overall narrative chronology; it is insignificant in the ages
of life scheme, as we shall see. Similarly, in the *Mort*, the fifteen years
between Lancelot's age after the tournament at Teneborc and that
when he fights Gawain is not improbable.

Second, precise age in years is not the principal concern of the author or authors of the *Prose Lancelot*, a fact which the chronological

precision makes obvious by contrast. Indeed, there are real discrepancies, if not impossibilities, that have crept in with some indications
of age for other personages. For example, Hector is younger than
Claudin during the invasion of Gaunes, yet older than Lancelot. But
Ban died of grief just after Lancelot's birth, and thus after the adultery
which occurred, therefore, before Lancelot's birth. In fact, Hector's
conception occurred at the time of Arthur's coronation (Micha 4:
223). But later, Hector, Lancelot's older half-brother, is unhorsed
by Claudas's son, Claudin, because Hector is "plus . . . juesnes et
tendres" (Micha 6: 140, "younger and less hardened"); yet Claudin
is not yet twenty-seven years old (Micha 6: 48) and thus younger
than Lancelot who, by Lot's calculations, is over twenty-eight (Lot
63–64). Such discrepancies bear out the presumption that the ages
of life scheme, not the number of years in a life, interests the au-
thor(s) more.

Now, the number of ages in medieval age of life schemes varies
considerably. Seven, the number we know today, is not so common
as three, four, six, or even ten, as Burrow shows. In the *Prose Lancelot*
itself we may discern about six fairly distinct ages, or designations for
ages, although the potential numerical equivalents are not fixed.
Some personages mature or advance faster and thus enter different
ages earlier. There is also rather great variation in usage of some attributes, especially *enfant* and *jeune*. Finally, topical variations and
evaluations occur within the specific ages from person to person. I
shall deal with these factors in turn, then apply the general findings
to Lancelot's own life. Let us begin again with numerical ages other
than Lancelot's and see how they are variously identified within the
cursus aetatis.

Bors and Lionel are respectively nine and twenty-one months old
when Claudas seizes their father's lands (Micha 7: 32). Hervis de Rivel
is still able to fight at eighty (Micha 8: 67). Galehaut becomes a knight
at twenty-five and dies at thirty-nine (Micha 1: 2). Ban commits adultery when he is fifty (Micha 2: 37; cf. 9: 354). Bors is twenty-one when
he rides in the cart (Micha 2: 93). The "Damoisele de Grant Aage"
("Damsel Advanced in Years") appears to be seventy years old (Micha
2: 273). Mordred is twenty when he first appears (Micha 2: 408). Three
women "de divers aages" ("of different ages") whom Guerrehés encounters at a fountain are, respectively, forty, sixty, and twenty years
old (Micha 4: 24). A marriage is contracted between two children
when he is six and she five (Micha 4: 180). A lady about a hundred
years old appears in another episode (Micha 4: 204). The daughter of
a giant is fifteen; her child is the biggest person in the country at
fourteen, and he becomes a knight at fifteen (Micha 4: 251–252). Bors

is baptized when he is no more than four months old (Micha 4: 274). Bademagu is admitted to the Round Table when he is forty-six (Micha 5: 5–6). A child's legitimacy can be tested when he is less than two years old, then knighted and crowned at eighteen (Micha 5: 87–89). A valet is said to be ten years old (Micha 5: 126). Bors sees Galahad when the latter is said to be ten months old (Micha 5: 254), and Bors's son is no more than two when Lancelot sees him for the first time (Micha 5: 295–296). While Arthur is preparing to invade Claudas's lands, "il ne pooit mie avoir plus de .L. anz" (Micha 6: 5–6, "He couldn't be more than fifty years old"), which makes him slightly younger than Bademagu, who is also in the invading army; it is A.D. 426[7] and Claudas's son, Claudin, is not yet twenty-seven (Micha 6: 48). Esclamor, who commands Claudas's fifth line of battle, is twenty years old (Micha 6: 86). Perceval is no more than fifteen when Agloval finds him at home (Micha 6: 183). On one occasion Arthur is served a meal by four knights who are, respectively, eighteen, thirty, forty, and eighty years old (Micha 6: 192). At about ten years of age Galahad leaves Corbenic for an abbey to be nearer to his father (Micha 6: 240–242). He remains there until he is fifteen (Micha 6: 243). At that time he comes to Arthur's court and the quest for the Holy Grail begins. When Perceval sees Mordrain during that quest, the latter appears to be 300 years old (*Queste* 82.27–28), but is actually over 400 (*Queste* 86.14–16). At the start of the *Mort* Guenevere is fifty (*Mort* 4.20–21). At the time of Lancelot's duel with Gawain, Arthur is ninety-two, Gawain seventy-six, and Lancelot twenty-one years younger than Gawain, that is, fifty-five (*Mort* 158.59–63). *Sauf erreur*, there are no more numerical ages in the *Prose Lancelot* editions currently available. The noncyclic *Lancelot* is essentially common with the cyclic version until Galehaut's departure from Arthur's court.[8] Thus, it agrees that Lancelot is eighteen when he goes to court but does not contain the later assertion that he was fifteen.[9]

Let us evaluate this information. By and large the age chronology is roughly plausible, although it does not always resist close scrutiny, as Ferdinand Lot demonstrated and we observed in the cases of Claudin and Hector. Likewise, if Arthur is in fact fifty at the time of the invasion of Claudas's lands, he could not be ninety-two at the time of the war with Lancelot in the *Mort* (Lot 62–63). Less than forty-two years pass between the two events. Furthermore, if in the *Mort* Lancelot is fifty-five when Arthur is ninety-two, Lancelot would have been only seventeen at the time of the first invasion, which makes him slightly younger than when he was dubbed. This may merely reflect the intervention of multiple authors or amplifying scribes. Yet given the accuracy of the chronology of episodes, it is astonishing.

One suspects that the ages are given not for the chronology but as part of a description of persons. They have topical, not temporal significance. At fifty, Guenevere is still the most beautiful woman in the world. Bademagu at forty-six is still able to fight with the best, "car il est encore en sa force et en son bon aage" (Micha 5: 5, "for he's still in his prime and at the peak of his powers"). Thus, age is a topical category that contributes to the description and identification of the "person."

Now, "person" does not convey any modern sense of individuality in Old French or in its rare occurrences in the *Prose Lancelot*. A passage from the *Mort* will clarify this point. Gaheriet remarks apropos of another knight: "il a bien persone d'ome qui poïst estre bons chevaliers" (*Mort* 23.38–39, "he does have the features of a man capable of being a good knight"). His "person" here identifies a type, a role, a mask, if you will; it is not a wanted-by-police description. In this passage, the words identify the person as a type (a knight) and evaluate how well he conforms to that type ("a good knight"), after qualifying the judgment—"qui poïst estre"—if actions and interior description bear out the judgment. Similarly, Bademagu's age tells us something about him as a knight in the prime of life. Age is a feature that identifies the type.

Lancelot's ages are given in the same way. Even the same numbers recur, often merely in variations of fives and tens, with nothing specific between his twenty-eighth and fifty-fifth years. We see him at three, ten, eighteen or fifteen (knighthood), seven years later (twenty-five or twenty-two, Micha 1: 353), and no older than twenty-six (Micha 4: 165). The discrepancy between eighteen and fifteen presents no real problem, since both fit into the period when one is usually knighted. In the *Prose Lancelot*, the dubbing of knights customarily occurs from about fifteen to about twenty-five.[10] Thirty is too late according to Agloval: "trop seroit granz domages, se si biaux anfes . . . usoit sa jouvente entor sa mere . . . ; et se il passe l'aage de jovente et il vient en l'aage de .XXX. anz, que il ne soit dedenz celui terme acoustumez de chevalerie, ja puis ne porra venir a bonté d'armes" (Micha 6: 184, "it would be a great misfortune for such a handsome young man to waste his youth by staying with his mother; and if he leaves his youth and reaches thirty years of age, he will never thereafter achieve excellence in arms"). The reference to *jouvente* locates age in the context of the *cursus aetatis*, not, as it were, the *cursus annorum*. *Jouvente* appears to end, or to be an age too late to begin practicing knighthood, at thirty. Does thirty mark the end of *jouvente* in the *Prose Lancelot*? What are the ages of life in the *Prose Lancelot*?

The language is indeed slippery. A coherent terminology seems at first to elude us. But, taking into account context, the usage in matters of age does evince an overall coherence that we can appreciate and use to evaluate conduct that is appropriate to or even prescribed for specific ages or conduct that is inappropriate and decried. For example, Agloval's reflections on Perceval's age identify one age, its limits, and conduct appropriate to it: *jouvente* comes to an end at about thirty. Prior to that age is a time for the training and dubbing of knights. To wait beyond that limit would be wrong. Later, at court, Perceval is located in a larger spectrum of ages. Four knights who serve at Arthur's meal in Karadigan are distinguished by their four ages (".IIII. aage," Micha 6: 192): eighteen, thirty, forty, and eighty. Perceval himself sits together with the "juesnes," a group that would include the eighteen-year-old knight serving Arthur, but, presumably, exclude the thirty-year-old serving knight who, in Agloval's estimation, would have passed the "aage de jouvente" ("age of youth"). The *jeune* Perceval also "avoit la chiere simple[11] et resambloit bien simple creature" (Micha 6: 193, "had a guileless look and seemed a totally unpretentious person"); later there is anxiety about his fate alone in the woods because he had not yet attained the "age d'ome" ("manhood"), and may have to endure more travail than befits his age—he is *tendre*, not *dur* or *fort* enough (Micha 6: 198).

Let us pause a moment to reflect on the rhetorical context of the *cursus aetatis*. Burrow and Dove both point out that most writers in the High Middle Ages acquired their knowledge of the age topos from the rhetorical tradition (Burrow 2–10; Dove 28–30). Among the ancient sources available to medieval writers were Cicero and Horace. They transmitted the commonplace to later times, in which it continued to flourish. In fact, Matthew of Vendôme identifies age—*aetas*—as a topos. One example contrasts nicely with Perceval—"Ab etate, ut apud Ovidium: 'A iuvene et cupido credatur reddita virgo' " (*Ars versificatoria* 1.82, "Using the topos of age, as in Ovid: 'Could one believe a maid would return a virgin from a lusty youth' ").[12] *Iuvenis* marks the age and explains conduct (cf. *Ars* 1.115), as does *vir* ("man") elsewhere in Matthew (1:82). Number of years is not essential to the identification, although it is, of course, implicit. Ovid's young man and Perceval differ because Perceval has a virtuous simplicity, Ovid's "youth" an uncontrollable sexual drive—he is *cupidus*. Perceval's simple manner is therefore not synonymous with his being *nice*, a trait mentioned only once (*Queste* 112.26). Lancelot calls himself *nice* when he first came to court, but says that he changed when he fell in love with Guenevere (Micha 5: 3). In another passage, Matthew of Vendôme, still following Horace, insists that one assign attributes in complementary groupings. Thus, Ovid's *iuvenis* is *cupidus*, just as Perceval's virginity squares with his simplicity in spite of his age. As Horace recommended:

> Ne forte seniles
> Mandentur iuveni partes pueroque viriles,
> Semper in adiunctis evoque morabimus aptis.
>
> (*Ad Pisones* 176–178, from *Ars* 1.43)

(Lest the features of an old man be assigned to a youth or those of a mature man to a boy, we shall maintain attributes appropriate to each age.)

How does this injunction square with Arthur's, Gawain's, and even Lancelot's "virility" on the field of battle at, respectively, ninety-two, seventy-six, and fifty-five years of age? Burrow identifies the representation of age in terms of upward and downward transcendence (Burrow ch. 3), which, in topical invention, admits as opposite upward and downward degeneration. The former occurs on either the *puer senex* model, when a younger person acquires the physical or spiritual strength of an older person, or when an older person is capable of the achievement of tasks normally fit for a younger person. The obvious examples of the former are Galahad and Perceval—so different from the normal "*iuvenis cupidus virginum*" among Arthur's knights, especially those in King Lot's family. Galahad's extraordinary beauty and achievements immediately place him before all others in the Grail quest despite his fifteen years (*Queste* 23.7–21), a position he maintains until his death. Similar achievements on the mundane sphere are evident in the strength of Arthur, Gawain, and Lancelot despite their ages in the *Mort*. They manifest downward transcendance as older men with the strength of youth.

In the *Lancelot Proper* there are similar examples of transcendence. Bertholais the Elder provokes astonishment and even disgust when, in advanced age, he offers to defend the claims of the False Guenevere in battle. Gawain doesn't like this at all: "si li ennuie molt de ce qu'il le voit si viel" ("it distresses him to see the man to be so old"). And Dodinel "le tint a grant desdaing" ("scorned it") and "a craché par despit environ lui" ("spat in disgust"), then exclaimed derisively: "Sire, j'ai pensé qui fera la bataille encontre cel chevalier: Rioul de Caus qui n'est mie trop jovenes, et cil Rioul fu prisiés d'armes ançois que vostre peres fust chevaliers et plus a de dis ans qu'il ne leva de lit. Si les metés ensemble, se vos volés veoir bataille de deus homes mors" (Micha 1: 30–31, "My lord, I've thought of someone to fight this knight. Rioul of Caus isn't too young; he was renowned in arms before your father became a knight and has been bedridden for ten years. Pit them against one another if you want to see two dead men fight"). Bertholais, unmoved by the laughter and scorn, maintains his offer. Despite the commonplaces of advanced age—white hair, pale, lined face marked by old wounds, long beard—the old knight "a les bras lons et les espaules bien formees et est si bien fes de tos menbres que miels nel puissiés deviser; si estoit merveilles grans et corsus et drois et espers en son estant plus que l'en ne peust cuidier de si viel home" (Micha 1: 24, "has long arms, his shoulders are well-formed, and he is so well shaped that you couldn't imagine anyone better. And he was amazingly tall and muscular, erect and agile—more so than you might expect from such an old man"). Bertholais has the physical shape of a knight in the prime of life.

Bademagu is also such a knight. At the time of the first invasion of Gaul in the *Lancelot Proper* "il est encore en sa force et en son bon aage come cil qui n'a mie plus de .XLVI. anz" (Micha 5: 5–6, "he is still in his prime and at the peak of his powers, being no more than forty-six years old"). Mary Dove has shown that the "perfect age" falls in the middle of life (Dove 19; on women, see ch. 3). This seems to be the case in the *Prose Lancelot*. The "young knight" (*jeune*) rarely has the experience or the moral or physical strength found in knights between, say, thirty and the midfifties. Thus a young "bacheler" like Lambegue, "qui enfes estoit" ("who was a youth"), could not sustain the blows of his uncle Pharien, "qui grans chevaliers et fors estoit" (Micha 7: 168, "who was a big, strong knight"). Similarly, Mordred, when he appears on the scene as a twenty-year-old knight, cannot endure the great heat of day because he has not learned to bear great distress (Micha 2: 408). Later, Lancelot fears for Bors, who appears "jones anfes et tandres" (Micha 5: 19, "a young, unhardened youth") when he goes to fight the giant Malduit. Later still, Claudin is able to unhorse Hector because the latter "plus ert juesnes et tendres" (Micha 6: 140; cf. pp. 149–150, "was younger and less hardened") than his opponent who is nearing thirty. Perceval also provokes anxiety because of his "tenderness" (Micha 6: 198; but cf. pp. 199–200). But Perceval, like Galahad and Bors before him, is "upwardly transcendent": his "virtues," in the sense of the *Queste*, give him the strength and ability to achieve what his elders, but not betters, attain only after training, experience, and time. Others like Galehodin try to win the company of a renowned knight in order to learn from him while gaining the experience necessary to be a *preudome* in their prime: "je sui jones hom et sai encore poi des armes: si avroie mestier d'acointier moi d'.I. si prodome com il est, por ce qu'il m'en apreist et por ce que j'en amanderoie de lui et de sa compaingnie" (Micha 4: 195, "I'm a young man and still know very little about fighting. I need to seek the company of a man as valiant as he, so he'll teach me and so I'll increase my honor by his company").

The *preudome* in the *Prose Lancelot* is the ideal. The notion embodies something of Matthew of Vendôme's *vir, virilis*, including virtue and prime of life. Erich Köhler devotes an excursus to the *preudome* topic.[13] He concentrates on Chrétien's use of the word, but does bring in the *Prose Lancelot* somewhat. However, his focus on Chrétien precludes consideration of the age topos that is prominent in the *Prose Lancelot's* evaluation of the *preudome*.

It is noteworthy, first of all, that there was a distinction between the person who is *preu* and the *preudome*. Köhler identifies the distinction in Joinville's *Life of Saint Louis*. Joinville's distinction is analogous to that made in the *Prose Lancelot*. I shall therefore analyze it briefly here, then demonstrate the correlation between Joinville's usage and that in the *Prose Lancelot*.[14]

Joinville distinguishes between "*preudome*" and "*preu home*." The latter includes many knights both Christian and pagan.

> Diex donne grant don et grant grace au chevalier crestïen que il seuffre estre vaillant de cors et que il seuffre en son service en li gardant de pechié mortel; et celi qui ainsi se demeinne doit l'on appeler preudome, pour ce que ceste proesse li vient dou don Dieu. Et ceus de cui j'ai avant parlei puet l'on appeler preuz homes, pour ce que il sont preu de lour cors et ne doutent Dieu ne pechiés.
>
> (Andrieux-Riex 114; cf. Köhler 135 n. 7)

> (God bestows a great gift and high grace on the Christian knight by allowing him to be valiant in His service without incurring mortal sin. Such a person should be called a *preudome*, for his worth comes from God. Those whom I spoke of can be called *preuz homes* because they are valiant and fear neither God nor sin.)

The analogy with the *Queste* is obvious, I should think; but in the pre-*Queste* *Lancelot Proper* and in the *Mort* the distinction is less obvious and, in some parts, not obvious at all.[15] However, the distinction is there insofar as the text recognizes knights who are *preu* but have not yet attained the perfection—the prime of life—of the *preudome*. For example, Claudas tells the young Lambegue: "se tu vivoies par eage, tu seroies assés preudom" (Micha 7: 225; cf. Dufournet 148–153, "if you lived long enough you would be a very worthy man"). Kay later says that a "preudomme" (Micha 7: 300) is better equipped than a "joines hons" ("young man") by experience and strength to accomplish certain tasks. Thus, an older knight "mellé de caignes" ("greyhaired") can seem to be a "preudom" (Micha 7: 344).

A young man, although not yet a *preudome*, can therefore be "preu" (Micha 8: 256; cf. pp. 266–267, 272). This and the examples in the preceding paragraph occur as well in the noncyclic *Prose Lancelot*, no doubt in Joinville's sense of *preu home*—that is, a man strong enough to perform well in a joust. This excludes the mental equipment, the aristocratic *san*, possessed by the older *preudome*. The idea is implicit in these words addressed to Lambegue by Pharien:[16]

> Et se tu viens en bataille ou en poigneis de guerre ou en lieu ou la grant chevalerie soit assamblee, garde que ja n'i atendes plus jone ne plus viel de toi, mais fier devant tous les autres des esperons por faire .I. biau caup la ou tu poras ataindre, car a pris et a henor d'armes ne doit nus atendre ne jone ne viel por conquerre honor et pris, mais as grans consaus douner doivent li enfant entendre as plus viex.
>
> (Micha 7: 151–152)

> (If you get into combat, war, or in some great gathering of knights, do not wait on anyone younger or older than you, but spur on before all the others to strike a fine blow wherever you can. For when renown and honor are at stake, one should wait on neither young nor old to gain honor and renown in arms. But the young must defer to the oldest men in giving counsel.)

It is consistent with this counsel that even the mature knights on the Grail quest consult *preudomes*—usually hermits who have left knighthood, arming themselves not with sword and spear, but with the arms of the Lord which are used to say mass and administer confession.

Joinville insists on the efficacy of grace in distinguishing between the *preudome* and the *preu home*. Grace makes the *preudome* strong. Thus a hermit is "si vielz et de si grant aage que cil qui l'esgardent dient qu'il n'oïrent onques mes parler de nul si viel home; et neporquant moult estoit encore vertueus de son aage" (Micha 5: 219, "so old and on in years that those who observe him say that they have never heard tell of such an old man; and yet he was still very strong

The Ages of Life

	Petit ("small")	Enfant ("child")	Jeune ("young")	Preudome ("prime")	Vieux ("old")	Vieux et ancien ("old and aged")
Age (in years)	ca. 0–10	10–15	15–30	30–50	50–70	70+

for his years"). This would make him a *preudome* in Joinville's sense, his virtue giving him transcendental force. Another hermit who had left secular knighthood for the hermitage and the hair shirt, albeit old and white-haired, can, when called upon by his brother, take up arms again for a time and contribute decisively to the defeat of his brother's aggressor. He then returns to the hermitage to face more formidable attacks. Yet his strength—here we can confidently say his virtue—is such that swords cannot cut him nor fire burn him or his clothing (*Queste* 118–122). He has the transcendental virtue of a saint despite old age and white hair. He is a *preudome*, not merely a *preu home*.

Before concluding with Lancelot's biography, let us schematize the age vocabulary used in the *Prose Lancelot* as it emerges from references to age and the ages of life (see table). The different ages fit the topical suggestions in the examples adduced heretofore while taking into account possibilities for upward and downward transcendence and overlap. For example, "en eage d'estre chevalier" ("old enough to be a knight") may refer to an "enfant" or a "jeune," just as a "chevalier" ("knight") or an "ermite" ("hermit") covers more than one age. Similarly, "petit enfant" ("small child") may be, say, from five to twelve years of age, a person in the "meilleur age" ("prime") may be a "preudome" or even a "vieux," and another "d'eage" ("adult") or "de grant eage" ("advanced in years") may be in his or her prime or beyond.

One kind of designation is omitted. There does not seem to be a specific age for words like *seigneur, dame, pucele,* and *damoisele* ("lord, lady, maid, damsel"). Although these titles usually apply to the most obvious ages, they need not, as the following examples demonstrate: "la vielle damoisele au Cercle d'Or" (Micha 4: 362, "the Old Damsel of the Golden Circle") and the "Damoisele de Grant Aage" (Micha 2: 273, "Damsel of Great Age") who appears to be seventy years old. Elsewhere a vavasor addresses his children who are to provide Lancelot with lances at the Pannigue tournament as "seingnor anfant" (Micha 5: 218, "my young lords"). However, I have detected no confusion regarding *petit, enfant, jeune, preudome, vieux,* or *vieux et ancien.* There is only overlap which does not transcend the bordering category.

Now let us evaluate Lancelot's ages, his *cursus aetatis,* as they appear in the *Prose Lancelot.* As *petit* or *enfant petit,* Lancelot has remarkable qualities. Indeed, the "talents" or virtues with which the *Queste* hermit says he was born come to the fore. After ten years of age, having reached the "eage de bachelerie" (Micha 7: 71, "age of a bachelor in arms"), Lancelot began to exercise arms. He distinguishes himself in every way as a chivalrous *puer senex:* "ne faisoit il gaires choses qui n'apartenissent a boines enfanches" (Micha 7: 75; cf. p. 86, "he did virtually nothing unsuitable to good conduct in a young man"). He also speaks well and nobly (Micha 7: 76–77; cf. 7: 127).[17]

In the context imposed by the *Queste* then, Lancelot fails to realize his promise as *puer senex* when he arrives at Arthur's court at eighteen (or fifteen). He is now in his *jouvente* in Perceval's sense; but, unlike Perceval, he falls in love with Guenevere and becomes a *"iuvenis cupidus."* At least that is how the *Queste* hermit judges him (*Queste* 125.32–126.3). The moral psychology that explains Lancelot's degeneration is set forth by the hermit on the authority of the parable of talents. His love eats away, as it were, at his virtues. Together with the reports of the *preudomes* and the growing wrongs perpetrated by Round Table knights, Lancelot's love itself becomes the source of foolish excesses and even, in the *Agravain* section, of madness.

As the *Queste* author describes Lancelot's life, a royal way was open to Lancelot had he not sinned. He would first achieve the quest for the Holy Grail, a quest which takes place when he is in his early forties, that is, in his prime; then, like Perceval, he would take on the arms of the Lord to withdraw into a monastery or hermitage. Such exceptional accomplishments would be consistent with his promise as a *puer senex* and with the example of other *preudomes* who abandon knighthood for the hermit's life at that age. His upward transcendence would have been evident in the *Queste* and the *Mort.* He would have been a hermit throughout the *Mort,* rather than only at the end when, after his definitive separation from Guenevere, the passing of Arthur, and the end of Round Table knighthood (*Mort* 201–202), Lancelot becomes a priest and retires into a hermitage to await death. He dies there after four years or more (*Mort* 201. 46–47). Since he was fifty-five at the time of the duel with Gawain, he would then be about sixty, *vieux* but not yet *ancien.*

Scholarly opinion generally holds to the view that the *Prose Lancelot* is the product of several hands, each writing according to a different conception of the morality of Lancelot's love for Guenevere. My reading has been from the point of view of the whole work as we know it through Micha's, Pauphilet's, and Frappier's editions. But however one imagines the execution of the three branches of the *Prose Lancelot*—multiple authors writing independently, an *atelier* of scribes more or less subject to the wishes of a controlling architect, an evolution in the author's, authors', or architect's conception of the work, or even a single author—one cannot but admire the skill with which the earlier secular idealism is gradually undermined in favor of the harsh morality of the *Queste* hermits who condemn Lancelot and, through him and Guenevere, the Round Table. What appears to be upward transcendence in secular chivalry becomes degeneration according to the ethos of the *Queste*.

Allegory requires rereading, and that is the key to the ultimate triumph of the *Queste* ethos. With our awareness of the ages of life and the example of good knights at any given stage in the *cursus aetatis*, even in the earliest part of the cycle, we can recognize the moments in which Lancelot strays from the path of the life foreseen, but not predestined, for him. Lancelot comes upon his first hermit[18] during the Dolorous Guard episode, while wandering "mas et pensis" (Micha 7: 355, "downcast and preoccupied") because he fears Guenevere is angry with him: "Li hermites estoit de grant eage, si avoit esté chevaliers, .I. des plus biaus del monde, si s'estoit rendus en son millor eage por une perte qui avenue li estoit de .XII. fiex que il avoit eus, si les vit morir tous dedens .I. an" (Micha 7: 355, "The hermit was well on in years. He had been a knight—one of the most handsome—and had become a hermit in his prime because he had lost twelve sons, all of whom he had seen die within one year"). The misfortune adumbrates the *mescheances* of the *Queste* and *Mort*. In them Lancelot, too, loses not only Guenevere, but almost all his brothers in arms, after which he too chooses the hermitage. Viewed from the end of the *Mort*, his encounter with the first hermit is not unlike Julien Sorel's encounter with the newspaper clipping in the church he stops at on the way to the Rênal house (in Stendhal's *The Red and the Black*). Both are warnings.

The ages of life enunciated in the *Prose Lancelot* suggest a narrative coherence extending from Lancelot's birth to his death. Signs of moral and aristocratic transcendence mark the *puer senex* before he arrives at Arthur's court. Then he falls in love with the queen. On this new path, Lancelot gradually declines from what he was as he follows a different way from that which he was supposed to take. Growing folly and confusion in love counterpoint warnings that Lancelot does not heed about his state and that of the Round Table as the great quest approaches. He still believes in the *Agravain* section that his sin with Guenevere permits him to achieve greater good than would have been possible without her love (Micha 5: 3). If Lancelot were right, sin would bring more good than would virtue! In the *Queste* the truth is revealed. A hermit *preudome* explains that the origin and causes of Lancelot's degeneration lie in his love for Guenevere, whereupon Lancelot makes a sincere effort to atone for his sin and to eschew love. But when he returns to court, he quickly backslides. Already approaching old age, his love is more foolish and less careful than it had been before the quest. Lancelot does not become a hermit until all further contact with Guenevere is impossible.

This analysis and evaluation of Lancelot's life—what he did and what he should have done at its various ages—does not prove the coherence of the *Prose Lancelot*, but it is consistent with the evaluation of his biography at the various stages of the plot. It is a gradual undermining of a secular conception of chivalry based on love in favor of a new chivalry based on virtue. The *Prose Lancelot* authors—or author or architect—learned from Chrétien's *Charrette* how to reveal narrative truth gradually and slowly. As the Lancelot-Grail cycle develops, bringing together in one great complex structure the main twelfth-century Arthurian themes,[19] narrative truth is gradually and slowly revealed as time passes and ages succeed one another.[20]

Notes

1. Matilda Tomaryn Bruckner, *Narrative Invention in Twelfth-Century French Romance: The Convention of Hospitality (1160–1200)*, French Forum Monographs, 17 (Lexington, Ky.: French Forum, 1980); Katalin Halász, *Structures narratives chez Chrétien de Troyes*, Studia romanica Universitatis Debreceniensis de Ludovico Kossuth nominatae: series litteraria, 7 (Debrecen, Hungary: Kossuth Lajos Tudományegyetem, 1980); Donald Maddox, *The Arthurian Romances of Chrétien de Troyes: Once and Future Fictions*, Cambridge Studies in Medieval Literature, 12 (Cambridge: Cambridge University Press, 1991).

2. "Patterned Diversity: Hierarchy and Love in the Prose 'Lancelot'," dissertation, University of Wisconsin at Madison, 1988; see *Dissertation Abstracts International*, 49A (1988–1989): 1796.

3. Two recent studies provide good introductions to the topic as well as additional bibliography: J. A. Burrow, *The Ages of Man: A Study in Medieval Writing and Thought* (Oxford: Clarendon Press, 1986); Mary Dove, *The Perfect Age of Man's Life* (Cambridge: Cambridge University Press, 1986). See as well Arnulf Stefenelli, *Der Synonymenreichtum der altfranzösischen Dichtersprache*, Proceedings of the Österreichische Akademie der Wissenschaften: philosophisch-historische Klasse, 251.5 (Vienna: Böhlaus, 1967): 56–74; Micheline de Combarieu, "Le *Lancelot* comme roman d'apprentissage: enfance,

démesure et chevalerie," in *Approches du Lancelot en prose,* edited by Jean Dufournet, Unichamp 6 (Paris: Champion, 1984): 101–136.

4. Ferdinand Lot, *Etude sur "Le Lancelot en Prose,"* Bibliothèque de l'Ecole des Hautes Etudes, 226 (Paris: Champion, 1918): 29–64; Micha, *Essais sur le cycle du Lancelot-Graal,* Publications romanes et françaises, 179 (Geneva: Droz, 1987), ch. 4; Elspeth Kennedy, *Lancelot and the Grail: A Study of the Prose Lancelot* (Oxford: Clarendon Press, 1986): 201, especially n. 26 (p. 361) which contains additional bibliography.

5. See Albert Pauphilet, *Etudes sur "La Queste del Saint Graal"* (Paris: Champion, 1921): 163–167; Jean Frappier, *Etude sur "La Mort le roi Artu," Roman du XIIIe Siècle,* 2d ed., Publications romanes et françaises, 70 (Geneva: Droz, 1968): 351–360.

6. He has been a knight for seven years at Micha 1: 353, and he is no more than twenty-six years old at Micha 4: 165.

7. Or A.D. 435; see Micha 6: 5–6, note to section 9.

8. See Elspeth Kennedy, ed., *Lancelot do Lac: The Non-Cyclic Old French Prose Romance,* 2 vols. (Oxford: Clarendon Press, 1980), vol. 2, ch. 2; *Lancelot and the Grail,* 7–8.

9. Kennedy vol. 1, 138.37–38, 139.2–3, 139.14; cf. 602–603.

10. Bors is knighted at twenty-one (Micha 2: 93), Perceval at fifteen (Micha 6: 183, 191), Galahad at fifteen (Micha 6: 243), Galehaut at twenty-five (Micha 1: 2); others become knights at comparable ages (Micha 4: 252, 5: 89).

11. Cf. Micha 6: 183 and Galahad in *Queste* 2.30–31. *Simple* and *simplece* are not negative attributes in these passages.

12. Franco Munari, ed., *Ars versificatoria,* vol. 3 of *Mathei Vindocinensis opera,* Storia e letteratura: raccolta di studi e testi, 171 (Rome: Storia e letteratura, 1988); Munari keeps the same section numbers as Faral's earlier edition.

13. Erich Köhler, *Ideal und Wirklichkeit in der höfischen Epik: Studien zur Form der frühen Artus–und Graldichtung,* 2d ed., supplement to the Zeitschrift für romanische Philologie, 97 (Tübingen: Niemeyer, 1970), pp. 129–138.

14. See as well Nelly Andrieux-Reix, *Ancien français: fiches de vocabulaire* (Paris: PUF, 1987): 112–118. To her references, add Glyn S. Burgess, *Contribution à l'étude du vocabulaire pré-courtois,* Publications romanes et françaises, 110 (Geneva: Droz, 1970): 91–103; Köhler's excursus (see n. 13); Jean Dufournet, ed., "Un personnage exemplaire et complexe du *Lancelot:* Pharien," *Approches du Lancelot,* 137–156; and Pierre Gallais, *L'imaginaire d'un romancier françaisde la fin du XIIe siècle: description raisonnée, comparée et commentée de la "Continuation-Gauvain" (Première suite du "Conte du graal" de Chrétien de Troyes),* 4 vols., Faux titre 33, 34, 36, 39 (Amsterdam: Rodopi, 1988–1989): 1543–1545, 1801–1802.

15. See the examples for the noncyclic *Lancelot do Lac,* ed. Elspeth Kennedy, vol. 2, 475.

16. On the relation between Pharien and Lambegue, see Dufournet 148–153.

17. In this Lionel and Bors are Lancelot's equals (Micha 7: 145–146; cf. 7: 193–194; 7: 197).

18. See Micha 9: 59, s.v. *"ermite."*

19. Elspeth Kennedy shows how the noncyclic *Prose Lancelot* sets an example for such thematic intertextuality in *Lancelot and the Grail*, especially part 1.

20. I am very grateful to Elspeth Kennedy for her informed comments on and corrections of the first version of this paper. She is, of course, in no way responsible when I inadvertently trip or obstinately bump against obvious beams.

4. The Narration of Youthful Exploits in the *Prose Lancelot*

François Suard
Translated by Arthur F. Crispin

Youthful Exploits:
Limits of the Narrative and the Models Used

While it is relatively easy to determine the moment when the narrative of youthful exploits[1] begins—since any mention of the hero, however young he may be, points to and foreshadows his future fame—the end of this period is less easily determined.

Indeed, at what moment and based on what criterion should the end of the hero's youthful exploits be proclaimed? Should it be when he is knighted? Or after his first heroic deeds?[2] Should his initiation in love (which, as we know, was of major importance for Lancelot) be taken into account, and at which point should we consider it completed? And finally, should Claudas's attack against Lancelot's parents and cousins—redressed only at the end of the romance[3] and taking place at the time of Queen Elaine's last visit to her son Lancelot and her nephews Bors and Lionel—remain outside the theme of youthful exploits, although the victory over the despoiler and the severing of the relationship with the mother[4] clearly contribute, at some level, to bringing our heroes into adulthood? Using such reasoning, it would be easy to consider the *Lancelot Proper* in its entirety as a narrative of youthful exploits. However, the romance warns us against such conclusions by showing us, at certain moments in the story, that the hero has stepped out of youthful exploits, even though his adventures have barely begun: victor at the Dolorous Guard, and lover of Guenevere, Lancelot is already an accomplished knight when he becomes involved in the adventure of the cart (Micha 2: 11–13). The same is true for Bors when he confronts the giant Malduit (Micha 5: 18–23), and for Lionel when he plays the role of skillful mediator between Lancelot and the maiden who heals him (Micha 4: 151–155).[5] This paradoxical connection between situations that are typical of youthful exploits and characters who have already entered adulthood allows us to discover in the work the presence of several types of youthful exploit narratives, which are concentrated at times but spread out through the romance at other times. This explains why some youthful exploit themes may show up late in the romance, at a time when the heroes have clearly gone beyond the youthful exploits stage.

First, we recognize a model of the *epic* type, present at the beginning and at the end of the romance. Still outside the group of knights, the young man reveals his valor through remarks full of wisdom, like little Gui in the *Chanson de Guillaume*: "Cors as d'enfant e raisun as de ber" ("You are like a child, but you have great wisdom").[6] He also gives a hint of his strength and courage by resorting to acts of violence against those who are disrespectful toward him or who try to prevent him from engaging in battle too soon. Here he might be compared with Aymeri in *Girart de Viane* or Ogier in the *Chevalerie Ogier*.

Contaminated by a model of *folkloric* type, a variant of the epic scheme prevents the future hero from revealing his bravery to his family. As a result of treason or of someone despoiling him of his rightful inheritance, the hero is forced to flee into exile and prove himself in the service of a foreign ruler (for example, Mainet with the emir Galafre[7] or Beuve de Hantonne with the king of Armenia).[8]

A second model is exclusively of the *folkloric* type and endows the hero with a fabulous origin, making him the son of a human being and a fairy. This is the case for Tydorel, born out of the union of a water sprite and a queen; he must later discover the identity of his real father. As for Yonec, son of Muldumarec,[9] he is called upon to avenge the man-bird who fathered him. In fact, in this case we also detect connections between different models, since the story of Yonec involves the theme of despoliation later redressed by vengeance.

The third model is of the *romantic* type. It exists in works which, in the manner of the *Roman d'Alexandre* or Chrétien's *Conte du Graal*, give major importance to the hero's childhood. First outlined in the history of Alexander, the conqueror of Greece and of the Persian empire, this approach is stressed in the Perceval plot, which, as we know, includes three sorts of youthful exploits: chivalrous exploits— from the questioning of the knights in the forest to his knighting by Gornemant; amorous exploits—starting with the kisses stolen from the maiden in the tent to the "reveries"; and finally, what could be called accrediting exploits, preparatory to the Grail adventure— awareness of failures, useless wanderings, conversion—whose ending Chrétien did not give us.

These three models have certain elements in common, particularly the element of the *puer senex*[10] who, through his words or actions, questions the apparent order of things, underscoring its deep flaws. Above all, they share a double object: to suggest a critical observation of the romance's action and of the characters in the romance through a frequently contentious confrontation of the young hero and his milieu, and to anticipate, based on elaborate foreshadowing, the revelation of the hero.

Thus, in the *Prose Lancelot*, youthful exploits are at the same time a narrative and the promise of a narrative. One can imagine the broad range of possible readings, at various stages of the plot, afforded by the introduction into the text of an essentially multifocused narration. We shall now examine a few of these readings.

Youthful Exploits: The Beginning of the Story

Bound to a biographical perspective by the desire to build a coherent whole around a few essential characters, the author naturally concentrates the tales of youthful exploits at the beginning of his work. These narratives foreshadow the exceptional bravery of the three men who, in various degrees, are the mainstays of the *Lancelot Proper* as well as the Lancelot-Grail: Lancelot and his cousins, Bors and Lionel.[11]

The theme of the *puer senex* has a significant place in this part of the romance, as is shown, for example, by the exemplary remarks made by Lancelot to the vavasor whose horse was taken and who, as a result, would be unable to defend his honor at King Claudas's court: "Nus haus cuers ne se doit esmaier de perte qu'il puisse recovrer" (Micha 7: 76, "no noble hearted man should worry about a loss he can make good"). This causes the vavasor to ask himself: "qui chis enfes estoit qui iert si jones et qui si hautes paroles li avoit dites" (Micha 7: 76, "who was this child who was so young and yet spoke such noble words to him").

Acts of violence also occur, such as Lancelot lashing back at his tutor after the latter had struck him and, more significantly, his greyhound (Micha 7: 82–83), or the brawl initiated by Lionel and Bors in Claudas's palace, which results notably in the death of Claudas's son, Dorin (Micha 7: 118).

The parallel development of the three stories of youthful exploits and the different levels of influence of the models used in each case allow the author to make subtle distinctions between the three cousins. Lionel seems to harbor the greatest violence: "Et che fu li plus deffernés cuers d'enfant qui onques fust que Lyonel" (Micha 7: 108, "And Lionel had the wildest heart of any youth"). At the same time, he is the one who most resembles Lancelot: "ne nus ne retraist on-

ques si naturelment a Lancelot" (Micha 7: 108, "but no one more resembled Lancelot").

In Micha 7: 81–82, Lancelot violently breaks off with his tutor and
justifies himself to the Lady of the Lake, saying that "cuers d'omme
ne puet a grant honor venir, qui trop longement est sous maistre ne
sous maistresse" (Micha 7: 85, "a man cannot aspire to high honor if
he stays too long under the tutelage of a master or mistress"). Bors
and Lionel, on the other hand, waste away under the protection of
Ninianne while deprived of their tutors (Micha 7: 173); the lady must
summon Lambegue and Pharien, and when the latter, Lionel's tutor,
is unable to come, the child is most upset.

We can see that differences between the three youths are used by
the writer to problematize a question: how far can the traditional
model of chivalrous education dispensed by a male tutor be followed?
The fact that Ninianne, a woman, gives Lancelot a splendid lesson
in chivalry (Micha 7: 248–255) raises questions about traditional education but does not entirely negate it, since Bors and Lionel remain
totally dependent upon it.

The relationship between nature and nurture is subject to reconsid-
eration. Contrary to his cousins, Lancelot does not know his identity,
but his noble nature—his heart—draws him relentlessly toward the
high calling of which he is still unaware. He says, referring to the
royal lineage which Ninianne denies him after the dispute with his
tutor, "Mes cuers l'osast bien estre" (Micha 7: 85, "My heart would
dare aspire to it").

Still, his noble nature must be subjected to education, and his desire to become a knight (explained in Micha 7, chapter 21a) is aroused
by the speech of the Lady of the Lake, which introduces to him a
history—that of chivalry—which will soon be his and, through the
metaphoric interpretation of the warrior's weapons, the duties of
knighthood. This could not have been revealed by the heart alone.
Thus, nurture retains its importance, but the question is raised of
who may dispense it.

Replaced entirely by the Lady of the Lake in the case of Lancelot,
the traditional tutor is supplemented in the cases of Lionel and Bors.
At the moment when Lionel grieves over the absence of Pharien, he
discovers the wound that Saraïde (Ninianne's envoy to Claudas) received while saving his life. From now on, he will belong to her,
for "Ele m'a si chier acaté que bien me doit avoir gaaignié par tant
de mal" (Micha 7: 187, "She bought me so dearly that it is right she
win me after so much trouble"). Much later, the same Saraïde gives
Bors, already engaged in knightly life, a solemn appointment "de
diemenche en .VII. jors a l'issue de la forest de Roevent" (Micha 2:

162, "a week from Sunday at the exit of Roevent Forest"): it is by
carefully keeping this rendezvous that the hero is able to come to the
aid of his tutor Lambegue, who is on the edge of death (Micha 2:
257–258).

In short, a hierarchy begins to emerge, giving preeminence to the
education dispensed by the fairy or her attendants. Rejected in the
case of Lancelot, the traditional tutor retains importance for Bors and
Lionel, though they, too, are obviously influenced by the fairy-like
universe.

It must also be noted that the overlapping—or contamination—of
different models of narration of youthful exploits also results in delaying the ending of various sequences and in modifying their meaning.
This is the case, for example, with the dubbing of Lancelot, who
comes to the court with the white armor given him by the Lady of the
Lake: [12] King Arthur only dubs the hero (Micha 7: 277); it is the queen
who, at Lancelot's request, sends him a sword (Micha 7: 298). Here,
the contamination includes the epic, the chivalrous, and the romantic
models; and the ending of Lancelot's youthful exploits is delayed,
since the theoretical end of his youthful chivalrous exploits (the dubbing) is inseparable from the beginning of his amorous exploits (his
relationship with Guenevere).

Nor does anything prevent nurturing from continuing even after
the hero has accomplished his first knightly feats. As dispenser of the
magic shields that allow Lancelot to win victory at the Dolorous
Guard (Micha 7: 320–322), the Lady of the Lake guides his chivalrous
path [13] and, particularly, his amorous one throughout the romance.
After the exhortation to pursue only a love capable of increasing his
honor—"ne metés vo cuer en amor qui vous fache aparechier, mais
amender, car cuers qui por amors devient perecheus ne puet a haute
chose ataindre" (Micha 7: 349–350, "don't set your heart on a love
that makes you weak, but on one that betters you, for a heart that
grows weak in love cannot aspire to high deeds")—comes the deliv-
ery to Guenevere of the cleaved shield, an erotic symbol in the sense
that it invites amorous fulfillment. Not only does it guarantee the
value of this love (Micha 8: 206–207; 8: 443–444), but it also on several
occasions heals Lancelot of madness, notably when Ninianne places
the hero on the road leading to the adventure of the cart.

Finally, still because of the overlapping of different models, we no-
tice discrepancies in the development of the various types of youthful
exploits: Lancelot matures as a warrior more rapidly than as a lover,
if only because of the intensity of the passion that prevents him from
being near Guenevere. This is made clear in the episodes that follow
the conquest of the Dolorous Guard, when Lancelot, thinking only of

being able to gaze at the queen, leaves her outside the castle to which he invited her (Micha 7: 352). He proceeds, then, to shun the court because of the displeasure inflicted on his beloved.

Thus, the concentration of narratives of youthful exploits at the beginning of the *Lancelot Proper* is somewhat deceptive. To be sure, the characteristic deeds of valor of the young hero appear in the first pages of the work as the promise of a narrative, but similar features are found further along in the romance; some of them are an indication of subtle manipulations by the author.

Youthful Exploits: Renewal of the Narrative

Two types of phenomena must be taken into account: the inclusion within the work, at various moments, of narratives of youthful exploits that do not relate to the three cousins and also the repetitions and plot twists found at the heart of the romance relating to the youthful exploits of Bors and Lionel.

First, it should be noted that the romance progressively introduces new characters whose presentations give rise to narratives of youthful exploits similar to those that we have studied. Several of these narratives are concentrated at the end of the *Lancelot Proper*, notably the introduction of Perceval, which takes up part of chapter 106 (Micha 6: 183–207). Galahad's youthful exploits are also narrated in the last part of the work, but they are fragmented: Lancelot learns of the birth of his son in chapter 93 (Micha 5: 139–140), then Bors sees the child at Corbenic in the arms of an old knight.[14] Galahad, still "a small child," is led to Arthur after the end of the war against Claudas (Micha 6: 172–173); in the final chapter of the romance (ch. 108), the ten-year-old expresses his desire to remain by his father and is entrusted to the abbess of a convent near Camelot (Micha 8: 242). He stays there five years, at the end of which time a hermit announces to Arthur that the moment has come to dub him.

The same fragmentation occurs in the last part of the narrative with regard to Helain, son of Bors and King Brandegorre's daughter. Lancelot sees Helain when he "could not be more than two years old" and learns from Helain's mother the circumstances of his birth (Micha 5: 295–297); later, in chapter 108, we find Helain again in Carlion, where Arthur and Bors have brought him and where his father is about to dub him a knight (Micha 6: 243).[15]

In addition to these interruptions, brought about by the late introduction of the youthful exploits of new characters, the text surprises us even more by progressively shifting Lancelot's story with regard to that of his two cousins. While Lionel and Bors, introduced at the beginning of the romance as contemporaries of the hero, are at that moment the subjects of youthful exploit narratives consistent with this chronological data, we soon realize that youth is going to last much longer for the king of Gaunes's sons than for Lancelot and is going to take place, for each of the young men, within a somewhat different framework.

Lionel is the first to draw our attention. Although his violent behavior at Claudas's court could already be construed as "boines enfanches" (Micha 7: 75, "youthful exuberance"), the Lady of the Lake sends him to Lancelot, "et li manda que il le retenist tant que il voldroit estre chevaliers" (Micha 8: 131, "and asked him to keep him in his service until he was ready to become a knight"). On several occasions, the young man behaves with the mixture of insolence and wisdom characteristic of young heroes, notably in chapter 64a, which is almost entirely devoted to him (Micha 8: 356–393), but also much later when, on the verge of being made a knight, he wants to set off alone to search for Lancelot, who is seeking Gawain at the time (Micha 1: 214–217). We find Lionel often at the side of Lancelot, wearing the typical costume of a squire, whether at tournaments or in battle: "Et Lyoniax chevalce dalés lui, armé de capel et de hauberjon comme serjans" (Micha 8: 437, "And Lionel rode beside him, dressed in a cap and cloak like a servant"). He is also the one who carries the queen's pennon during the action against the Saxons (Micha 8: 437), and he is on several occasions the messenger of love between Lancelot and Guenevere.

The "second childhood" of Bors is different and more surprising. We lose sight of him in chapter 22a, at the time of the parting of Lancelot and the Lady of the Lake (Micha 7: 270), only to meet him again much later, in chapter 40, long after Lionel's youthful exploits, in the guise of an enigmatic knight riding in the infamous cart and therefore scorned by the whole court, with the exception of Gawain. He challenges King Arthur by seizing his horse and knocking down four knights (among them, the seneschal Kay) before being proclaimed by the Lady of the Lake as the first cousin of Lancelot and the brother of Lionel, "jovenes enfes de .XXI. ans et fu chevaliers novials a Pentecoste" (Micha 2: 93, "a youth of twenty-one, newly knighted at Pentecost"). He presently names himself "Bors the Exiled" to the king.

Thus appears, with a string of provocations and violence, a hero of youthful exploits who has, however, already been dubbed a knight and whose promotion is unusually swift, since Arthur "retint le chevalier compaignon de la Table Roonde" (Micha 2: 93, "made him a knight of the Round Table").

Nevertheless, Bors's youthful exploits do not cease, even after such a dazzling endorsement. Twice, the Lady of the Lake tests the quality of nurturing which she herself has given him: he agrees to stop pursuing a knight as soon as Ninianne's envoy requests it, and later he submits to her request that he drop his sword while fighting Gallidés (Micha 2: 155, 159).

Along with these feats that vouch for Bors's gallantry, others indicate his inexperience. The circumstances under which he begets Helain, or Elyam le Blanc, future emperor of Constantinople (Micha 2: 188–198), subject him entirely to the passion of King Brandegorre's daughter and to the wiles of a mistress acquainted with magic. Above all, the vow that he takes together with the twelve knights is certainly a careless vow, a young man's "boast": "jamais ne finerai devant que j'aie veue la roine Genievre et por l'amor de vos le prendrai je bien el conduit a .IIII. chevaliers, quel qu'il soient, fors que Lancelos del Lac n'i soit" (Micha 2: 192, "I'll not stop until I have seen Queen Guenevere, and for love of you I'll challenge any four knights for her, excepting only Lancelot of the Lake"). Indeed, this vow leads him in spite of himself to do violence to the queen and to oppose Lancelot; he will pay for this temerity with a serious wound (Micha 2: 273).

Nevertheless, he is decisively marked by the nurturing he has received, not only from the Lady of the Lake, but also from Lancelot, who even intervenes in his education when, in chapter 43, he gives him the same advice that Ninianne had given earlier: "je li mant que ja chevaliers ne croistra son pris de trop longuement demorer en un lieu, ne je ne le pris mie miels, bien le sache il, de ce qu'il demore por noient a la cort" (Micha 2: 130,[16] "I tell him that no knight increases his worth by staying too long in one place, and know you well that I do not esteem him the more for staying at court for any reason").

Finally, as Lancelot had received his sword—the essential element of the knight's dubbing—from Guenevere's hand, so Bors receives his from Ninianne, and it is Galehaut's sword (Micha 2: 261).

These manipulations of youthful exploits allow the author to achieve various effects, all aimed at the enrichment of the text and the diversification of his characters. The regular introduction of the youthful exploits of new heroes into the romance constantly delays the conclusion of the work and promises new narratives. For example, Perceval and Galahad are destined to a glorious future with the quest for the Grail; with Mordred, the progress of fate is also inscribed in the text, but it leads to the destruction of the Arthurian world.[17]

As for the "shifted" adventures of Bors and Lionel, they sustain for a long while the major themes of the narrative of youthful exploits and create within the *Lancelot Proper* an interesting system of echoes. One must smile at the blunders of Lionel who, fascinated by knights preparing for battle, stands in the way on the field where Gawain must fight his adversary: "il n'avoit onques veu bataille de .II. chevaliers: si fu si angoisseus de veoir que il se mist tous a cheval sor cheus qui tenoient la damoisele" (Micha 8: 356–357, "he had never seen a combat between two knights; he was so eager to see it that he rode his horse right up upon those who were holding the maiden"). As the fight continues, he refuses to recognize Gawain as the jouster who is unable to overcome his enemy swiftly: "car il ne demorast mie devant si grant poeple com il a chi por .I. seul chevalier conquerre" (Micha 8: 358, "for he would not take so long to defeat a great crowd of people as this man to vanquish a single knight").

Another amusing episode is that in which the same Lionel tries to rush off discretely in search of Lancelot, riding "sor .I. grandisme cheval qui tost le porte" (Micha 1: 214, "on a huge, swift horse"); Galehaut barely manages to stop him, and not without a fight.

Insolent and victorious over their adversaries, Lionel and Bors are also excellent lesson-givers. Bors shames those who had scorned him for riding in a cart, so that at the end of chapter 40, the whole court considers it a point of honor to step into that vehicle with the queen, "ne des lors en avant, tant com li rois vesqui, ne fu nus hom dampnés mis en charrete" (Micha 2: 94, "and from then on, as long as the king was alive, no condemned man was placed in a cart"). At the end of the romance, Bors explains why it is impossible for him to accept the crown of the kingdom of Gaunes: "car si tost come je avrai reaume, il me couvendra laissier toute chevalerie, ou je voille ou non, et ce seroit plus grant honor, se je estoie povres hom et bons chevaliers, que se je estoie riches rois recreanz" (Micha 6: 170, "for as soon as I had a kingdom, whether I wished it or not I would have to abandon knightly exploits, and it would be a greater honor for me to be a poor man but a good knight, than if I were a rich but recreant king").

Lionel is not far behind when it comes to offering advice. When he recovers his stolen horse, he berates the knight-thief and asks him to promise Gawain "que jamais ne metra main a home desarmé, se sor soi desfendant ne le fait" (Micha 8: 366, "never to lay a hand on an unarmed man, except in self-defense"). He also knows how to keep Lancelot from being overly rash while fighting the Saxons. After having begged him in vain not to let himself be killed for no reason, Lionel beseeches him in the name of Guenevere: "Je vous di de par ma dame que vous n'alés avant ne par la foi que vous li devés" (Micha 8: 473, "I tell you by my lady and the faith you owe her not to go forward"), and Lancelot immediately reins in his horse.

But it is Lionel's relations with Lancelot, different enough to constitute an element of characterization, that interest us here more particularly. In dealings with his cousin, Lionel is like a "youth" next to an
experienced knight. We have seen him dressed as a squire in the presence of Lancelot, but his role as messenger between the hero and
Guenevere is particularly noteworthy. During the first stay in Sorelois, he is dispatched by Galehaut to the queen to tell her of Lancelot's
melancholy (Micha 8: 323–324), and Guenevere sends him back to her
friend with the mission of giving him ".I. pigne mout riche dont tout
li dent sont plain de ses cavex et la chainture dont ele estoit chainte et
l'aumousniere" (Micha 8: 408, "an expensive comb whose teeth were
filled with her hair, the belt around her waist, and her almspurse").

After having interrupted, in chapter 70a, the fight between Lancelot and Gawain, it is Lionel who conveys to Lancelot the amorous
invitation from the queen. Later, when the hero, poisoned by water
from a spring, is able to recover thanks only to the care of the healing
maiden, Lionel finds a prudent formula that reconciles Lancelot's fi-
delity to Guenevere with his appreciation for the maiden: "des ore
mais poez faire de lui comme de vostre chevalier et de vostre ami, se
il vos plaist" (Micha 4: 153, "henceforth you can treat him as your
knight and friend, if you please").[18]

Bors's status is different and more complex.[19] His youthful exploits
extend far beyond the usual period, since the episode of the cart and
his boasting to King Brandegorre's daughter and its consequences
take place when he is already a knight. On the other hand, these feats
tend to make Bors less the companion of Lancelot than his double
and sometimes his adversary. Indeed, while he repeats Lancelot's
gesture of climbing into the cart "por l'amor de Lancelot qui por cele
dame i monta" (Micha 2: 93, "for the love of Lancelot, who climbed
in because of that lady"), he differs from his cousin by repeating, as
the result of a rash boon, Meleagant's gesture: "Maintenant gete la
main et aert la roine par le frain et dist: 'Dame, je vos preing et vos
ne me poés eschaper legierement'" (Micha 2: 269, "He immediately
seizes the queen's horse by the reins and says: 'My lady, you are in
my power and cannot easily escape'"). Friend to, then rival of, Lancelot, the young Bors is thus sometimes the double and sometimes
the opposite of his cousin.

In the Grail adventures, Bors is also the one who must go farther
than Lancelot or at least place himself in a different context, since he
is progressively admitted, at Corbenic, to the secrets of the Grail and
to the quest in which Perceval and Galahad will also participate. The
mark of this election is the prophecy made by one of the queen's

ladies-in-waiting, who regains her speech on that occasion—"ele n'avoit onques parlé" (Micha 6: 191, "she had never before uttered a word")—and assigns him a place, like Perceval, beside the Perilous Seat.

Does Lancelot's exclusion from this ultimate phase of the Grail adventure, occasioned by his own lust (Micha 1: 53) as well as that of his father (Micha 2: 36–37), vitiate his status as a worthy knight? This question, delicate yet decisive for the appreciation of Lancelot's stature in the romance as a whole, can receive some elucidation through the examination of his youthful exploits as preparatory to the quest of the Grail.

Youthful Exploits: All Roads Lead to Lancelot

From the very beginning, the superiority of Lancelot over his two cousins is obvious. The child nurtured by the Lady of the Lake turns out to be a dispenser of nurturing himself, although he still does not know his own identity: "Lyonel, Lyonel, ne soiés pas esbahis ne desesperés, se dans Claudas a vostre terre en baillie, car vous avrés plus d'amis que vous ne quidiés au recovrer" (Micha 7: 270,[20] "Lionel, Lionel! Don't be upset or in despair that Sir Claudas has taken over your lands, for you will have more friends than you think when you recover them"). He has become a teacher, while his young cousins continue an apprenticeship which, for him, has ended.

But how do his youthful exploits compare to Perceval's and Galahad's? The youthful exploits of those two characters, who are called to play such an important role in the quest for the Grail, are distinctly different from those of Lancelot and his cousins. In speaking of Galahad, the principal quester, the expression "youthful exploits" can be used only for the successive biological stages that reveal the growth of the child. None of his actions or remarks is significant, except for his assertion of the wish to stay with his father: "Il fera sa volenté, mais ou que il aille, je volrai estre si pres de lui que je le voie souvent" (Micha 6: 241, "he will do as he will, but wherever he goes, I want to be near enough to see him often").

This proximity of father and son must be taken into account in the interpretation of the respective status of both characters in the *Queste*. But youthful exploits, in the traditional sense of the expression, are replaced here by predictions which, from the moment of Galahad's conception, accompany his development: "de ceste flor perdue fu restorez Galaad, li virges, li tres bon chevaliers, cil qui les aventures del saint Graal mist a fin" (Micha 4: 210–211, "from this lost flower [the virginity of King Pellés's daughter] blossomed forth Galahad, the virginal, the most excellent knight, who achieved the adventures of the Holy Grail").

Perceval, on the other hand, experiences true youthful exploits, with his running away from his mother in order to become a knight, then his parting with his squire, also done by ruse, and his first feat (the rescue of Patrides), which makes King Arthur deplore the loss of the "millor chevalier fors Gauvain" (Micha 6: 198, "best knight except Gawain"). But these rather abbreviated youthful exploits, concentrated in chapter 106, also include the theme of prophecy, which overlaps that of innocence. The "maiden who never lied" makes Perceval sit to the right of the Perilous Seat, but nothing in the attitude of the young man seems to justify such an honor: "entre les juesnes seoit Perceval qui avoit la chiere simple et resambloit bien simple creature" (Micha 6: 192–193, "Perceval, who had a childlike face and seemed a naïve creature, sat among the youths"). It is because he is made the butt of Kay's and Mordred's sarcasms that the young man leaves for his first adventures.

Finally, let us remember that Bors, who shares the fact of having had "traditional" youthful exploits with his brother and his cousin, is also marked with the sign of prophecy concerning the Grail (he will sit on the left of the Perilous Seat).

Thus, viewed from the perspective of the Grail quest, it is as if the theme of youthful exploits were being superseded, in various ways, by prophecy: no youthful exploits for Galahad; only brief youthful exploits for Perceval, emphasizing the mysterious character of the prediction; and broadly sketched youthful exploits for Bors, for whom prophecy affirms a higher destiny. In that way, two types of destinies seem to confront each other: that of the heroes who, displaying their noble natures through words and actions in the course of their youthful exploits, are predestined to the status of chivalric knight (Lionel and Lancelot), and that of the characters (Bors, Perceval, and Galahad) who, cast in the forefront by prophecy, are destined—whether or not youthful exploits foreshadow their merit—to the supreme adventure, that of the Grail quest.

Now, if we reexamine the close bonds between Lancelot and Bors (the link between the two groups[21]) established by the accounts of their youthful exploits, we see how Lancelot is promoted as the main character of the romance. The close relationship between Bors and Lancelot is that much more surprising because it asserts itself relatively late, as we have seen, progressively overshadowing the stated resemblance between Lionel and Lancelot.[22] We are alluding of course to Bors's deeds narrated in chapter 40. His climbing into the cart before slaying four of Arthur's knights is not only a gesture of friendship toward Lancelot but also a sort of complement to Lancelot's own action, the point being to convey to the court the exemplary character of the hero's challenge and to transform an element tied to the queen's request to Lancelot into a universally liberating act (the abolition of the custom of the cart).

The bonds between the two cousins are further strengthened by their each fathering a child destined to a great future, even though the matings which led to their sons' conceptions were in neither case desired. It is Bors, in chapter 48, who sets the pace. Having attracted the attentions of King Brandegorre's daughter, he is unable to thwart her lady-in-waiting's wiles and accepts the ring that makes him lose his mind (Micha 2: 196); his nurturing had fated him to remain a virgin (or so thought the Lady of the Lake, Micha 2: 198), but—and here we recognize another characteristic of youthful exploit narratives—nature instructs the young man and his lover in "[c]e dont il n'avoient onques riens seu" (Micha 2: 197, "what they had been unaware of"). For Bors, the night spent with King Brandegorre's daughter ends his virginity, but it does not end his chastity, since it is involuntarily and only once that the hero falls to the flesh. A great knight will be born from this union, the future emperor of Constantinople.

Foolishly, and because Lancelot cannot see through Brisane's ruse, filled as he is with the kind of desire which is not that of a young man blinded by passion but rather that of a fulfilled, yet hungry lover, Lancelot knows King Pellés's daughter "em pechié et en avoutire et contre Deu et encontre Sainte Eglyse" (Micha 4: 210, "in sin and adultery and in opposition to God and Holy Church") and begets "the virginal, the most excellent knight."

Aside from the differences that separate Bors and Lancelot and that are indispensable to the autonomy of each of these characters, we have to become aware of the kinship that the author wished to establish between them, notably in their male line. In that respect, each is the instrument of divine will,[23] which modifies human action while fully fitting within its ambiguity. Ninianne's surprise at learning of Bors's lost virginity is answered with the birth of Helain, "si haut fruit que de .II. si jovenes hantes ne descendi d'icel tens nul arbre plus puissant" (Micha 2: 198, "in our days no finer tree ever grew from two such youthful graftings"). To the reader's shock—was the unintentional lover of King Pellés's daughter not "*loials d'amors*" (Micha 1: 299,"faithful in love"), faithful to his lady in intention as well as in action?—Lancelot knows another woman "ausinc com Adam fist sa fame" (Micha 4: 210, "as Adam knew his wife"), but from this unexpected mating is born, through God's grace, the redeeming hero Galahad.

After the children are born, the double paternity continues to bring the two characters together, if only because the child of one is presented through the other's eyes. In chapter 18, Galahad is introduced to Bors as his "little relative," and Bors is struck by the baby's likeness to his cousin: "bien li est avis qu'il soit de Lancelot" (Micha 5: 254, "to him he looked just like Lancelot"). In chapter 99, it is Lancelot to whom Bors's son is introduced, and upon the narration of the circumstances of the child's conception, Lancelot recognizes his own adventure: "si se pense que tout ainsi li estoit avenu de la fille le roi Pellés, que ja avoit .I. enfant de lui si conme on li avoit dit" (Micha 5: 296, "he thought that the same thing had happened in the case of King Pellés's daughter, who had had a child by him, as he had been told").

We should also note the sort of chiasmus that arises between the two cousins and their sons with regard to the Grail quest: the father's (Lancelot's) exclusion is balanced by the son's (Galahad's) election, and vice versa (Bors-Helain). The distribution of roles in the supreme adventure is, to say the least, paradoxical: as the author chooses (Galahad and Bors), he continues to connect the chosen to those cast aside, and particularly to Lancelot, father of the major hero and the double of one of the three questers. Strictly speaking, may one even speak of exclusion in the case of Lancelot? I do not believe so, for the romance leads us rather to the recognition of the undeniable triumph of desire symbolized by this hero.

Long before the end of the *Lancelot Proper*, in chapter 85, the romance has indicated the special quality and incomparable value of the type of chivalry that derives its strength from love: "Sachiez que je ja ne fusse venuz a si grant hautesce com je sui, se vos ne fussiez, car je n'eusse mie cuer par moi au conmancement de ma chevalerie d'amprendre les choses que li autre laissoient par defaute de pooir" (Micha 5: 3, "Know that I would never have attained the great honor I did, had it not been for you, for I would never have had the courage alone, when I first became a knight, to undertake the deeds that others did not have the strength to achieve"). And the romance has a final episode, itself connected to youthful exploits—Galahad's—that manifests the overwhelming power of love and the essential centrality of Lancelot. We recall that at the end of chapter 105 (Micha 6: 171), King Pellés's daughter leads Galahad to Camelot. This visit, which one would expect to be focused entirely on the *Queste del Saint Graal* (since it involves its main hero), results instead in a repetition of the scene that had ended in the conception of Galahad: Brisane's spells bring the hero once more to the young woman's bed. This time, however, the circumstances are entirely different:[24] Pellés's daughter is seduced by Lancelot, whom she "tant l'amoit conme fame porroit plus amer home" (Micha 6: 171, "loved as only a woman could love a man"). To appreciate this scene to the fullest, must we not recognize that the author, at the very moment when the Grail quest is about to begin, indicates its limitations by turning our attention toward love as an essential element of his narrative, thereby suggesting a kind of reconciliation between earthly chivalry and the Grail?

Indeed, for the woman who was the bearer of the Grail, it is as if Lancelot's desire for her—while dreaming of another—is purchased at the expense of the joy she should have felt in giving birth to the messianic child; she thinks only of Lancelot and easily consents to Brisane's ruse. She thus becomes the storm center when Guenevere catches the lovers and forces Lancelot to leave the court, causing despair and anger, as Bors tells her, "Dame, por quoi nos avez vos si traïs, fet il, que vos mon signor Lancelot qui ert li plus prodome dou monde et qui plus vos amoit avez si vilainnement chacié de cort?" (Micha 6: 179, "'My lady,' he said, 'why have you betrayed us by banishing so villainously from the court my lord Lancelot, who was the noblest knight in the world and loved you more than anyone?"). Later, having accomplished heroic deeds even during his period of madness, Lancelot is healed by the Grail and stays for a long time at the Isle of Joy with Pellés's daughter, whom he has forgiven, before returning to Guenevere.

Thus, it seems to me that the arrival of Galahad and the promise of the Grail adventures turn the reader's attention, through the love of Pellés's daughter and its consequences, back to Lancelot and to everything for which he stands in the romance: passionate love, to which the young woman falls prey, and outstanding chivalric prowess, on which rests the salvation of the Arthurian world. For that matter, passion—Amite's as well as Lancelot's—does not preclude the beneficent effects of the Grail, which heals Lancelot and, at a certain level, even suggests a possible reconciliation.

Thus, the forms and functions of the narratives of youthful exploits are many in the *Lancelot Proper*. At the beginning of the work, they announce the worth of the main heroes, opposing good youthful exploits (for example, those of the three cousins) to the bad ones (of Mordred, for example); and with the occasional recourse to prophecy, these sequences allow us to maintain our distance from the action of the romance and to question received ideas, in either a purely diverting or a more didactic manner.

Situated principally at the beginning of the romance—but sometimes, even dealing with the same characters, farther along in the narrative—stories of youthful exploits are both the performance of astounding feats and the promise of future adventures, thus opening multiple chronological levels to the reader. Also, a complicating strategy is actually used with regard to Lionel and Bors, since the author does not hesitate to dissociate the two young men from their cousin Lancelot, although he had initially made them contemporaries. Furthermore, he creates specific bonds between each of them and Lancelot, and these bonds are modified as the narrative progresses. After the companionship between the eldest (Lancelot) and the youngest (Lionel), who most resembles him, it is the confrontation between the hero and Bors—who is both Lancelot's twin and his rival—that is underlined in the narration of youthful exploits.

In the final analysis, it is the character and status of Lancelot that gain the most from these relationships and from these divergent narrative rhythms. A "youth," like his cousins Bors and Lionel, at the beginning of the romance (Micha 7), Lancelot quickly becomes an older "brother" whose chivalric, if not amorous, education is completed while Lionel is still only a squire (Micha 8 and 1) and while even Bors, who is already a knight, is still behaving like a hero of youthful adventures (Micha 2). Toward the end of the narrative, the arrival of new characters belonging to the next generation (Perceval and, particularly, Galahad) confuses the chronology, since even Bors, who belongs to the initial generation, is called upon to be a Grail hero.

This multiplication of characters, as well as the increased attention given to the supreme adventure (that of the Grail), far from excluding the figure of Lancelot from the story line, keeps him constantly present in the mind of the reader. Indeed, it is in Lancelot that the mystery of the election to knighthood is best expressed, with its blend of the driving power of adventure and mad desire, which innocents like King Pellés's daughter may some day know. Scenes and characters in the romance all lead back to Lancelot because the tragic demands of love and valor are reconciled in him with the beginning of the Grail adventure: indeed, only a son of Lancelot will be able to complete that quest.

Notes

1. The expression "youthful exploits" has been chosen to translate the French *enfances*, a technical term referring to the preparatory and initiatory deeds of a young man before he is officially knighted.

2. This is the choice reflected in certain manuscripts of the noncyclical version, fixing the end of Lancelot's youthful exploits after his fight against

Alybon and the latter's return to Arthur's court. See the edition by Elspeth Kennedy (whom we thank for this information), vol. 2, p. 47, par. 182, 26–27: "Et ci faillent les enfances de Lancelot" ("And here end Lancelot's youthful exploits").

3. In Micha 6: 105.

4. Indeed, Elaine dies shortly after visiting her family (Micha 5: 169).

5. One must compare his shrewdness here with the violence of his beginnings (see *infra*).

6. François Suard, ed. and trans., *La Chanson de Guillaume*, Classiques Garnier (Paris: Bordas, 1991): v. 1637.

7. See J. Horrent, *Les versions françaises et étrangères des Enfances Charlemagne* (Brussels, 1979).

8. See L. Jordan, "Ueber Boeve de Hanstone," *Zeitschrift für romanische Philologie*, supplement 14, 1908.

9. See the lais, *Tydorel*, in *Les lais anonymes des XIIe et XIIIe siècles*, edited by P. M. Tobin (Geneva: Droz, 1976), and *Yonec*, in *Lais de Marie de France*, edited by Laurence Harf (Paris: Lettres gothiques, 1990).

10. See Ernst Robert Curtius, *European Literature and the Latin Middle Ages*, translated by Willard Trask (Princeton, N.J., 1973).

11. The biographical perspective is also tied to romance narrative, which, like chronicles, aims at narrating the events from the beginning and is constantly looking for an origin: "En la marche de Gaule et de la petite Bertaigne avoit .ii. rois anchienement . . ." (Micha 7: 1, "In the borderland between Gaul and of lesser Brittany, there were once two kings"); see Emmanuèle Baumgartner, "*La prose du Lancelot,*" *Romania* 105 (1984): 1–15.

12. We recall that Ninianne strongly refuses to allow Arthur to give the young man any armor other than what he is wearing (Micha 7: 267–268).

13. In the episode of the Dolorous Guard, she forbids him to immediately join the king's household: "Mais bien gardés que vous ne remaigniés ne au roi Artu ne a autrui, devant que vous soiés conneus par vos proeches en plusors terres" (Micha 7: 321, "But be careful not to stay in the service of King Arthur, or of any other person, until you have become known for your valor in several lands").

14. He is less than a year old at the time (Micha 5: 254).

15. For other characters, their situation within the text is even less systematic. Mordred is introduced in chapter 60 as the youngest brother of Gawain; later, his portrait is given, in which his physical beauty contrasts with the ugliness of his acts (Micha 2: 411), after which the text tells us some of his misdeeds that foreshadow the Salisbury tragedy, notably the murder of the hermit who revealed to him his incestuous birth (Micha 5: 219–222). Short explanations are also given of Galehodin, the nephew of Galehaut who has been designated by him as his successor (Micha 1: 82). In chapter 88, Galehodin decides to seek out Lancelot's company, for he is certain that the hero will "mielz a conseillier que uns autres ne feroit" (Micha 4: 195, "give me better counsel than any other could"). The notion of nurturing again points us to the theme of youthful exploits.

16. See Micha 7: 269, 321.

17. Lancelot knows Mordred's future and reveals it to the queen, but she does not believe him and does not tell the king. Yet, had she talked, the king "l'eust chacié fors de sa cort et ainsi remainsist la guerre et la bataille qui fu puis es plains de Salibieres" (Micha 6: 61, "would have thrown him out of his court, and so the war and battle in the plains of Salisbury would not have taken place").

18. Lionel's cleverness is not rewarded with a good role in the rest of the romance. A beneficiary of Lancelot's prowess rather than a protagonist, we see him fight his brother Bors in the *Queste del Saint Graal* (*Queste* 191–192); in the *Mort Artu*, he is made king of Gaunes by Lancelot (*Mort* 125, 164) and then is killed during the battle of Winchester against Mordred's sons (*Mort* 197, 255).

19. Bors too is a messenger of the queen to Lancelot, but in a more passing manner (Micha 4: 365–377); still, the point is to prepare a tryst between the hero and Guenevere.

20. See also Micha 7: 193.

21. After Lancelot, it is Bors who has the best youthful exploits, but he also benefits from prophecy.

22. See also in chapter 15 (Micha 2: 215), the exclamation of Galehaut, who associates Lionel and Lancelot: "Ha, Ha, cuers sans frain, certes, certes voirement estes vos ambedui cosin!" ("Ah, Ah! Unbridled hearts, indeed you two are truly cousins!").

23. See Micha 2: 198 and 4: 210–211.

24. See my article "La conception de l'aventure dans le *Lancelot* en prose," *Romania* 108 (1987): 244 ff.

5. The *Mort Artu* and Cyclic Closure

Norris J. Lacy

A particular weight of responsibility rests upon the *Mort Artu* or, indeed, upon the final component of any cycle: it must to some extent stand on its own, particularly in a loose-knit set of works, and yet it must evidently provide proper closure for the cycle. Most commonly, critics have admired the *Mort Artu* when considering it apart from the cycle at whose end it stands. They have praised it for its taut dramatic structure and its narrative economy; but of course, it is not an independent romance—at least it is not only that—and it has by no means been universally praised as a fit conclusion to the Vulgate.

In most cases, critics who find fault are doubtless reflecting the influence of Jean Frappier, whose final paragraph on the subject of the *Mort Artu* (in Loomis's *Arthurian Literature in the Middle Ages*)[1] tells us that the author "commands a style dignified and at times vivacious and dramatic. But it is not adequate to the richness and beauty of the theme. This 'Twilight of the Gods' needs all the resources of an orchestra and the thunder-peal of organs; one has to be content with a flute."[2]

There can be no point in arguing that the *Mort Artu* does provide the "thunder-peal" Frappier wants, for it clearly does not do so. However, we may legitimately deny that thunder is required and suggest, on the contrary, that the flute provides an appropriate embellishment of the romance's theme and an effectively crepuscular conclusion to the cycle. "This is the way the world ends," wrote Eliot, "not with a bang but a whimper."[3] This—to stretch a point only slightly—is also the way the Vulgate ends.

In fact, paradoxical though it may appear, I agree entirely with Frappier that the climax of this enormous Arthurian epic requires something more than a perfunctory, factual account of events. However, the key word here is "climax," and I would argue that the cycle's climax can be located not in the *Mort Artu* but long before. The *Mort Artu*, as I read the work, is the cycle's conclusion but not its climax.

The apogee of Arthurian chivalry and the climactic moments of Arthurian history are not located there or even in the *Queste del Saint Graal*, which had dramatized, more than anything, the moribundity of the Arthurian world. Rather, if we seek a genuinely *Arthurian* climax, we must look all the way back to the *Lancelot Proper*; but, of course, where we find the climax we also find the first evidence of the social and ideological decay (specifically, but not exclusively, the love of Lancelot and Guenevere) that will require chivalry to be superseded in the *Queste del Saint Graal* and dismantled in the *Mort Artu*.

By its design, then, the *Mort Artu* is not climax but anticlimax of the cycle, not climax but closure. Nevertheless, as an individual romance it must also present its own trajectory and its own conclusion. It thus offers a dual perspective—it is both retrospective and prospective, looking back to and concluding the cycle, while also looking ahead and meticulously preparing for the final battle in which Arthur's reign will be ended and his Round Table undone.

The predominant direction in the early pages of the romance is retrospection, but the predominant tone is far removed from the joy that might be expected to follow the achievement of the Grail, simply because that quest is not an Arthurian triumph but instead a demonstration of Arthurian inadequacies. Indeed, the opening folios are characterized by a morose preoccupation with the cost of that achievement. Mentioning the Grail quest only in passing, the author loses no time in fixing the tone: his first foreboding lines announce his intention to record the deaths of his characters, and he says that "en la fin est escrit conment li rois Artus fu navrez en la bataille de Salebieres et conment il se parti de Girflet qui si longuement li fist compaignie que aprés lui ne fu nus hom qui le veïst vivant" (*Mort* 1.10–14,[4] "the end tells how King Arthur was wounded in the battle at Salisbury and how he was separated from Girflet, who stayed with him so long that he was the last one to see Arthur alive"). He further notes that a great number of Arthur's best knights (thirty-two in all) have died, all in combat. Gawain himself had killed eighteen knights, demonstrating not his heroism but his sin (admitted by himself: "par mon pechié" [*Mort* 3. 24, the "consequence of my sin"]). That sin, compounding the sin into which Lancelot quickly lapsed again with the queen (*Mort* 4. 1–10), confirms that the Arthurian world is battling not an enemy from without but itself. The Round Table is now rotting wood beneath a polished veneer.

The loss of Arthur's knights is a theme replayed at intervals during the romance. When Lancelot rescues the queen, his knights pursue Arthur's and kill seventy-seven out of eighty of them, including Gawain's brothers (*Mort* 94. 20–55). The Round Table itself has lost seventy-two—almost half—of its members (*Mort* 107. 26–28). Arthur must choose replacements, and the few who are mentioned—largely unknown and obviously of lesser distinction, though just as surely the best the realm now has to offer—illustrate the sad fate of the Round Table society.

Specifically, Lancelot's seat at the table is occupied by "a knight named Eliant"—not just "Eliant," which would indicate that he was at least notable enough to have his name recognized—and Bors's place is assumed by one Balynor (*Mort* 107. 32–33). Both are praised as kings' sons and good knights, but there is no pretense that they equal their predecessors at the Table. Moreover, we are then told that the seats once held by Hector and by Gaheriet are now taken by "a Scottish knight" and by "a knight who was the nephew of the king of North Wales"; their names, obviously, do not even merit mention.

Not only the personnel of the Round Table, but also their activities, will change. A crucial observation is made in a familiar passage early in the text: "les aventures del roiaume de Logres estoient si menees a fin qu'il n'en avenoit mes nule se petit non . . ." (*Mort* 3. 39–41, "the adventures of the kingdom of Logres had been ended, so that scarcely anything more could occur . . ."). Here is a double key to the text. First, this is a romance without adventure; and, second, the fact that this is a contradiction in terms (since adventures, virtually synonymous with Arthurian history, are the lifeblood of romance) illustrates a narratorial dilemma. How could we expect the author of such a romance to provide a dramatically or rhetorically intense conclusion when his point is precisely that this literary world is suddenly deprived of the marvelous, unpredictable, and exciting challenge of adventures?

As E. Jane Burns and others have noted,[5] an adventure is, by both etymology and convention, an incident that cannot be known in advance. Logically, then, if adventures disappear, the outcome of present events may become predictable. This simple fact explains much about the character of the *Mort Artu*: its increasingly linear structure, its increasing emphasis on literary causality, the inability of the characters (or their lack of will) to set or alter the course of events, and the author's simple announcement—in his very first lines—of the way all this will end.

We are reminded on more than one occasion that adventures have ended. One of the most plaintive illustrations of this absence occurs when the body of the maiden of Escalot arrives at Camelot (*Mort* 70). Arthur and Gawain gaze at the fabulously beautiful boat that comes to Camelot without apparent guide, and the latter wistfully remarks: "se ceste nacele est ausi bele dedenz com dehors, ce seroit merveilles;

a poi que ge ne di que les aventures recommencent" (*Mort* 70. 22–24,[6] my emphasis, "if this boat is as beautiful inside as out, it will be remarkable. *I'm almost convinced that adventures are beginning anew"*). The affliction from which the Arthurian court suffers is a moral failing, but one of its critical symptoms is the disappearance of adventures.

As adventures give meaning to the actions and endeavors of the court, they also stimulate stylistic and narratorial interest. But when the Grail quest is completed and adventures are no more, the author is deprived of the rhetoric and the register appropriate to their narration. He is reduced to a more direct and unadorned expression, a restricted vocabulary, and a subdued style. The lack of stylistic variety accurately reflects the lack of variety and depth of event. In other words, seen as an expression of a world deprived of adventure, a rhetorically impoverished style is appropriate. The thunder-peal of organs could be nothing more than misplaced bombast.

The second interpretive key provided by the opening lines of the *Mort Artu* resides in Arthur's reaction to the disappearance of adventure. When he sees that adventures are no more, Arthur announces a tourney at Winchester, because he does not want his knights to "give up bearing arms" (*Mort* 3. 43). Thus, when adventures do not present themselves (which is to say, when one of the most fundamental conventions of romance is suspended), the king has to try to re-create them with tourneys. But in fact, he is not creating adventures but fabricating *surrogate* adventures. And they are a poor substitute at that, being mere diversion.

However, they are no less deadly for being diversion. Knights deliver "granz cox destre et senestre et a abatre chevaliers et a ocirre chevax et a esrachier escuz de cox et hiaumes de testes . . ." (*Mort* 20. 3–5, "fierce blows left and right, striking down knights and killing horses and tearing shields from necks and helmets from heads"). A squire is killed (*Mort* 21. 11–12), and the critically wounded include Lancelot (*Mort* 21. 14–17). The fact that Lancelot's adversary is his comrade Bors, who simply failed to recognize him, further underlines not only the mindless destruction of tourneys in general but, especially, the futility of Arthur's attempt to reanimate his world by announcing tournaments repeatedly: at Winchester, soon afterward at Teneborc, then at Camelot.

Curiously, the Arthur who had been distraught because his knights killed one another in the quest seems unperturbed by the further destruction wrought in the name of sport. Instead, as soon as one tournament ends, another is announced, implying a sad and perhaps desperate effort to avoid facing the reality of this realm in which all adventures have already been played out.

An additional point is particularly relevant here: the author emphasizes the gradual withering of the Arthurian world by portraying a diminished monarch and an increasingly impersonalized cosmos. Significant is Arthur's bland reaction to terrible news. When he learns of Lancelot's and Guenevere's sin, he becomes pale but says only "ce sont merveilles" (*Mort* 86. 32–33)[7]—nothing more. Elsewhere, Arthur appears not bland but indecisive and weak, and this is a weakness that goes far beyond the characteristics we observed in earlier texts (e.g., Chrétien's *Yvain* or *Perceval*, or even the earlier romances of the Vulgate Cycle). Here, he is virtually helpless. When Gawain tells Lancelot that Arthur wants him (Lancelot) to leave the land, the latter asks Arthur if that is true. Arthur replies, lamely, "Puis que Gauvains le velt . . . il me plest bien" (*Mort* 119. 49–50, "Since Gawain wishes it . . . so do I"). We could argue that, with his brothers dead, Gawain is considered an aggrieved party who has the right to demand redress or punishment, but the fact that Gawain may be justified in his demand does not alter another fact: that Arthur is not in charge, and this episode and others emphasize the extent to which control of events has slipped away from an increasingly impotent monarch.

The romance insistently underlines the fact that not only Arthur, but other characters as well, are incapable of guiding the course of events. Even groups and factions tend to be depersonalized in the *Mort Artu*. When Arthur's and Lancelot's forces face each other for what could be a cataclysm, we might expect the author to emphasize the ensuing human tragedy by referring repeatedly to the antagonists by name and to underline the depth of their former love. Yet, he rarely, if ever, does so. Instead of identifying the armies by naming their leaders—which would have been clearer and much simpler—he refers repeatedly to "the army in the city" and "those outside."

The author's method implies that he is making an effort *not* to identify the war as a personal conflict between Arthur and Lancelot; it is instead one army against another one, two largely impersonal forces pitted against each other in a combat that is no longer a matter of choice, planning, or personal enmity. Emphasis is now on the irreversible forces shaping events; what will now happen is beyond the control of the individuals involved. They, at one time in at least partial control of their destiny, have now become pawns who move as other forces dictate.

These forces themselves merit some discussion. The reader knows that they have been set in motion largely by the adultery of Lancelot and Guenevere; but the author gives them a specific name and origin: they are the workings of Fortune. The *Mort Artu* offers a half-dozen extended discussions or dramatizations of Fortune, whereas the enormously longer *Lancelot Proper* mentions the word only a few times, and it never occurs in the *Queste del Saint Graal*. In the conclusion of the cycle, though, it is entirely appropriate: adventures are no more, the marvelous is virtually absent, the quest for the Grail has been completed, and Christianized concerns are largely foreign to this world. It is thus a romance world without romance. The text has been carefully constructed so as to emphasize that the impending downfall of Arthur and his world is inevitable, and the Wheel of Fortune effectively translates the author's vision.

Gawain, grieving over Gaheriet (*Mort* 100. 52–62), laments: How could Fortune, who had endowed him with all good qualities, permit his awful and vile destruction? Similarly, Arthur later blames Fortune for Gawain's death; Fortune, he says, is the most traitorous thing in the world: "por quoi me fus tu onques si debonere ne si amiable por vendre le moi si chierement au derrien? Tu me fus jadis mere, or m'ies tu devenue marrastre . . ." (*Mort* 172. 47–50, "why were you once so generous and kind to me, only to make me pay so dearly in the end? You once were my mother, but now you have become a [cruel] stepmother . . ."). Soon afterward, Arthur uses the same image while speaking to Girflet: "Fortune qui m'a esté mere jusque ci, et or m'est devenue marrastre, me fet user le remenant de ma vie en douleur et en courrouz et en tristesce" (*Mort* 192. 21–24, "Fortune, which until now has been a mother to me, has now become a stepmother, making me spend the rest of my life in grief and pain and sorrow").

When Yvain is killed, Arthur exclaims, "Ha! Dex, por quoi soufrez vos ce que ge voi . . ." (*Mort* 190. 2, "Oh, God, why do you permit what I am seeing . . ."). Sagremor answers that it is Fortune's doing, not God's: "Sire, ce sont li geu de Fortune; or poez veoir qu'ele vous vent chierement les granz biens et les granz honors que vous avez eü pieça, qu'ele vos tolt de voz meilleurs amis; or doint Dex que nos n'aions pis!" (*Mort* 190. 5–9, "Sir, these are Fortune's games; now you can see that she's making you pay dearly for the great benefits and honors you've enjoyed before, by taking away your best friends. May God grant that nothing worse may happen to us!").

In yet another passage, Arthur laments, "Ha! Dex, tant m'avez meintenu en grant enneur, et or sui en pou d'eure abessiez par droite mescheance, que nus hom ne perdi tant comme j'ai perdu" (*Mort* 103. 10–13, "Oh, God! You have sustained me so long in great honor, and have now cast me down so quickly that no man has ever lost as much as I"). But he immediately corrects himself and notes that he has sustained this loss not through the justice of God, but through Lancelot's pride; it was the fault of the man "que nos avons eslevé et escreü en nostre terre par meintes fois, ausint come s'il fust estrez de nostre char meïsmes" (*Mort* 103. 26–29, "whom we nurtured and enriched in our land many times, just as if he were our own flesh and blood").

Railing against one's treatment by the deity would be surprising in this text, simply because God is not the motive force in the romance. In fact, it would be difficult to reconcile the presence of God with the function of Fortune's Wheel. On the other hand, as this passage implies, Fortune is by no means incompatible with the force of human frailties and sins, specifically, the pride of Lancelot. Obviously, pride can unleash forces, emblematized by the Wheel of Fortune, that cannot be deterred. Incidentally, Fortune is first mentioned when Bors says that she fostered the love of Lancelot and Guenevere only for their ruin (*Mort* 59. 15–17). In retrospect, then, Fortune's tragic legacy has remote roots.

Arthur and those around him no longer have even the illusion of control. Deprived of adventure, they are also deprived of the will to resist their destiny, represented by the turning of the Wheel. As the cycle of the Vulgate is coming to an end, Fortune's Wheel is completing its revolution, and as it continues its descent, the author finds a style and a presentation that are entirely appropriate.

That events are largely beyond human control is confirmed by a compelling series of explicit announcements. The first such announcement is made to Lancelot by Bors: "Sire, fet Boorz, sachiez qu'il [Arthur] a nouveles oïes de vos et de la reïne. Ore esgardez que vos ferez, que nos somes venu a la guerre qui ja ne prendra fin" (*Mort* 89. 6–9, "Sir, you should know that [Arthur] has been told about you and the queen. Now be careful what you do, for we're facing the war that will have no end"). Soon after, he repeats his warning: because Lancelot has betrayed Arthur with the queen, "or verroiz la guerre commencier qui jamés ne prendra fin a nos vivans" (*Mort* 90. 87–88, "now you will see the war begin that will never end in our lifetime").

Bors's second announcement is preceded by a statement that, while no less revealing, has been noted by very few critics (except E. Jane Burns).[8] Bors points out that this tragedy has befallen them because they are no longer able to keep matters under wraps: "ore est la chose descouverte que nos avions tant celee" (*Mort* 90. 86–87, "what we had hidden for so long is now known"). This is a key passage and one of the clearest indications that events are now beyond their control. It might moreover be taken as a suggestion that the Arthurian world rests on a fragile illusion, perhaps from the beginning, certainly now. That world functions only as long as illusion is maintained and unpleasant truths are concealed. The trouble is that the recognition of problems requires response to them.

The one point at which I would take exception to Burns's excellent commentary is when she attributes the crisis to the lovers' inability to maintain the gap "between what others think to be the case and what really happens between this knight and his lady" (Burns, 153). But Bors did not speak of what the *lovers* had hidden until now, but what "we" (he, Arthur, all of them) had once been able to conceal: "que nos avions tant celee."

This passage, first of all, goes far in explaining Arthur's oddly understated and nearly neutral reactions to repeated evidence of the lovers' sin: they were an indication neither of the author's rhetorical poverty nor of the king's indifference but rather of an urgent need to avoid open acknowledgment of the truth. The evasion of truth permits the avoidance of action. Once Arthur has incontrovertible proof and no alternative to acknowledging it, he must act against Lancelot and the queen. Moreover, he presumably understands—at least Bors does—that the crisis is not simply personal: not only must he take action against his wife and his friend, but his ethic requires him to destroy the system governed by that ethic. Therein lies much of the tragedy and pathetic irony of the *Mort Artu*. When truth must be faced, the Arthurian world is forced to destroy itself—in "the war that will have no end."

Lancelot, learning that he inadvertently killed Gaheriet, soon echoes Bors's prediction: "Or poons nos bien dire, fet Lancelos, que jamés n'avrons pes au roi Artu ne a monseigneur Gauvain pour amour de Gaheriet, car or commencera la guerre qui jamés ne prendra fin" (*Mort* 96. 11–15, "Now we can be sure that we'll never have peace with King Arthur or with Gawain, because of their love for Gaheriet, for now will begin the war that will have no end"). It is notable that Lancelot conveniently ignores Bors's statement about the cause of the war: for Bors, it is adultery; for Lancelot, it is the death of Gaheriet.[9] More important for present purposes is the fact that several characters speak of this war in identical terms and that they refer to it not just as *a* war, but as *the* war that will have no end, as though the future is already formed. That is, the use of the definite article in conjunction with the future tense implies the characters' awareness, no less than the narrator's and the reader's, of the specific catastrophic form that the future will inevitably take.[10]

Passions and events have simply brought them to something already known to be in the offing. There is an awful sense of foreboding, as if the apocalypse is already set and the characters are helpless participants in an inevitable process—which is exactly what Fortune implies. On the Wheel of Fortune, Arthur is beginning his descent, and by definition and tradition, a reversal of the Wheel's movement is inconceivable. Thus, again, Arthurian characters are not in control.

In some instances the text announces not only the finality of war but its precise outcome as well: "Einsint fu la guerre emprise qui puis torna au domage le roi Artu . . ." (*Mort* 105. 11–13, "Thus was the war undertaken that later brought about King Arthur's downfall . . ."). The last announcement in the text, before the battle of Salisbury, is the most specific reference to the end of the Arthurian age: Caradoc states that "c'est la derreniere [bataille] qui i sera au tens le roi Artu" (*Mort* 184. 74–75, "this is the last battle that will take place in the time of King Arthur").

Thus, portents of the future are offered not only by some of the characters but also by the intrusive narrative voice, which announces the tragedy from the start. Later, the narrator juxtaposes within a few lines (*Mort* 129) the information that Arthur required people to swear allegiance to Mordred and the fact—for it is presented not as prediction but as simple fact, known from the "story" that is the source of this narrative—that Arthur will be defeated on Salisbury Plain. This is one of the primary effects of the *Mort Artu* references to *le conte*: it generates an extratemporal perspective and thus juxtaposes present and future to create foreboding irony.[11]

In addition, the future is indicated by prophetic dreams, as when Arthur dreams that Gawain announces his (the king's) death at Mordred's hand (*Mort* 176. 18–20) or when he dreams of the Wheel of Fortune and the narrator states, "Einsi vit li rois Artus les mescheances qui li estoient a avenir" (*Mort* 177. 1–2, "Thus did King Arthur see the misfortunes that were to befall him"). By this point in the text, the retrospection that we noted earlier has disappeared entirely, and every textual detail now points forward, toward the conclusion of the romance and the final dissolution of the Arthurian world.

The narrator clarifies and focuses his apocalyptic vision by fashioning a universe characterized by the progressive loss of contingency.[12] That is not to suggest that truth cannot be misunderstood or events misinterpreted: the Lady of Escalot's letter, for example, is taken by the queen as proof that Lancelot loved the former, an interpretation contrary to the truth. Yet, portents, dreams, and authorial interventions are themselves entirely reliable and unambiguous in the *Mort Artu*. In the *Queste*, there was always the risk, sometimes realized, that the interpretations offered by holy men would be incorrect or misleading—to us as well as to characters—simply because they might not be holy men at all: they might be the devil impersonating those with the power to interpret. In the *Mort Artu*, pronouncements that anticipate the future do not require interpretation. Nor, of course, can those events, once pronounced, be evaded. Everything in this text follows inexorably from events and forces in effect long before the author of the *Mort Artu* set quill to vellum.

The result of this increasing clarity is an effect of diminishing options: as predictions multiply (either from the mouths of characters or in the form of dreams), we realize more and more clearly that there is little for the characters to do but play out the sad drama to its preordained end. At that end, there is of course a vicious and bloodthirsty war, the war that will have no end. That war, narrated in abundant detail and spread out over nearly half the text,[13] is a most curious cataclysm: it does not bring about the end of the Arthurian world but instead noisily punctuates a destruction accomplished long before.

Yet, we should not minimize the importance of the war: the tension between its length and intensity, on one hand, and the impotence of the participants, on the other, defines the fundamental character of the *Mort Artu*. If, for most of us, war is by its nature mindless, this one is literally so: its brutality is all the more cruel because no one is planning and prosecuting it. Once it is begun, it simply happens. And just as it is the war that will have no end, it is also a war that can have no winners.

In fact, in depictions of warfare, the author's rhetoric generally does seem, to me, equal to his task, whether he is simply announcing that after the deaths of valiant men, their lands would lie waste and barren (*Mort* 181. 51–58), or showing how knights "fierent si granz cox qu'il font baignier les espees parmi les hiaumes jusques es cerveles" (*Mort* 182. 3–5, "struck such great blows that they bathed their swords in the brains within enemy helmets").

The author's style is thus fuller and more evocative in scenes that involve crowds, violence, and destruction than in the presentation of human emotions or passions. In the latter situations, he depicts subdued reactions rather than great rages, and he does so through an unusually restricted vocabulary and a register that is significantly lower than in the *Queste*. Even more than in the preceding romances, coordinating conjunctions string clauses together in parallel fashion, emphasizing consecutiveness and creating a leveling effect: in this text, the movement is primarily horizontal or linear, and not vertical. Propositions are thus equal and level, and we move from one to another without a sense that the author is providing explanation or justification: he is simply recounting, and the style contributes often to the impression that the death of a knight is of no greater importance than a routine conversation, that a tourney is as portentous as a war.

Curiously, a part of this leveling effect is cancelled by an increasing emphasis on cause and effect. It is customary to note, as I did above, that the *Mort Artu* is distinctive for its use of a tightly linked chain of causes and effects, for its emphasis on temporal sequence, and for its fundamentally linear structure. In a brief study done years ago, I suggested, however, that such a description is hardly applicable to the early sequences of the romance. The predominant structure in those early parts is patterning, a frame or "ring" structure that interlaces episodes and thus obscures linearity.[14]

Only after more than a third of the text (i.e., around section 85 of Frappier's 204 sections) does this spatial, patterning effect yield to a more direct and linear organization that permits and reinforces sequence and causality. It is in fact at that point that the text finally and completely abandons the kind of interlace that establishes structural simultaneity throughout the Vulgate Cycle. At this point, the text assumes a linear form in which motivations are often elucidated; for example, the author explains that Arthur was easily convinced by the pope's order to take Guenevere back *because* he loved his wife so much (*Mort* 117. 18). Modifying his method in midcourse permits the author to emphasize more graphically the subordination of human efforts to larger, inexorable forces. The change in organizational method, in other words, marks a surrender to inevitability.

To summarize, this romance is in a sense most remarkable for what is *not* there; that is, what the *Lancelot Proper* and the *Queste* have rendered impossible if not, indeed, inconceivable. A catalog of what is lacking from the *Mort Artu* universe includes adventures, the *merveilleux chrétien*, the efficacy of human will, the interlaced narrative lines that added richness and texture to the preceding members of the cycle, and, of course, a good many of the most illustrious inhabitants of Arthur's world. There remains little beyond the falling of dominoes tipped over by forces set off long before and controlled by Fortune rather than by either divinity or humanity.

Although Frappier admitted that the romance was "dramatic," it is difficult to find any real drama in it. The drama of the cycle occurred earlier, and we are now witnessing its harvest. The end of this romance, and of the cycle, is preordained and announced at the beginning, and while there is pathos (e.g., when Arthur and Lancelot recall their love for each other and express their regret that they now oppose each other), there is no drama, because no one is able to stay history's course and Fortune's Wheel. Can we be surprised that in a chivalric world without chivalrous ideals and aspirations, without adventure, without drama, without freedom—can we be surprised that a flute is the narrator's instrument of choice?

This is the flute song of old age, sadly recording the loss of Arthurian idealism and vigor. But the question, ultimately, is whether the flute song is a *fitting* way to end. For some modern sensibilities, the answer is no. But if we conceive of the Vulgate Cycle as the full turn of Fortune's Wheel, the full record of the Arthurian world's precedents, foundation, glory, inevitable decline, and death, then that answer may change.

Were this genuinely the climactic Arthurian moment, the "Twilight of the Gods" that Frappier sees, then with Frappier we should judge the author's linguistic resources entirely inadequate. But there are no gods in this twilight: long before this text opened, the characters (including Arthur) had been reduced to the status of simple human beings who, with limited options and diminished influence, must accept and endure what they are powerless to change. An unsettling effect is therefore generated if we bring to the text an assumption that it should be clothed in a heroic style and should offer a bombastic conclusion. Neither is possible, or, at least, neither is appropriate. A restricted lexical range, a sober style, a subdued rhetoric—all these prove to be the most effective expression of this understated apocalypse, of this sadly autumnal story of the death of King Arthur, of his finest knights, and of his world.

Notes

1. Oxford: Clarendon Press, 1959, p. 313.

2. Another assessment, more descriptive than judgmental, is provided by Alfred L. Kellogg in *Chaucer, Langland, Arthur* (New Brunswick: Rutgers University Press, 1972): 11. He describes the *Lancelot Proper* as "immense and brightly colored," emphasizes the "emphatic piety" of the *Queste*, and characterizes the *Mort Artu* as "compact, sober."

3. The final two lines of "The Hollow Men," in T. S. Eliot, *The Complete Poems and Plays, 1909–1950* (New York: Harcourt, Brace, 1958): 59.

4. The Old French text is quoted from Jean Frappier's edition, *La Mort le Roi Artu* (Geneva: Droz, 1964). Quotations from Frappier's text are cited not by page number but by section and line number. Translations are my own.

5. See, for example, E. Jane Burns, "La Répétition et la mémoire du texte," in *Jeux de mémoire*, edited by Bruno Roy and Paul Zumthor (Montreal: Les Presses de l'Université de Montréal, 1985): 65.

6. Here the word *merveilles* could be taken either figuratively (meaning only "remarkable") or literally, as an indication that marvels as well as adventures are still possible, but see below, n. 7.

7. The expression here seems to mean little more than "how remarkable!" Note that the *word* "merveilles" is used in the text, even though actual marvels are absent; the word is limited to its figurative sense of something striking or extraordinary—but not literally marvelous.

8. In her *Arthurian Fictions: Rereading the Vulgate Cycle* (Columbus: Ohio State University Press, 1985): 151–152.

9. Of course, the attribution of an event to two different causes is by no means unusual in medieval texts. Adultery is the distant or ultimate cause; the killing of Gaheriet is the proximate cause (or provocation). Similarly, the final tragedy of the story may be traceable to Mordred's treason, but the adulterous passion of Lancelot and Guenevere remains the ultimate cause.

10. Arthur, too, shares this sense of the irreversibility of history: he "dist que, se la reïne revenoit, que ja por ce la guerre ne remeindra entre li et Lancelot, puis qu'il l'avoit emprise" (*Mort* 117. 20–22, "said that, even if the queen returned, the war between Lancelot and himself would not cease, now that he had begun it").

11. This extratemporal dimension is further accentuated by the occasional use of past tenses to relate future events. An example is the passage, cited above, concerning the forthcoming battle in which Arthur *was* killed.

12. This is a statement that requires clarification, since the text repeatedly emphasizes "accidents." For example, Lancelot killed Gaheriet without recognizing him. Before that, Arthur had commanded Agravain to go to the pyre, in case Lancelot should try to rescue Guenevere (*Mort* 93. 60–69). Without explaining why, Agravain had asked Arthur to order Gaheriet to accompany him, and Arthur does so. If Agravain had not requested the presence of his brother, *and* if Lancelot had not killed Gaheriet, then the war would not have been provoked. But of course, since the war was inevitable (being rendered so long before by Lancelot's treason with the queen), then such "accidents" are similarly inevitable occurrences. That is, what appear to be accidental or unmotivated events are in fact essential steps in the process by which a thoroughly determined historical sequence is moving inexorably toward its conclusion.

13. To be precise, it occupies 120 pages out of 263 in Frappier's edition, if we measure from the declaration of war to the end of the battle at Salisbury.

14. For example, early sequences tend to be organized into an *abcdcba* pattern that relates subsequent episodes backward to link them up with others that correspond to them. See my article "Spatial Form in the *Mort Artu*," *Symposium* 31 (1977): 337–345.

6. Autobiography and History in the Vulgate *Estoire* and in the *Prose Merlin*

Rupert T. Pickens

The *Estoire del Saint Graal* starts out with an extraordinary prologue that is nearly ten quarto pages long in the Sommer edition.[1] There a clerkly—and clerical—narrator gives the history of the book he is about to translate in his vernacular account of the Grail, and he tells the story of his personal involvement with that book. Thus the Lancelot-Grail romance inscribes from its very beginning a reflective and self-referential discourse that accounts for its own origins—a specularity that penetrates the text down to the closing words of the *Mort Artu* some two and a half thousand pages later.[2] One could well argue that, as a unifying theme, the story of the romance's origins rivals in importance the history of the Grail which it parallels and in which it is so intimately bound up.

It is also significant that the initiatory *mise en abyme* of the Vulgate *Estoire* takes the form of autobiographical narrative: the Lancelot-Grail begins as autobiography. The primacy of autobiography is certainly true in a material sense, in terms of the way the romance is read linearly, from start to finish. The *Estoire* prologue, in the first words of the Vulgate romance, begins with a conventional exordial displacement of the authorial voice in the third person: "Chil ki se tient & iuge au plus petit et au plus peceor du monde. Mande salus au commenchement de ceste estoire A tos cheaus ki lor cuers ont & lor creance en la sainte trinite" (Sommer 3. 1–4,[3] "He who condemns himself as the least man in the world, and the most sinful, greets, at the start of this history, all those who put their faith and trust in the Holy Trinity"). When the narrator turns to the history of his book, however, "Chil ki se tient & iuge" becomes the divided "I" of conventional autobiographical discourse, the narrated "I" and the narrating "I": "iou li plus pechieres de tous les autres peceors estoie en .j. lieu le plus souage que iou ne voel faire connoistre . . ." (Sommer 4. 2–4, "I, the most sinful of all sinners, found myself in the most desolate place I would ever wish to describe . . ."). The text continues in this autobiographical mode through the next several pages until the clerkly/ clerical voice turns to the content of the book that he has depicted himself as having received and begun to translate, and at this point his voice becomes that of the conventional narrator of historical discourse. Indeed, he is the narrator of sacred history: "Al ior que li salueres du monde sousfri mort fu mors destruite & nostre uie restoree. A icel ior estoient moult poi de gent qui en lui creoient fors si desciple" (Sommer 12. 30–32, "On the day when the Savior of the world suffered death, death was destroyed and our life restored. On that day there were few people who believed in Him except His disciples"). Thus, in the *Estoire*, autobiography is accorded primacy in that it precedes history materially. As we shall see, throughout the Lancelot-Grail romance as a whole, autobiography precedes historical discourse textually as well.[4]

As E. Jane Burns has cogently argued in discussing the complexities of narrative voice in the Lancelot-Grail, shifts in focus are an essential feature of the romance's very textuality.[5] The shifts she has in mind are far more radical than the one we have just observed, when the autobiographer became the narrator of historical discourse. Four major displacements in the "I" narrator occur from branch to branch in the Vulgate romance, sometimes within the same branch: from the book written by Christ in the *Estoire* to Merlin's dictation and Blaise's transcriptions in the *Merlin* to the chronicles of the Queen's knights later on and then to the related Grail knights' histories and, finally, to Walter Map's translation of these chronicles in the *Queste del Saint Graal* and his *Mort Artu* addendum. Moreover, the personal identities of the myriad succession of narrators appear to be subsumed in the anonymity and quasi impersonality of the narrative text itself, *li contes* that succeeds and absorbs every one of their individual texts.[6] Thus, in its vast corpus, the Vulgate romance as a whole embodies and exemplifies a *mouvance* that eventually brings into question conventional assumptions about the textual organization of narrative; moreover, to the extent that narrative shifts are produced in conformity with apparent changes in clerkly perspective from branch to branch, they also exemplify processes of *translatio* that are implicit in *mouvance* and explicit in the adaptation of Latin texts in the vernacular (Burns, 27–34).

My discussion will therefore focus on the essential generic transformation that constitutes the basis of that *mouvance* and that *translatio* and on the process whereby one narrative voice appropriates and succeeds another in the generation of historical narrative from autobiography. Simply put, one narrator's autobiography becomes another voice's third-person narrative. And the process is replicated throughout the romance as a purely secular and vernacular textuality succeeds and ultimately supplants sacred history. The process is begun, and the outcome is already adumbrated, in the Vulgate *Estoire* prologue itself, but the *Prose Merlin*[7] proves pivotal in more than one sense. In terms of the Lancelot-Grail plot, the *Merlin* significantly promotes the secularization of Grail history and thereby energizes the forces of *mouvance* and *translatio;* so the *Merlin* exemplifies what Burns calls "the poetics of rewriting."[8] Not only does the *Merlin* figure in the Lancelot-Grail romance itself, however, but it also constitutes—primarily, in terms of the *Merlin's* external literary history—a part of the so-called Robert de Boron trilogy, the nature of which can be perceived independently of the Lancelot-Grail romance.[9] By no means is Robert de Boron entirely "translated out" of the Lancelot-Grail, for his remains an authoritative voice; thus the *Prose Merlin,* as part of the Lancelot-Grail romance, clearly bears the signs of its earlier, pre-Vulgate association with Robert de Boron's verse *Estoire.* In heightened specularity, the Lancelot-Grail text internalizes and incorporates a fragment of its external history, that is, its "real-time" development as a *translatio*—and, we must admit, a considerable amplification—of Robert de Boron's verse *Estoire* and *Merlin.*

Very obviously, then, in real time the Lancelot-Grail romance developed through processes of rewriting and conjoining a series of core texts, texts by Chrétien de Troyes, Robert de Boron, Wace, and many others. And this real-time writing project is reflected fictionally in the Lancelot-Grail text at a multiplicity of levels: first, in commentary attributable to the voice of the *conte* narrator which portrays the *conte* as the product of *translatio* and conjoining; second, within the basic plot, where characters are depicted as translators, rewriters, and transmitters of text that is most often depicted as the original core of the very work we are reading; and finally (and this is a textual layer whose constituent strands are much more difficult to trace), in the myriad translations and rewritings referred to as having taken place in time and space separating the present moment of the *conte* narrator's narration in the present and the distant events that constitute the romance's plot, which is itself so concerned with the production and transmission of text.

The *Estoire del Saint Graal's* initial autobiography, as its length alone might suggest, is remarkably complex. For our purposes, it suffices to highlight two features: how the autobiographical account establishes an authorial voice and how it exemplifies processes of translation. The narrator opens his discourse by referring to himself as the world's worst sinner, as we have seen, and he exhorts those to whom he addresses his discourse to believe firmly in the Trinity. Invoking the fear-of-detractors topos, he vows to remain nameless for three reasons: first, he dreads being considered presumptuous in conveying such a lofty *estoire* as that of the Holy Grail; second, readers who know him might value his work all the less; third, if errors creep into his text in the course of transmission, critical readers will blame him instead of the careless copyists. The narrator's use of the unreliable scribe topos is especially interesting because the verb he uses to signify "to transmit a text in writing" is, precisely, *translater* (Sommer 3. 21).

The narrator remains indefinite about the discursive present and does not date the *présent de l'énonciation* when he identifies himself as the unnamed narrating "I," when he enters into communication with his addressees, when he names his text *L'Estoire del Saint Graal*, when he speculates about his text's future in transmission, and so forth; but he is explicit in dating the events in his autobiographical discourse, situating the narrated "I" as a priestly hermit living in an isolated *locus amoenus* during the period from Maundy Thursday through Easter Monday in the year A.D. 750 or, as he specifies, 717 years after the Passion of Our Lord.[10] During the night from Maundy Thursday to Good Friday, he is visited by the living Christ, who leaves with him a book written in His own hand. Later Christ's book is referred to as *L'Escripture du Saint Graal* (Sommer 120. 6), also as "la sainte escripture" (Sommer 119. 10) and "la sainte estoire uraie" (Sommer 119. 13) in contradistinction to our narrator's text, on the one hand, and, on the other, to the *conte* that contains it.

Christ's book, which will become the source of the narrator's *Estoire*, has, as an object, extraordinary powers. It is small enough to fit into a man's hand (Sommer 5. 2), and yet, for a book its size, it contains an extraordinary amount of writing (Sommer 5. 28–29); it can revive a man who appears senseless and drive a devil from his body (Sommer 11. 1–27). It is closely associated with the *corpus Domini*: at one point, after reading it, the clerical narrator stores it with the reserved sacrament (Sommer 8. 3); later, after Christ has taken the book away from him, he finds it on an altar (Sommer 11. 7–8). Equally as important, the narrator must undergo an extended mystical quest to regain the book, which Christ later hides from him, apparently in order to prove him worthy of copying it (Sommer 8–12). For, in effect, Christ's book is given to the narrator not to keep or to pass along intact, but to transcribe in another book (Sommer 12. 21–29)—that is, to return to the language of the narrator's introductory statements, he is given the book to *translater*.

The anonymous narrator's mediatory role between Christ's text and the *translatio* he makes of it is further strengthened by the fact that

Christ's book is written in no human tongue, but in what we may call the language of heaven. Christ does not give the narrator His book to copy until after he has learned to read and to speak that heavenly language. When Christ asks him, "Pues tu entendre et apercevoir qui iou sui" (Sommer 4. 22, "Can you comprehend and perceive who I am?"), his reply invokes the ineffability topos: "ne sui mie encore poissans de dire ce dont toutes les mortex langues estoient encombrees del dire" (Sommer 4. 24–25, "I lack as yet the power to say what all mortal tongues are hampered [*entravé*] in speaking about"). This answer thus suggests a direct link between his inability to behold the heavenly ("Et iou li respondi que mi oeil estoient mortel si ne pooie pas esgarder si grant clarte" [Sommer 4. 22–23, "And I answered him that my eyes were mortal and I could not look at such bright light"]) and his powerlessness to express what he might have seen.

But Christ grants the narrator the gift both to comprehend and to speak the language of heaven. In the narrator's vision, Christ breathes on him; immediately it seems as though his eyes see a hundred times more clearly than before, and he feels before his mouth "unes grans merveilles de langues" (Sommer 4. 27–28, "great wonders of tongues"). And when next he opens his mouth to speak, he spews forth a stream of fire, while, awestruck, he cannot utter ordinary words. The heavenly language is thus spoken in fire, we might say Pentecostal fire, and it is no meaningless apocalyptic ornament in the narrator's account that henceforth every heavenly visitation is announced by an air-splitting thunderbolt.

Christ warns the narrator that the book written in His hand must be read by the tongue of the heart and not spoken aloud by the tongue in the head. Indeed, if Christ's handwriting were to be read aloud by a human tongue (the verb used is *nomer*, Sommer 5. 9), all creation would be destroyed as the four elements exchanged their properties (Sommer 5. 7–11). Despite the knowledge Christ instills in him, however, the *Estoire* narrator, as a mortal, can hardly know the heavenly language perfectly. When he hears choirs of angels singing a hymn of praise, a song they repeat seven times, he understands the acclamation at the very end, but can make out no other words in the hymn. Referring to the hymn's closing, he observes: "Ceste loenge entendi iou bien, mais en tout l'autre n'entendoie iou nient" (Sommer 6. 21–22, "I understood this praise well, but I comprehended nothing in all the rest").

So when the *Estoire* narrator undertakes to write down in another book what he finds in the exemplar written by Christ—when he undertakes to translate Christ's book—we understand that it is not merely a process of reproducing the book in an act of automatic textual transmission, but a process of rendering in human language what he finds inscribed there in Pentecostal fire.[11] Moreover, as we also understand that the *Estoire* narrator has limited proficiency in the fiery language of heaven, his project is flawed from the very beginning: although he is an elect mediator, he regards himself ever as the lowest of God's sinners. This phase in the history of the Vulgate *Estoire del Saint Graal* text we might call a first-degree *translatio*.

Just as the *Estoire* begins as autobiography and continues by inscribing an important shift as the autobiography's narrated "I" gives way to the third-person narrated "Other" of historical discourse, so we can observe from the very first lines of the narrated history a more advanced phase in the transformational process. Christ appears as a character in the *Estoire* narrator's historical discourse, his *translatio* of the book written by Christ. The book written by Christ in heavenly language is therefore in some sense autobiographical. We have already seen that the account begins with the Crucifixion, and it continues with Christ's ministrations to Joseph of Arimathea in prison and other instances of His intervention in human affairs. Thus the first historical discourse in the Lancelot-Grail romance also exemplifies the rule of generic transformation: autobiography precedes history. In terms of the history of the Vulgate *Estoire del Saint Graal* text, such a step represents a second-degree *translatio*.

The narrative status of that *Estoire* narrator's text within the framework of the Lancelot-Grail as a whole is not perceived so readily, for the time of its production lies in that intermediate layer between the time of the plot and the moment of its narration. We recall that the narrator is precise in dating the events of his earlier life, but he does not account for the time when he composes his story. However, the simple fact that the narrator's autobiography and his historical discourse are juxtaposed, indeed conjoined, and the fact that the one directs our reading of the other, both suggest the effects of yet other degrees of *translatio* following both the act of translating and transmitting Christ's book, to be sure, and, as well, the production of the autobiographical framework—thus a process of *translatio* to the third degree. Moreover, as a branch of the Lancelot-Grail romance, the Vulgate *Estoire* is necessarily subsumed in the all-embracing *conte*—a *translatio*, then, to the fourth degree. In fact, as we shall see, the Vulgate *Merlin Continuation*, by identifying the anonymous *Estoire* narrator, locates his mystical involvement with *translatio* relative to a specific moment in Arthurian history.

Meanwhile, to return to the Vulgate *Estoire*, two subsequent references which foreshadow the transition into the *Prose Merlin* suggest a relationship between the *Estoire* narrator's text and Robert de Boron.

The Vulgate *Estoire* twice calls Robert de Boron to witness: "ensi le tesmoigne mesires robers de Borron qui a translate ceste estoire en franchois de latin" (Sommer 195. 33–35, "so testifies my lord Robert of Boron, who has translated this history into French from Latin"). The second appeal is more emphatic: "Car messires robers de borron qui ceste estoire translata de latin en franchois & la uraie estoire le tesmoigne, car sans faille chis le translata" (Sommer 280. 12–14, "For my lord Robert of Boron, who translated this history from Latin into French, and the True History testifies to this; for without any doubt, he is the one who translated it"). Textually, the commentary in these references is not attributable to the *Estoire* narrator's voice, for it is a question of a *translatio* lying in the distant future with respect to plot-time—a stage in the text's development following the events associated with third-degree *translatio* during that vague intermediate time between the events of the plot and the moment of narration. Robert de Boron is, in fact, a modern translator who worked in the recent past with respect to the organization of the Lancelot-Grail romance. We are therefore justified in associating the commentary on Robert de Boron with the voice of the *conte* narrator, who is his near contemporary.

These passages are specific and unambiguous about a previous state in the history of the *Estoire* narrator's text. The text was at one time in Latin, and the Latin text is the *translatio*, or a version of that *translatio*, from the heavenly language that is to be ascribed to the autobiographical narrator of the Vulgate *Estoire*'s prologue. Moreover, as we are reading a text written in French, we identify this vernacular text with yet another stage in the process of *translatio* beyond the conjoining of the clerical narrator's autobiographical discourse and his historical discourse; this is precisely the fourth-degree *translatio* associated with the more global *conte*.

So the Vulgate *Estoire* comments upon its own source in referring to Robert de Boron. The question may arise, however, as to whether the Vulgate *Estoire* ascribes authorship of one or another of its own *translationes* to Robert de Boron. I would suggest, in opposition to most other scholars' understanding of the references (above, n. 6), that it is worth considering a response in the negative. Here the Vulgate *Estoire* does not seek to arrogate or to appropriate to itself the authorial identity of Robert de Boron. On one level, the references constitute a conventional appeal to Robert de Boron's authority as that of another translator—I would stress, another modern translator—who, like the translator-narrator of the *conte*, bears witness to the priestly autobiographer's initiatory *translatio* of Christ's own fiery words. Furthermore, the Vulgate *Estoire*'s second and more developed reference to Robert de Boron specifically states that both Robert de Boron's independent *translatio* and the Lancelot-Grail's *translatio* of the Latin text attest to what is true in "la uraie estoire." This, we have seen, is another term the Vulgate text uses for Christ's *Escripture du Saint Graal*. Both Robert de Boron's *translatio* and that of the narrator of the Lancelot-Grail's *conte* are several removes from the copy of Christ's book executed by the priestly autobiographer in the *Estoire*.

The Vulgate *Estoire* does not name Robert de Boron among its translators but specifies that he has produced a parallel *translatio* of the Vulgate *Estoire*'s source-text. This assertion, which does not reflect the truth of what we believe to be the real-time history of the Vulgate Cycle, serves fictionally, nevertheless, to validate the independent status of the Vulgate *Estoire* as a text distinct from Robert de Boron's *Estoire du Graal* and its translation into prose, the *Joseph d'Arimathie*. Yet, in the words of the Vulgate *Estoire*'s epilogue, the Lancelot-Grail proceeds openly to embrace and to incorporate Robert de Boron's *Merlin*. So, in the transitional commentary linking the Vulgate *Estoire* to the *Prose Merlin*, it is the voice of the *conte* narrator that informs us of the necessity to add the *Merlin* branch to the *Estoire del Saint Graal*, and the *conte* continues with particular emphasis to inscribe Robert de Boron as the authoritative voice in that source: "Et commenche messires robers en tel maniere comme vous porres oir sil est qui le vous die" (Sommer 296. 19–21, "And my lord Robert begins just as you will hear, and it is indeed he who tells it to you").

In embracing Robert de Boron's *Merlin*, the Lancelot-Grail absorbs what can be numbered among the most beautiful and most fortunate of Robert de Boron's inventions: the symbiotic relationship that binds the seminal narrator Merlin and his scribe Blaise. For in the Vulgate *Merlin* the book of Blaise, called the *Livre du Graal* (Sommer 28. 15; cf. Micha 290. 60), and the circumstances of its periodic dictation and inscription constitute, in an unusually extended and interlaced *mise en abyme*, a force more powerful than the Grail itself, which remains hidden throughout the *Merlin* and functions, in fact, solely as the object of Merlin's discourse. Merlin's frequent returns to Blaise throughout the branch constantly refocus attention on the processes of *translatio* within the romance's historical discourse, and this reflects the frequent, signatory statements "here the *conte* falls silent/here the *conte* begins speaking" that punctuate the romance's discursive present and draw attention both to the *conte*'s narrative voice and its organization of narrated material.

Scholars have noted that the Vulgate *Estoire* was written to parallel the *Merlin*, though in terms of our reading of the Lancelot-Grail as fiction, we should be interested in how the *Merlin* reflects the opening branch. In any case, the two branches are mutually illuminative. Christ figures prominently in the *Estoire* prologue; Merlin is conceived as a diabolical Antichrist, but becomes Christlike thanks to his mother's constant faith in God and especially to his baptism, when God endows him with the superhuman powers and knowledge that are his diabolical heritage, but turned to God's service. Further, Christ and the Christlike Merlin are featured as producers of text—the former in fiery writing and the latter in dictation—that a scribe "translates" into a book destined to be subject to retranslation and rewriting in the production of the Lancelot-Grail itself. The essential difference between Christ and man, even an extraordinary man like Merlin, as originator of mediatory text is pointed up in the *Estoire* narrator's somewhat puzzling preoccupation with the doctrine of the Trinity.

We recall that, in his prologue, the Vulgate *Estoire* narrator greets his audience in the name of the Trinity. He then describes himself as a priest of nearly exemplary beliefs, except that he has been unable to accept the doctrine of the Trinity. Indeed, coextensive with his involvement with Christ's book about the Grail are a series of mystical experiences all focusing on the Trinity; finally, the Holy Ghost bears him, like St. Paul (2 Cor. 12), up to the Third Heaven and then even higher, where he actually beholds the Trinity in glory (Sommer 7. 4–26). Having seen the reality, he understands and thus accepts the doctrine. The Vulgate *Estoire*'s prologue is otherwise concerned with processes of textual origination and translation, so it appears to reiterate the fundamental fact in medieval textuality. Only God can originate text, and Christ is mediator of divine text in communication with humankind; but as God, Christ communicates about Himself: Christ as original autobiographer has authored the sacred book of Grail history written in His hand. Mortals, however, need to have that text translated; as man, Christ provides means to facilitate that translation. Human beings, even mortals with extraordinary powers like Merlin, originate nothing; for them, communication is a process of transmission and translation of matter received. Human autobiography, therefore, although undertaken in imitation of Christ, is also derivative because it bears witness to oneself as narrated "Other" (see Vitz 126–148).

In imitation of Christ and as a reflection of the Vulgate *Estoire* narrator, Merlin also produces an autobiography that is translated into historical discourse as Blaise inscribes it and as it is transmitted and ultimately conjoined with the Lancelot-Grail's *conte*. Christ and His Incarnation are at the center of sacred history and early Grail history as recounted in His book. Likewise, Merlin's "incarnation" as event and Merlin as participant are important components of later Grail history and in the history of Britain. The text of the *Merlin Proper* (that is, the text common to Robert de Boron's trilogy and to the Lancelot-Grail) portrays Merlin's autobiographical account in a way that is stylistically quite arresting; it is portrayed in "emergent direct discourse"; that is, when a sustained indirect discourse suddenly shifts to direct (the switch to italics marks the approximate point of "emergence"):[12]

> Apres li dist [a Blaise] des diables comment il orent parlement de ce quil auoient perdu lor pooir quil soloient auoir sor les hommes. & si li conte comment li prophete lor auoient mal fait. & por ce auoient porparle quil feroient .j. homme. & disent *quil me feroient & tu las bien oi & seu par ma mere & par autrui la paine & lenginge & puis la folie dont il sont plain mont il perdu & tous autres biens.*

> (Sommer 19. 19–24)

> (Afterward he told Blaise about the devils and how they had gathered to talk about having lost the power they exerted over men. And he told them how the prophets had done them harm, and that is why they came to an agreement that they would make a man. And they said *they would make me, and you have heard it all and learned from my mother and others about their efforts and trickery, and then, in the folly they are so full of they have lost me and all their other gains.*)

At the diegetic level, that is, within the story, Merlin dictates the very events we have just read, and Blaise inscribes them in the book that is to become the source-text of which we are reading a *translatio*. The stylistic effect of the "emergent direct discourse" is a product of that recent *translatio*, as the indirect discourse at the opening represents the voice of the *conte*'s narrator. In this instance, the narrator allows autobiography to emerge from history in a display of stylistic prowess. Merlin's words are translated into historical discourse thanks to Blaise's inscription. And Merlin's frequent successive visits to Blaise's writing desk reinforce the Lancelot-Grail's fundamental discursive process: as participant in and eyewitness to the events he narrates to Blaise, Merlin produces an autobiographical text that is transformed subsequently, if not immediately, into historical discourse in the course of translation.

At this point, it may prove informative to pull back and examine the special status of the *Merlin* from another point of view before returning to a discussion of the book copied by Blaise. The Vulgate

Merlin functions very differently from the Vulgate *Estoire* as a text by Robert de Boron, or attributable to Robert de Boron, which in real time made its way into the Lancelot-Grail romance through various processes of translation and amplification. The Vulgate *Merlin* is divided into two parts. The first part, called the *Merlin Proper*, appears in Alexandre Micha's 1980 edition (above, n. 9) and embraces the first eighty-eight pages or so of Sommer's 1908 quarto edition (above, n. 7); the *Merlin Proper* is found in some fifty-one manuscripts. The second part is known as the *Merlin Continuation* or, to use Sommer's term from his introduction, the *Livre d'Artus*.[13] The Vulgate *Merlin Continuation*, more than four times longer than the first part, is found in only twelve of the fifty-one manuscripts.[14]

The twelve manuscripts with both the *Merlin Proper* and the *Merlin Continuation* are the ones of greatest interest in the present context because they transmit the Lancelot-Grail cycle; thus, in them the *Prose Merlin* (*Merlin Proper* plus *Continuation*) is associated with the Vulgate *Estoire* as its predecessor in the cycle, and it is followed by the *Lancelot Proper*. The thirty-nine manuscripts without the *Merlin Continuation*, on the contrary, are associated with the "Little Grail Cycle" attributed to Robert de Boron that is introduced by his verse *Estoire*, or rather its prose translation, the *Joseph d'Arimathie*; two of these manuscripts conclude with the *Didot Perceval*. One of the particularly interesting features of the *Prose Merlin* generally is that the text of the *Merlin Proper* is, *grosso modo*, shared by both Grail cycles. It is as though, given the independent status of the two cycles in the manuscript tradition, they intersect in the course of the *Merlin Proper*, diverge when the *Continuation* begins, and then proceed to their divergent conclusions. As we have seen, the Vulgate *Estoire* acknowledges the existence of its rival and extols it as an exemplary work by another modern translator.

Alexandre Micha notes some variations in the text of the *Merlin Proper* consistent with its identification with one or the other of the cycles ("Les Manuscrits" 145–174), but, when one examines Micha's established Robert de Boron prose text (what he calls the α text) and Sommer's Vulgate *Merlin Proper* (Micha's β), it is apparent that the differences between the two versions are slight in comparison with the enormous gap that separates Robert de Boron's *Estoire/Joseph* from the Vulgate *Estoire* that descended from it in real time. What is striking, in fact, and what seems significant, therefore, is the remarkable cohesion of the α and β texts in the midst of all the rereading and rewriting, in real time and in plot-time, that have been discussed thus far. It is as though the manuscript tradition respected and somehow celebrated the integrity of Robert de Boron's *Merlin Proper*, thereby preserving it from significant change in *mouvance*. Similarly, we recall William Roach's observation that medieval scribal tradition honored the text of Chrétien de Troyes's *Conte du Graal* in stark contrast to the profound modifications that characterize the various redactions of the *Continuations*.[15]

There are, however, significant differences between the α and β texts of the *Merlin Proper*. Most important is the fact that references to Robert de Boron occur only in manuscripts that also manifest Robert de Boron's *Joseph*, and they are not found in the manuscripts that incorporate the *Merlin Proper* into the Lancelot-Grail romance. Thus, the "Little Grail Cycle" continuously and consistently ascribes itself to Robert de Boron's authorship. In the Lancelot-Grail, however, the *conte* narrator appeals to Robert de Boron's authority and extols his *Merlin* as a worthy translation and a branch required by the Vulgate project, but then, as Robert de Boron's work is absorbed, his name is utterly forgotten; the name Robert de Boron does not recur after the closing transition in the Vulgate *Estoire*.

One passage that is important for other reasons as well offers still more interesting differences. When Merlin starts dictating his book to Blaise and begins his account of early Grail history, the details in his retrospective discourse according to the α text are consistent with Robert de Boron's *Estoire/Joseph*. In the α text, Merlin speaks of Alain and the adventures of Petrus (Micha 73. 68–70). Alain and Petrus are Grail companions in Robert de Boron's text who do not recur in the Vulgate *Estoire*; accordingly, Merlin does not include them in his account according to the β text. Conversely, Merlin's discourse in the β text refers to Nascien and his companions (Sommer 19. 18). Nascien is an invention of the Vulgate *Estoire* translator, and his name occurs neither in Robert de Boron's *Estoire/Joseph* nor, significantly, in the α text of the *Merlin Proper*.

This passage also bears a significant exception to the remarkable consistency in the Vulgate *Merlin*'s "real-time" rewriting of Robert de Boron, and the example points to profoundly different functions ascribed to Blaise's project in each of the two Grail cycles. Turning to the future, Merlin announces, according to both the α and the β texts, that Blaise will eventually join the company of the Grail and finish his book in the presence of the Grail (Sommer 19. 33–20. 8; Micha 75. 93–107). In other words, eventually the history of the Grail and that of the book where that history is manifest will be conjoined absolutely. Despite what Merlin promises here, this is most assuredly not the fate reserved for Blaise and his book in the Vulgate Cycle. The prediction is consistent with eventualities in the Robert de Boron cycle, however, where, in the *Didot Perceval*, Blaise takes his book and joins the new Fisher King, who is Perceval, at the Grail castle.

Merlin soon reiterates his prophecy with renewed emphasis— again in both the α and the β texts—and he reveals the title Blaise's book will have: the *Livre du Graal* (Sommer 28. 15; Micha 101. 63–64). Moreover, here Merlin for the first time intimates that, henceforth, Grail history will be conjoined not only with the writing of Blaise's book but also with the history of Arthur's reign in Britain: "Et saces que nule vie de roiaus ne de sages ne fu onques si volentiers oie comme sera cele del roy artus & des gens qui a cel tans seront & regneront" (Sommer 28. 10–12, "And know that no life of a king or a wise man was ever more gladly heard than will be the life of King Arthur and the people who will live and rule in that time"). Indeed, it is the function of the *Merlin Proper* in both Grail cycles to "translate" the history of the Grail into British history. However, to repeat, the Lancelot-Grail, unlike the "Little Grail Cycle" of Robert de Boron, does not fulfill the promise of an ideal intersection of history and commentary.[16] In the Lancelot-Grail, Grail history and the writing of Grail history do not converge in time and space.

Blaise's inscriptions are essential in the fictional transmission of Grail history, but as the *Prose Merlin* progresses far into the Vulgate *Continuation*, other fictionalized texts and books gradually emerge as alternate sources of the *conte* narrator's knowledge of British history.[17] One is an apparent source-text called "li contes des estoires" (Sommer 136. 30) or, in the plural, "li conte des estoires" (Sommer 221. 31–32). The context of the latter occurrence is particularly noteworthy. On the one hand, the "conte des estoires," which provides information about a cousin of Perceval the Welshman, is clearly distinguished from the Lancelot-Grail's *conte*, which will speak later about Perceval and/or his mother, "car il lieus nen est ore mie" (Sommer 221. 33, "for it is not now the place to do so"). On the other hand, the passage is important because it identifies the anonymous narrator of the Vulgate *Estoire*; it sets the circumstances under which he translated Christ's book well into the diegetic future, and it ascribes to him a role in organizing the text of the book copied by Blaise. Nascien, a knight of the Round Table, distinguishes himself in the battle between Leodegan and King Rion. In an extensive commentary, the voice of the *conte* narrator informs us that, later, Nascien became a hermit priest and then was visited by Christ, who gave him "la sainte estoire" (Sommer 222. 3) to copy: "& tant en escrist quil aiousta al liure blaise qui par merlin en fist ce quil en fist" (Sommer 222. 4–5, "and he kept writing until he added [his transcription] to the book of Blaise who did with it what he did because of Merlin").

It is clear that the Lancelot-Grail has begun to subvert the central role as source-text ascribed to the book of Blaise by Robert de Boron's "Little Grail Cycle." In identifying very specifically the book Robert de Boron undertook to translate as he produced his *Estoire/Joseph*, the Vulgate *Estoire* proposes, indeed imposes, a rereading of Robert de Boron's *Merlin* as well as of his *Estoire/Joseph*; in so doing, the Lancelot-Grail effectively acknowledges its own enterprise of rewriting Robert de Boron in real time. We recall that, in the *Estoire/Joseph*, Robert de Boron describes his *Estoire du Graal* as a *translatio* of a Latin source, a *livre* (Nitze 3457–3514). This much accords with the Lancelot-Grail commentary about the common source of both the Vulgate *Estoire* and Robert de Boron. In his *Merlin* (or in the prose translation we possess of the *Merlin*), however, Robert de Boron for the first time turns explicitly to the history of his own source-text, which is the book dictated by Merlin and written down by Blaise; henceforth, the history of the book written by Blaise is to be coextensive with the history of the Grail. In that extraordinary *mise en abyme*, furthermore, Robert de Boron inscribes Merlin, dictating to Blaise, as the author of the book Robert de Boron translates in his *Estoire/Joseph*.

Merlin starts dictating, in fact, at the very point where the Vulgate *Estoire*'s clerical narrator begins his historical discourse: "si . . . comença a aconter les amors de Jhesu Crist et de Joseph tot ensi com eles avoient esté . . ." (Micha 73. 63–65,[18] "so he began to recount the love between Jesus Christ and Joseph just as it had been"). According to the fiction of Robert de Boron's trilogy, I repeat, Merlin is thus unambiguously the originator of the *Joseph/Estoire* source. In the rereading imposed by the Lancelot-Grail, however, Merlin does not author the source-text common to Robert de Boron and the Vulgate *Estoire*, for the book written by Blaise as dictated by Merlin cannot contain that which, according to the voice of the *conte* narrator, Nascien later added to that book. As, nevertheless, Blaise's book clearly manifests an early Grail history, we understand that Merlin's "invention" of that text, as portrayed in the common *Merlin Proper*, is a version of those events that is necessarily inferior to the *translatio* produced by Nascien, the knight-turned-hermit whom Christ trusted to translate His book.

The Vulgate *Merlin Continuation* invents yet another and ultimately, perhaps, more important source-text to serve the Lancelot-Grail romance. This is the book, founded at Gawain's behest, in which the knights of Arthur's court are to have their adventures written down when they return to court after a year's questing, for a complete and truthful inscription of their adventures is to be an essential function of the kind of questing knight-errantry established when Gawain and his companions attach themselves to Guenevere as the queen's knights who are to succeed—in a perfect example of *translatio imperii*—the barbarous knights of the original Round Table. Arthur embraces Gawain's enterprise and chooses four clerks to record henceforth their tales of adventure (Sommer 321). Theirs is the book eventually hidden at Salisbury—written in Latin, to be sure—that Walter Map was given to translate by King Henry II.

What the Vulgate *Merlin* thus portrays is the establishment of an idealized secular knighthood and a secular textuality that is appropriate to the inscription of that knighthood and its values, however religious such values may be at times. The Lancelot-Grail romance itself, in the ultimate *translatio* produced by the *conte* narrator, of course vernacularizes that already secular textuality. This process is portrayed, in reflection and specularity, at many textual levels in the Lancelot-Grail.

The progressive humanization and weakening of Merlin exemplify the triumph of secularized and vernacularized textuality;[19] for the emergence, in the *Merlin Continuation*, of other source-texts besides the book of Blaise—a "conte des estoires," Nascien's book, the chronicle of the queen's knights—occurs simultaneously with Merlin's growing love for and his gradual entrapment by Viviane (Sommer 211–213, 376, 421, 450–452). In some sense, Viviane is a female Blaise, "chele qui bien estoit endoctrinee de clergie" (Sommer 421. 39, "she who was inculcated with sound learning"); in fact, her knowledge of writing is one of the unusual things about her as a child that draw Merlin's attention to her (Sommer 211). As Merlin's pupil, moreover, she writes down all the lessons he gives her, and as he is ever more helplessly seduced by her, the secrets he reveals to her are ever more powerful. Indeed, as in the kinds of *translatio* we have observed in process at every level in the Lancelot-Grail, it is through the act of transcribing that Viviane appropriates to herself and absorbs Merlin's words, Merlin's powers, and eventually Merlin himself.

Just before Merlin goes to Viviane and yields to her forever, he visits Blaise for the last time and dictates the story of Arthur's victory over the Romans (Sommer 421–422). This is the last time Blaise is depicted as the clerkly transcriber of Merlin's authoritative autobiographical dictation. The book of Blaise thus fades away, at the diegetic level, as a significant reflection of the translator's enterprise and, at the level of the *conte*'s narrative organization, as a primary source-text. Those grand and grandiose predictions that Merlin made for

Blaise's project and its merger with Grail history are not realized in the Lancelot-Grail, as they are in the Robert de Boron cycle, but are undercut by the serio-comic, conventionally *fabelesque* downfall of the man of powerful intellect who is brought low and imprisoned by the forces of love. However, what makes Merlin a more poignant figure than, say, the philosopher in the *Lai d'Aristote* or, more pertinently, the Hippocrates of the Vulgate *Estoire* (Sommer 170–182), is his clairvoyant knowledge of his doom and, at the same time, his unwillingness or inability to avoid it.

After Merlin's final farewell to Arthur, Gawain leaves the court in quest of him and discovers him at Viviane's stronghold; there Merlin speaks to Gawain as a disembodied voice. Gawain asks him: "Comment puet ce a force auenir qui esties li plus sages homs del monde" (Sommer 461. 35–36, "How can such a thing have happened to you, the wisest man in the whole world"). And these are among Merlin's last recorded words: "Mais li plus fols . . . quar iou sauoie bien ce quauenir mestoit. E iou fui si fols que j'aim plus autrui que moi. et si apris a mamie par quoi iou sui enprisones. ne nus ne me puet desprisonner" (Sommer 461. 35–38, "But I was the most foolish of men. For I knew clearly what was to happen to me, and I was so foolish as to love someone else more than myself. And so I taught my lady-love how to make me her prisoner, and now no one can free me from captivity"). Merlin is rendered impotent by love and, most significantly, by a process of *translatio* that has at the same time dissipated the powers of the project of transcription undertaken by Blaise.

Merlin's last words are inscribed not in the book written by Blaise but in the chronicle of the queen's knights in a *translatio* of renewed vigor made from Gawain's own autobiographical account of his quest (Sommer 464. 9–11). The weakening and ultimate disappearance of the Merlin figure are thus emblematic of the gradual disengagement of the domain of historical writing from the sacred world of mystical experience, evoked in the *Estoire* prologue, and its transfer—its translation—to the reenergized secular realm of Arthurian knighthood. As the romance of *Merlin* realizes this shift, however, the process whereby narrative is generated remains a constant principle: Gawain's fully secularized story again shows that one subject's autobiography inevitably becomes another's impersonal history.

Notes

1. H. Oskar Sommer, ed., *The Vulgate Version of the Arthurian Romances, Edited from Manuscripts in the British Museum*, 1: *Lestoire del Saint Graal* (Washington: Carnegie Institution, 1909; Reprinted New York: AMS Press, 1969).

2. On specularity, reflexivity, and *mise en abyme*, see Lucien Dällenbach, *Le Récit spéculaire: Essai sur la mise en abyme* (Paris: Seuil, 1977). Translated by Jeremy Whiteley and Emma Hugues under the title *The Mirror in the Text* (Chicago: University of Chicago Press, 1989).

3. References to Sommer's editions of the Vulgate *History* (above, n. 1) and Vulgate *Merlin* (below, n. 7), as well as to Alexandre Micha's edition of the prose *Merlin* attributed to Robert de Boron (below, n. 9), show the page number or the page followed by the line number. Translations of the *Estoire*, by Carol J. Chase, and the *Merlin*, by Rupert T. Pickens, have recently been published in *Lancelot-Grail: The Old French Arthurian Vulgate and Post-Vulgate in Translation*, edited by Norris J. Lacy, vol. 1 (New York and London: Garland, 1993).

4. On medieval autobiographical writing, see Evelyn Birge Vitz, *Medieval Narrative and Modern Narratology: Subjects and Objects of Desire* (New York: New York University Press, 1989), especially ch. 1–5.

5. E. Jane Burns, *Arthurian Fictions: Rereading the Vulgate Cycle* (Columbus: Ohio State University Press, 1985), especially pp. 1–54. See also her "The Teller in the Tale: The Anonymous *Estoire del Saint Graal*," *Assays* 3 (1985): 73–84.

6. Burns, *Arthurian Fictions*, ch. 1. Other important studies of narrative voice and textual authority, especially in the *Estoire* and the *Prose Merlin*, include Alexandre Leupin, *Le Graal et la littérature: Etude sur la Vulgate arthu-rienne en prose* (Lausanne: L'Age d'Homme, 1982), especially ch. 1; and Leu-pim, "Qui parle? Narrateurs et scripteurs dans la *Vulgate* arthurienne," *Di-graphe* 20 (1982): 81–109; Emmanuèle Baumgartner, *L'Arbre et le pain: Essai sur "La Queste del Saint Graal"* (Paris: SEDES, 1981), especially pp. 33–45; and Baumgartner, "Les Techniques dans le roman en prose," *The Legacy of Chré-tien de Troyes*, edited by Norris J. Lacy, Douglas Kelly, and Keith Busby, Faux Titre 31, 37, 2 vols. (Amsterdam: Rodopi, 1987–1988) 1: 167–190, especially pp. 172–177; Larry S. Crist, "Les Livres de Merlin," *Mélanges de langue et littérature françaises du moyen âge offerts à Pierre Jonin*, Senefiance 7 (Aix-en-Provence: Publications du CUER-MA, 1979): 197–210; Michelle Szkilnik, *L'Archipel du Graal: Etude de "L'Estoire del Saint Graal"* (Geneva: Droz, 1991); Douglas Kelly, *The Art of Medieval French Romance* (Madison: University of Wisconsin Press, 1992), especially pp. 104–105, 136–140, 185–188; and Carol Chase's contribution to this volume, "'Or dist li contes': Narrative Interven-tions and the Implied Audience in the *Estoire del Saint Graal*."

7. H. Oskar Sommer, ed., *The Vulgate Version of the Arthurian Romances Edited from Manuscripts in the British Museum*, 2: *Lestoire de Merlin* (Washington: Carnegie Institution, 1908; Reprinted New York: AMS Press, 1969).

8. Burns, *Arthurian Fictions*, ch. 1. For a general study of the poetics of rewriting, see Daniel Poirion, "Ecriture et réécriture au moyen âge," *Littéra-ture* 41 (1981): 109–118. On rewriting in the Robert de Boron trilogy, see Rupert T. Pickens, "'Mais de çou ne parole pas Crestiens de Troies . . .': A Re-examination of the Didot *Perceval*," *Romania* 105 (1984): 492–510, and es-pecially "Histoire et commentaire chez Chrétien de Troyes et Robert de Bo-

ron: Robert de Boron et le livre de Philippe de Flandre," in *The Legacy of Chrétien de Troyes* 2: 17–39.

9. The "Little Grail Cycle" is a prose translation of verse romances by Robert de Boron. Robert de Boron's *Estoire dou Graal* and the first 504 verses of his *Merlin* survive in a single manuscript edited by W. A. Nitze in *Robert de Boron, Le Roman de l'Estoire dou Graal* (Paris: Champion, 1927). Some 39 manuscripts, however, contain prose translations of these romances, including the complete *Merlin*; to avoid confusion with the Vulgate *Estoire*, which derives from Robert de Boron's *Estoire dou Graal*, the prose version of the latter is usually referred to as the *Joseph d'Arimathie*. See William Roach, "The Modena Text of the Prose *Joseph d'Arimathie*," *Romance Philology* 9 (1955–1956): 313–342. Richard O'Gorman's critical edition of the *Joseph*, the first to account for all manuscript texts, is being published in Toronto by the Pontifical Institute of Medieval Studies. Alexandre Micha has critically edited the prose translation of Robert de Boron's *Merlin* in *Merlin: Roman du XIIIᵉ siècle* (Geneva: Droz, 1979). Two manuscripts complete the cycle with a *Perceval* followed by a *Mort Artu*; both manuscripts are edited by William Roach in *The Didot Perceval According to the Manuscripts of Paris and Modena* (Philadelphia: University of Pennsylvania Press, 1941). See also Alexandre Micha, *Etude sur le "Merlin" de Robert de Boron* (Geneva: Droz, 1980), especially ch. 1–3. Bernard Cerquiglini has edited the Modena text of the whole cycle in *Robert de Boron, Le Roman du Graal* (Paris: Union Générale d'Editions, 1981). On the relationship between the Vulgate *Merlin* and the Robert de Boron *Merlin*, see below in text.

10. Leupin notes the implicit symbolism in the symmetrical arrangement of the mystical numbers 7–1–7 ("Qui parle?" 85). One should add that the narrator's means of establishing the date from Christ's Passion requires adding to that number the pair 3–3 (the traditional age of Jesus when crucified), reflecting the perfection of the Trinity, in order to calculate the date: 717 + 33 = 750. As will be suggested below, the Vulgate *Estoire* narrator's concern with the doctrine of the Trinity may prove significant in terms of narrative textuality.

11. Following this logic, the first textual quotations the narrator takes from Christ's book, when he reads two rubrics, appear in his autobiographical account as translations from the heavenly language: "Qvant iou oi longement este en cel penser [contemplating his own sense of unworthiness in comparison to his ancestors' virtues and prowess described in the book] si regardai auant & vi quil i auoit escrit. Chi commenche del saint graal. & quant iou oi tant lut que miedis fu passes si trouai Chi commenche la grant paor" (Sommer 5. 36–6. 2, "After I had been preoccupied with this thought for some time, I looked up and saw what was written there: 'Here begins the account of the Grail.' And I read until it was past midday, when I found: 'Here it begins telling about great fear,' and I read on until I had seen things most dreadful").

12. The term "emergent direct discourse" was used by Samuel Rosenberg in discussion with the American team of translators under the general edi-

torship of Norris J. Lacy; publication by Garland began in 1993 (see n. 3 above).

13. The title *Livre d'Artus* is not to be confused with the text in Sommer's supplemental volume of the same name, which is, in fact, a unique, fragmentary continuation of the *Merlin Proper*; H. Oskar Sommer, ed., *The Vulgate Version of the Arthurian Romances, Edited from Manuscripts in the British Museum*, 7: *Supplement: Le Livre d'Artus* (Washington: Carnegie Institution, 1913; Reprinted New York: AMS Press, 1969).

14. For a detailed analysis of the manuscript tradition, see Alexandre Micha, "Les Manuscrits du *Merlin* en prose de Robert de Boron," *Romania* 79 (1958): 78–94, 145–174.

15. William Roach, et al., ed., *The Continuations of the Old French* Perceval *of Chrétien de Troyes*, 1: *The First Continuation* (Philadelphia: The University of Pennsylvania Press, 1949): xxxiv.

16. Both of which Emmanuèle Baumgartner sees conjoined, in another sense, in the personage of Galahad (*L'Arbre* 141–154).

17. In addition to the books discussed below, the *Merlin Proper* mentions a book of Merlin's prophecies, which Uther orders to be written down henceforth (Micha 164. 1–3; Sommer 48. 13–18). Because the prophecies regard the future and are not records of the past, they do not figure among the historical source-texts, and the book drops from sight in the *Prose Merlin*. It assumes importance only in the unique *Continuation, Le Livre d'Artus* (e.g., Sommer 158–164). See Crist, "Les Livres de Merlin."

18. In the Vulgate *Estoire*, the narrator's account of Christ's book begins with the day of the Crucifixion (Sommer 12. 30), but the *translatio* soon turns to Joseph of Arimathea: "Mais seur tous les autres dist li contes dun chevalier qui auoit non ioseph darrimathie . . ." (Sommer 13. 4–5, "But above all the others [who at that time were beginning to benefit from Christ's death] the *conte* tells about a knight named Joseph of Arimathea").

19. Leupin notes the importance of these events in "Qui parle?" (Sommer 97–100) and *Le Graal et la littérature*, ch. 1.

7. "Or dist li contes": Narrative Interventions and the Implied Audience in the *Estoire del Saint Graal*

Carol Chase

Written after the three major components of the Lancelot-Grail cycle—the *Lancelot Proper*, the *Queste del Saint Graal*, and the *Mort Artu*—the *Estoire del Saint Graal* serves nevertheless as an introduction to the other texts.[1] It recounts the early "history" of the Grail, telling how Joseph of Arimathea recovers the *"escuelle,"* or bowl, used by Christ and takes it from East to West—from Jerusalem to the new Promised Land, England. But it is also the story of the bringing of Christianity to Britain—a kind of Crusade in reverse.[2] The *Estoire* is thus the story of a voyage, or rather of multiple voyages, on the part of Joseph and his followers, his son Josephus, and two pagan rulers who are converted to Christianity early in the tale, Evalac-Mordrain and Seraphe-Nascien, all of whom converge in England. As Michelle Szkilnik has shown in her perceptive study of the *Estoire*, the sea replaces the forest as the essential space during an important part of the text; travel is by ship, with stopovers at islands, where the personages are tested. The journey thus also takes place on a spiritual level; and it can be seen as a metaphor for the narrative.[3]

A long prologue introducing the *Estoire* relates the circumstances of textual transmission.[4] The prologue is narrated by a hermit whose soul is transported to view divine secrets that reassure him about the only article of faith he ever doubted, the Trinity. Addressed by a divine voice and visited by Christ, who gives him a small book that He himself has written, the hermit becomes in turn a reader, a quester, and then a scribe. Following divine orders, the hermit seeks the book, which mysteriously disappeared; once he has found it, he begins to copy it. This is the text that the prologue introduces. However, later it is stated that yet another hand has intervened, for this work was translated from Latin by Robert de Boron.[5]

The *Estoire* thus accumulates authorities in baffling succession.

Commenting on the apocryphal nature of the attributions to Christ and to Robert de Boron, Alexandre Leupin describes this complex narrative framework as "a series of boxes within boxes," adding that it is impossible to determine which one is on the outside.[6] It seems as if the amassing of creators is an attempt to convince a possibly dubious public of the authenticity and veracity of this romance.

This assemblage also obscures the narrative voice. Though the hermit-scribe is clearly the narrator of the prologue, the text he copies is characterized by the same double presence found in the rest of the Lancelot-Grail cycle: "*li contes*" ("the story") and a first-person narrator (*je* and sometimes *nous*).[7] In addition, the work is punctuated by remarks addressed to the implied public—the fictional audience outside the text evoked and created by narrative intrusions.[8] Who is this first-person narrator? Is it the medieval scribe, the hermit, the translator, or Christ?[9] Moreover, how should the references to "*li contes*" be interpreted? If Christ wrote the *Estoire*, the allusions to "*li contes*" seem strange, suggestive of an oral tradition rather than of the book that is the purported source. Finally, what role does the implied public play, and what relationship is established with it by the ambiguous narrative presence?

In order to consider these questions, it is the intent of this study to examine narrative interventions in the *Estoire*, first outlining the general narrative framework and then investigating in detail a section of the text, that devoted to the Turning Isle. In this portion of the tale numerous intrusions that guarantee the truth of the story, comment on its organization, and address the implied audience interrupt the narrative. By analyzing these interventions, we can perhaps refine and extend the work already done by other critics[10] and better understand how the narrator conceives of his story, the nature of the narrative contract with the implied public, and the difficult issue of narrative voice. My approach relies on work on narratology; it will make use of the narrator's functions as defined by Gérard Genette.[11]

Like the other narratives in the Lancelot-Grail cycle, the *Estoire* uses the technique of interlacing to organize the numerous adventures. The formulaic statements, or transition formulas,[12] that mark off the segments are characterized by references to "*li contes*" and/or to the first-person narrator. They use verbs in the present tense that suggest oral performance, or alternatively, a backward and forward movement along a narrative road, a path that might be compared to the Christians' voyage and the spiritual path they are constantly urged to take. Two standard versions of the formula appear:

Si se taist a tant li contes ici endroit de lui [Mordrain] et parole de Nascien. Chi endroit dist li contes. . . .

(Hucher 2: 404–405)

Mais or laisses le contes a parler de lui et retorne au duc Ganor.

(Hucher 3: 146)[13]

Numerous reminders and announcements evoke a listening audience. These references, which help the public to organize the narrative material and follow the story,[14] have a communicative function. They also seem to serve as attempts to gain the audience's adherence.

Studies of the role played by *"li contes"* in the Lancelot-Grail cycle have stressed the effacement or the evacuation of the narrator and the importance of *"li contes"* as the *sujet de l'énonciation*[15]—even though they have sometimes pointed out that references to *"li contes"* coexist with those to a first-person narrator and/or to an implied audience, as in the following example from the *Estoire*:

> Par cele maniere que je vous ai devisé fu la maisons [de Hippocrate] establie premierement si rice et si biele comme jou vous ai contet. Apres fu desertée trop malement, si comme jou vous deviserai, mais çou n'iert mie ichi endroit, quar a tant s'en taist li contes orendroit que assés en a parlet et retorne as messages dont vous avés oït.[16]

> (In the way I have told you, [Hippocrates's] house was first built, as splendid and beautiful as I have recounted. Then it was devastated, as I will tell you, but this is not the place, for the story stops speaking about it, since it has spoken enough about it, and returns to the messengers you have heard about.)[17]

Recently, however, Emmanuèle Baumgartner has suggested that the use of *"li contes"* does not mean that the narrator has disappeared or renounced his prerogatives.[18] In the example cited above, *"je,"* or the "I" narrator shares with *"li contes"* the function of organizing the text in interlaced episodes, but retains the function of communicating with the implied public. In order to establish differences between these two instances, the terms *"li contes"* and "I" narrator will be maintained, while a third locution, the "narrator-poet" will refer to the voice that produces statements not specifically attributed to either of the other two.[19] The "narrator-poet" is not the real writer of the text, but rather the instance that the text poses as taking charge of the narration. Though this is usually referred to simply as the narrator, it will be useful here to make a differentiation between the three instances.

The section on the Turning Isle begins when the converted pagan, Nascien, is carried there by God from the prison where he was being held. As Michelle Szkilnik has shown, islands play a particular role in the *Estoire*.[20] It is on islands that the faith of a number of the main characters is tested; Nascien is no exception to this. In the Christians' voyage from East to West, islands involve a detour and a stopover. Similarly, they are an occasion for narrative digression:[21] each island has a "story" attached to it, which is enchased in the narrative. The section containing Nascien's stay on the Turning Isle therefore begins with a long account of the origin of the island. The arrival of Solomon's ship occasions another lengthy description of the boat and its provenance. The entire passage is characterized by a large number of narrative interventions. Many of these are brief reminders or references to the implied audience, such as the following, taken from two pages of text (emphasis is mine):

> . . . en tele maniere comme *vous orrés* . . . (Hucher 2: 432)
> . . . et *vous avés bien oï* chaen ariere ke li contes dist que . . . (Hucher 2: 432)
> Qant li masse dont *je vous* [ai] *parlet* vint flotant jusques au liu u li aymans estoit, si s'arestut, car li force del aymant le retint par çou que ele estoit fierreuse, ensi comme *vous avés oï* . . . (Hucher 2: 433)[22]

The frequency of these rapid references to the implied audience reveals the intrusive presence of one of the narrative instances, which constantly communicates with the implied public; this can be seen as an attempt to ensure the audience's adherence to what is being recounted.

A number of longer and more important interventions evince a similar concern. The first of these interventions occurs immediately after the transition formula; it introduces the description of the origin of the strange island where Nascien finds himself. The name of the island seems to provoke the narrative intervention, which begins by asserting that the island is rightfully called the Turning Isle:

> Cele ille si est apielée tournians par droite raison, car il est verités que ele tournoie, mais pour çou que la maniere de son tournoie-

ment ne est pas couneüe de tous chiaus ne de toutes celes qui
parlé en ont oï, et pour çou est il raisons que cis contes en demonstre la veritet, quar dont seroit il uns enlacemens de paroles,
se il de cascune doutance dont il parleroit ne moustroit apiertement raison et counissance, autressi comme font une maniere de
gent qui dient maintes paroles et les vauroient affremer a voires, et
si ne puent traire avant nul tesmong, fors que tant seulement que
dire l'ont oï as autres; mais de ceste maniere mauvaise se escuse
chis contes, kar il ne traist auques parole nule avant, u il puisse
apiercevoir doutance, que il ne le face de tout en tout en apert
counoistre. Et pour çou est il a droit apielés l'estoire des estoires.

Or repaire l'estoire a raconter la droite maniere del ille u Nas-
ciens fu portés que li païsant si, comme je vous ai dit, [apielent]
l'ille tournoiant. Il est verités prouvee [que] au coumencement de
toutes coses . . .

(Hucher 2: 428–429)[23]

(This island is rightly called turning because it is true that it turns.
But everyone who has heard about it does not know how it turns,
and it is right that this story show the truth, for if it did not clearly
show the reason and knowledge about every doubtful thing it
mentions, it would only be words interlaced together, just like
some people who speak many words, claiming their truth, but
who cannot cite any support [or produce a witness], except that
they have heard it from others. This story eschews this bad way,
for it does not set forth any doubtful statement without explaining
it with utter clarity. That is why it is rightly called the Chronicle of
Chronicles.

Now the chronicle stops to recount the true ways of the island
where Nascien was carried, which the local people call, as I told
you, the Turning Isle. It is proven truth that at the beginning of all
things . . .)

I have quoted this passage at length because it contains a number
of important clues to the narrative contract. An insistence on truth
dominates the passage: words for truth (*"verités," "veritet," "voire"*)
and knowledge (*"counoistre," "counissance"*) occur over and over and
are opposed to those expressing doubt (*"doutance"*) and ignorance,
which will be cleared up by the description contained here. A web of
vocabulary associated with proof, reason, and demonstration is connected with the affirmations of verity (*"demonstre"*; *"moustroit apiertement raison et counissance"*; *"face de tout en tout en apert counoistre"*;

"provee"). The words *"raison"* and *"droit"* also recur, insisting on the "right," "proper," or "straight" nature of the name and essence of the island and of the story itself. The narrator contrasts his own tale with interlaced words, which he likens to the statements of people who can only say they have heard them from others without being able to call on a single witness. This story will not follow this bad (or evil) method, for wherever there might be any doubt, everything will be made known.

These assurances are based on medieval views of language. In an attempt to understand how words had meaning, medieval theorists looked to their origins. Through etymology or through physical property, words were felt to be connected to their referents and to the original moment of naming. Thus, they signified properly and were true.[24] The name of the Turning Isle is designated as proper, for it corresponds to the physical property of the island, which turns. The actual description of the Turning Isle will be based on its origins and on its physical properties. Likewise, the name of this story is correct and proper: it is rightly called the *"Estoire des estoires"* (Chronicle of Chronicles, Story of Stories, or even History of Histories) because it removes all doubt and makes everything known. The name and properties of the story reflect the pretensions to divine origins of this text and suggest that it is truthful.

The insistent affirmations of truthfulness and the web of vocabulary associated with proof and demonstration, as well as the reference to people who make statements without being able to produce a witness, suggest a judicial mode. The narrative stance almost seems to be that of someone giving testimony before an audience of skeptical jurors.

This vocabulary can also be seen as belonging to the registers of historical truth or of religious faith. Michelle Szkilnik points out that in the theological debates in the *Estoire* the expressions *"prover"* and *"voir apertement"* are used both by Christians and pagans, but with different values. For the Christians this vocabulary is part of the discourse of faith—the statements made about the virgin birth and the Trinity are in and of themselves proof—while for the pagans these words belong to the discourse of reason—they are seeking a logical demonstration for the articles of faith. Szkilnik further suggests that the act of faith the Christians ask of the pagans is the same as that the narrator wishes the public to make.[25]

In this passage there is only one reference to the "I" narrator, who communicates fleetingly with the implied public (*"comme je vous ai dit,"* "as I told you"). The audience is otherwise present in the third person, for the description of the island is aimed at those who do not know how the island turns. The public is perceived as having possible doubts—that will be cleared up by this story—much like the hermit whose doubts about the Trinity were effaced when his soul was transported to view divine secrets. The story is thus subtly compared to celestial revelation.

The rest of the passage is filled with insistent impersonal statements (*"il est verités," "est il raisons," "il est verités prouvee," "est il . . . apielés"*) and references to the *"contes"* (or alternatively, *"l'estoire"*). Two of these allusions are to *"this* story" (*"cis/chis contes"*); both are followed by a series of pronouns that refer back to it, and one is introduced by an impersonal expression. The impersonal expressions are used to present statements as if they emanated from an authoritative source. The demonstrative pronouns present "this story" in much the same way as I might write about "this study." It is thus the "narrator-poet" who makes these assertions, distancing himself so that it seems as if *"li contes"* is in charge. In fact, the narrator-poet shares responsibility with *"li contes"* in this passage, which is largely devoted to the function of guaranteeing the text. The *"contes,"* which is "true" and "proper," as contrasted with the "interlacing of words" or words without meaning, thus functions along with the narrator-poet to testify to its own truth.

However, the assertions of truth are tautological; they gloss over the fact that this double narrative voice is in fact the sole surety of the truth it purports to set forth. Like the Turning Isle, *"li contes"* turns; its announcement that it will relate the *"droite maniere"* of the island, is in fact a narrative pirouette. The Turning Isle can thus be seen as a metaphor for the narrative itself.

In the text that follows, it is explained that the origin of the Turning Isle goes back to the creation of the world. By inserting the "history" of the Turning Isle into the biblical tradition and joining its origin with the Creation, the narrator implies that what he is recounting is part of the revealed truth.[26] When the Creator separated the four elements (sky, air, water, and earth), there was matter left over that came from the sky, the earth, and the water but could not be reintegrated. At this point the narrator once again intervenes, this time to respond to a possible objection on the part of the implied audience about the fourth element, the air:

Et pour çou que auquns ne desist, "autressi estoit li airs amoncelés comme chil trois, pour coi n'en parole dont chis contes? Il est voirs prouvés que avec ces trois esconcirrés, ot auqune cose de l'air" et

a çou s'acorde bien li contes, mais il dist que si petit en ot que ja
pour cest mestier n'en deüst estre parole tenue.

(Hucher 2: 431)

(Someone might say, "Air was piled up in the same way as these
three; why doesn't this story speak about it? It is proven truth that
along with these three things that were amassed, there was a bit
of air as well." The story agrees with this, but it says that there
was so little that it is not necessary to speak about it.)

In this passage the implied audience plays a more active role—
asking a question about the story and even using the impersonal expression *"il est voirs prouvés"* that the poet-narrator so often uses to
guarantee the truth of his assertions. The question is presented hy-
pothetically; it is asked about *"this* story" (the demonstrative pronoun
again), while it is *"li contes"* that responds, agreeing with the objection but minimizing its importance. The verb used in the response
(*"deüst,"* from *devoir*) suggests a duty to speak about certain things.
Here, this duty has not been neglected, for it is not necessary to speak
about the air, since there was so little of it. *"Li contes"* thus takes on
the function of communicating with the audience here; the "I" narrator is absent. Yet behind the demonstrative pronoun used to refer
to the "story," the narrator-poet is present, in a deictic posture.

After this intrusion the description of the origins of the Turning Isle
is completed. The island's composition—a combination of ferrous
matter from the earth, rusty matter from the water, and fiery matter
from the sky—made it come to a stop above a place in the sea where
there was magnetic material. But it is attracted both to the earth and
to the sky; therefore, it turns. This description closes with a mini-
formula:

En tele maniere comme vous avés oït tournoie l'ille. Or vous
a li contes deviset pour quel raison li païssant l'apielent l'ille
tournoiant.

(Hucher 2: 433)

(In the way you have heard, the island turns. Now the story has
told you why the local people call it the Turning Isle.)

In a rational and logical tone the narrator-poet speaks directly to the
audience, summarizing what it has just heard and emphasizing the
propriety of the island's name. The transition formula functions in

the usual way to organize the narrative and communicate with the implied public.

Nascien's first night on the island follows. Nascien falls asleep and has a vision; when he awakens, he feels the island trembling, then sees one side rising, while the other descends into the water, though it is not a small island. At this point the narrator-poet intervenes yet again to furnish the precise measurements of the island, calling on truth itself as a witness:

> Et ne pourkant si n'estoit pas l'ille petite. Anschois avoit, chou tiesmongne la verités, [.XII. C] et quatre vins estas [de lonc et de lé en estoit neuf cens et douze] . . .

> (Hucher 2: 439)

(And yet the island was not small. Rather, the truth attests that it was twelve hundred eighty stadia long and nine hundred twelve stadia wide.)

The narrator-poet explains that a stadia is one-sixteenth of a league, then addresses the implied audience:

> Ensi poés aconter que en cel ille avoit quatre vins lieues tout reondement . . . que il ni faloit riens. Mais se plus i avoit, pour çou n'en ment mie li contes, kar il ne garandist ses paroles de nule plus, mais del mains tout. Kar chou tiesmongne li contes, si comme vous orrés deviser cha avant, que toutes les aventures dou Graal ne [seroient] ja seües par nul houme mortel; assés en couvient trespasser; mais en la sainte estoire qui fu envoié en tiere par la bouce de la veritet, chou est de Jhesu Crist, en celui ne trouvera on ja un mot de faussetet, kar chil seroit de trop forsenet hardement plains, qui oseroit ajoindre menchongne en si haute estoire com est l'estoire que li vrais crucefis escrist de la soie propre main; et pour chou doit ele estre tenue en gregnour hounour, car nous ne trouvons lisant en nule divine escripture, que onques Jhesu-Crist, li vrais fiex Dieu, escresist li tres dous sires de sa propre main fors que seulement en deux lieus.

> (Hucher 2: 439–440)

(Thus you can calculate that this island was exactly eighty leagues long. But even if the island were longer, the story is not lying, for it does not guarantee its words against there being anything more, but against anything less. For the story testifies, just as you will hear told later, that all the adventures of the Grail will not be known by any mortal man. Many must be left in silence. But in the holy story that was sent to earth by the Mouth of Truth, that is, by Jesus Christ, one will never find a false word, for anyone who would dare to add lies to such a noble history as the one the True Crucified One wrote with His own hand would be too full of foolish daring. This story should therefore be held in greater honor, for we do not find as we read in any divine Scripture that Jesus Christ, the very sweet Lord, ever wrote with His own hand except in two places.)

We find the same insistence on truth in this passage as we have seen earlier, as well as the language of demonstration and proof: "*Ensi poés aconter,*" "*garandist,*" and twice "*tiesmongne.*" The assertions of truth are accompanied by strong denials of falsehood: the word "lie" appears both as a verb and a noun ("*ment,*" "*menchongne*"), as well as the expression "not a single false word" ("*ja un mot de fausse-tet*"). In addition, the text's authority is emphasized by referring to it as the "holy story that was sent to earth by the Mouth of Truth, that is, Jesus Christ," and as the "noble story . . . that the True Crucified One wrote with His own hand." In both cases words for "truth" are used in the denotations for Christ, overdetermining the repeated statements of veracity. The word "*estoire,*" which is used elsewhere interchangeably with "*li contes,*" seems to refer here to the written source.[27]

The "I" narrator is also present, not only addressing the public directly, but also as a guarantor who can read and thus verify divine Scripture. This appearance of the "I" narrator is in the first person plural ("*nous*"). How should this plural be interpreted? The evocation of the act of reading and of another writer foolhardy enough to add material suggests that "*nous*" refers either to the "I" narrator plus other readers of Scripture or to the "I" narrator plus a literate portion of the public. In addition, the impersonal pronoun "*on*" appears, seemingly referring to the implied public. The narrator-poet is also present, making impersonal assertions. All these narrative instances have a testimonial function.

The size of the island is first guaranteed by "truth." Then the public is called upon to make its own calculations. Finally, "*li contes*" guarantees that there are no fewer stadia, but it does not guarantee that there are no more. This statement is then applied to the contents of the story itself, for "all of the adventures of the Grail will never be known by mortals." The Grail's feats are thus comparable to divine secrets, or even to Jesus, whose acts cannot all be told.[28]

The above passage introduces a description of the two things that Christ wrote during his lifetime: the Lord's Prayer and the judgment regarding a woman caught in adultery. This is followed by a repetition of the somewhat sacrilegious suggestion that Christ also wrote this text, but here we learn that it was after the Resurrection. By presenting the Lord's Prayer as a written text (contrary to what the Bible states) and including the judgment, which was written in sand, the narrative creates a trinity of texts written by Christ, corresponding to the importance of the Trinity in the *Estoire*. At the closing of the section, another intrusion occurs, repeating a number of things said in the introductory intervention:

> En ces deux lieus que vous avés oï chi ramentevoir trouvons nous que Jhesu Crist, li vrais fiex Diu, escrist devant çou que il soufrist la mort en la glorieuse crois; mais coument que il esploitast en dementiers que il estoit envolepés en la mortel char, ja ne trouverés si hardi clerc qui die que il onques fesist escripture puis la surrection, ne mais seulement le haute escripture dou Saint Graal; et qui vauroit dire que il, puis la surrection, eüst autre escripture faite de sa propre main, il ne poroit avant traire nule divine auctorité. Et pour çou seroit il tenus a menteour; donques di je bien que chil seroit de trop fol hardement espris qui menchongne i vaurroit ajouster a si tres haute estoire comme est ceste que li vrais Diex escrist de sa main propre, puis que il eut jus mis le mortel cors et reviesti la cellestienne maïestet.

> (Hucher 2: 441–442)

(We find that Jesus Christ, the true Son of God, wrote in these two places you have heard recalled here before He suffered death on the glorious cross. But however He may have acted while He was wrapped in mortal flesh, you will never find a clerk bold enough to say that He ever wrote anything after the Resurrection other than the high writing (or scripture) of the Holy Grail. Anyone who wished to say that after the Resurrection, He wrote anything else with His own hand could not find any divine authority to back him, and so would be considered a liar. Thus, I say indeed that it would be a very foolishly bold thing for anyone to try to append a lie to such a noble story as this one, which the true God wrote with His own hand after laying down His mortal body and clothing Himself again in celestial majesty.)

The entire passage is based on a series of negations: the "I" narrator insists on the truth of his assertions by a series of denials and by accusing anyone who dared state otherwise of falsehood. The words "lie" and "liar" ("*menchongne*," "*menteour*") are repeated and contrasted with "true," which is again used in the denotations for Christ ("*li vrais fiex Diu*," "*li vrais Diex*"). In addition, the *Estoire* is referred to here as "*la haute Escripture dou Saint Graal*"; the word "scripture" confers authority and makes it a rival of *the* holy book, the Bible.[29]

In this part of the intervention, "*li contes*" is absent; only the "I" narrator appears, both as "*je*" and "*nous*" ("I" and "we"). As in the intrusion introducing the description of Christ's writings, the first-person plural is used as well as the singular, and a "clerk" is referred to, representative of literacy, but also of possible foolhardiness by daring to add a lie to the text. "*Nous*" seems to refer again to the "I" narrator plus other literate members of the implied public or of the clerkly order. The "I" narrator communicates with the implied public, who is also present, and takes full charge of the testimonial function.

Alexandre Leupin has commented on this section of the text, noting that the inauthenticity of the book that Christ is said to have written is unveiled by the very statements claiming its divine origins, which end up being circular and specular. Leupin also points out that the negative statements about foolhardy, lying clerks can be seen as a rhetorical figure consisting of projecting onto someone else something the speaker is forced to admit about himself. Thus, the remarks about the falsified additions can be seen to apply to the narrator, who is thereby revealed to be an interpolator.[30]

This intervention ends with an important variation on the transition formula:

> Mais or est drois que li contes soit ramenés a la droite estoire
> dont il est auques departis pour parler d'ices coses que il a ra-
> menteües, qui si fierent entre les paroles del estoire et si n'en sunt
> mie; mais la droite voie repaire a l'ille dont li contes a devisé et le
> lonc et le let.
>
> (Hucher 2: 442)

> (But now it is right that the story be brought back to the main line
> of the chronicle, which it left for a while in order to speak about
> these things that it called to mind and placed among the words of
> the chronicle and yet are not in it. The straight way returns to the
> island whose length and width were told by the story.)

The repetition of the word "*droit*," which appears three times, emphasizes the return to the "straight," "proper," or "true" line of the story from which the narrator-poet has just deviated. The imper- sonal expression "it is right" or "proper" (*"est drois"*) that intro- duces the transition formula reveals the presence of the narrator- poet; it is he who will lead *"li contes"* back to the "true story," or narrative material (*"droite estoire"*), from which it departed. A distinc- tion that is blurred elsewhere is again suggested between *"li contes"* and *"l'estoire"*; *"l'estoire"* seems to mean the material of the story, while *"li contes"* refers to some aspects of the narrator's functions. The passage also continues to betray the presence of an interpolator (the hermit? the translator? a scribe?) who stuck the preceding re- marks in between the words of *"l'estoire"*—things that are never- theless not there! The insertion of these things amidst the words is suggestive of the description of how the spindles from the Tree of Life are stuck into the bed in Solomon's ship to make a frame. In like manner, these things have been inserted to create a frame for the text. The material language thus seems to form a concrete space into which a digression can be placed.

This passage also presents the narrator-poet's vision of the narra- tive material as a "straight road" (*"droite voie"*).[31] This could also be interpreted as the "correct" or "proper" road. Medieval views of lan- guage may illuminate this. Grammar, the most basic of the seven lib- eral arts and the one devoted to language, was considered to possess the property of straightness. Isidore of Seville connects "the straight- ness of letters and roads"; John of Salisbury viewed grammar as a highway.[32] Both thinkers were highly influential throughout the Middle Ages. "The function of early medieval grammar is the delin- eation of straight paths, the creation of linear links between symbols, sounds, and letters, as well as between words and the physical prop- erties of things."[33] The narrator-poet's view of his material as a straight road thus suggests that he considers the events or episodes to be linked in a line, along which he moves and which he occasion- ally leaves—but to which he always returns. This vision may seem surprising to the modern critic. Burns, for example, has pointed out that in the *Prose Lancelot*, though it is affirmed that the narrative will follow a straight or direct road, the narrative path is anything but straight.[34] In the *Estoire* this conception of the narrative also corre- sponds to the spiritual path the Christians are constantly urged to take. Ideology thus conditions the way the narrator visualizes his ma- terial. Since the story is true, it must be straight.

In the preceding passages the narrative instances have insisted on the truth of the assertions before a seemingly skeptical audience. We have also seen that the material of the story is viewed as a *"droite voie."* We will see another side of the narrative stance as we stay with

Nascien on the Turning Isle. A ship arrives; Nascien approaches and reads an inscription written in Chaldean on the side of the boat warning that those who enter must be full of faith. This is the ship Solomon prepared to inform the last descendant in his lineage (Galahad) that he knew about his coming. Nascien boards and examines the objects within.

After carefully looking over the ship, Nascien finds a bed covered by a cloth. He raises the cloth and discovers a magnificent sword, which is pulled partly out of its sheath. This uncovering is analogous to the narrative pretensions of "uncovering the truth." In the next interventions, however, we will see a refusal to uncover something at this time. First, each color in the stone of the sword's pommel has a specific quality that will be described later:

> Car a cascune des coulours avoit une vertu que li contes devisera bien, la u il parlera de la force et de la virtu plus assés [que] chi.
>
> (Hucher 2: 446)

> (For each of the colors had a quality that the story will certainly tell about when it speaks more of its power and strength than here.)

This promise, however, is not kept; the qualities of the colors are never presented. The text goes on to describe the sword handle and the sheath and Nascien's hesitations about the material of which the sheath is made. Then, in another variation on the transition formula, a long list of things "*li contes*" will not tell at this time follows:

> Ne li contes ne le devise mie chi endroit ne de quel maniere ele estoit, car encor n'est mie venus ne liex ne li tans que il le doive deviser, ne l'espee coument ele fu forgié, ni en quel liu ne de quoi fu li fueres, ne de quel lieu il fu aportés. . . . Toutes ces coses ne descuevre mie li contes en ceste partie, mais qant chou venra a l'essaucement de l'espee que ele sera conneüe et que on l'apielera par son droit non . . . lors sera venus et li lieus et li tans que les manieres du fuerre et [de l'espee] et les virtus seront demoustrees apiertement. Mais a tant se taist li contes en cestui lieu et dou fuerre et de l'espee et si parole d'une autre cose.
>
>   Ci dist li contes chi endroit que el miliu dou lit, tout a droiture, avoit fichiet un fuisiel par devant qui tous estoit drois. . . .
>
> (Hucher 2: 451–452)

(And the story does not tell here what it was made of, for neither
the time nor the place has come when it should tell it, nor how
and where the sword was forged, nor what the scabbard was
made of, nor whence it was brought. . . . All these things are not
revealed by the story in this part. But the time and place will come
to show clearly the ways and the qualities of the scabbard and
the sword-belt when the glorification of the sword comes. Then it
will be known and called by its right name. . . . But now the story
stops speaking about the scabbard and the sword and speaks
about something else.

Here the story says that a spindle was placed upright in the
middle of the front side of the bed . . .)

In these passages "*li contes*" seems omnipresent. However, there
are several impersonal statements for which the narrator-poet is responsible. A series of negative statements note that certain things will
not be told at this point because they will be revealed when the
proper time and place come.[35] The verbs alternate between those referring to oral recounting ("*parler*," "*deviser*") and those suggesting
the revelatory role of the text ("*descuevre*," "*sera conneüe*," "*seront de-
moustrees apiertement*"). In addition, the verb "*devoir*" reappears, indicating the necessity or "duty" of telling things in a certain order.

At the end of this transition, a new segment opens in which the
spindles that frame the bed are described. Once again the audience is
addressed directly:

. . . sachiés vraiement que çou estoient naturaus coulours, sains
painture, car eles n'i avoient esté mises par nul houme mortel ne
de nule femme. Et por chou que en doutance en seroient tiex
gens, le poroient oïr conter et s'en tenroient pour engigniet se il
n'en savoient plus, pour chou s'en destorne a tant li contes de la
droite voie de sa matiere, que il en descuevre la veritet pour abatre
la doutance. Et chou est une cose qui ne fait mie a trespasser, ançois est moult delitable a escuter et a oïr . . .

(Hucher 2: 453)

(You should know that they were natural colors, not painted, for
they had not been put there by any mortal man or woman. And
because some people who heard about it might be doubtful and
consider themselves deceived if they knew nothing more, the
story turns aside from the straight road of its material in order to

reveal the truth and put doubt to rest. This is something that is not to be glossed over [or passed by] but is very delightful to hear . . .)

This introduces a long, enchased narrative about the Tree of Life and the preparation of Solomon's ship. The intervention begins with a formula that emphasizes the importance of what will follow ("*sachiés que*," "you should know").[36] As in the introduction to the description of the Turning Isle, the veracity of this material is emphasized by the repetition of words for "truth" ("*vraiement*," "*veritet*"), which are opposed to the term "doubt" ("*doutance*," repeated twice). It is suggested not only that some readers or listeners might be doubtful but also that they might feel tricked or deceived ("*engigniet*") if they did not learn more about the colors of the spindles framing the bed. "*Li contes*" thus makes another detour from the "straight road of its material" to reveal the truth and strike down possible doubt. This stopover on the narrative voyage is presented with vocabulary often used for digressions ("this is something that should not be passed by, since it is delightful to hear"). The pleasing and agreeable qualities ascribed to the text, however, are usually associated with romance, not the sacred history the *Estoire* purports to be.[37]

The vocabulary that characterizes the implied audience's viewpoint is extremely suggestive; the use of the word "*engigniet*" for the public's reaction, if it did not learn more, makes the ambiguous narrator into a possible source of trickery. While "*engin*" can be seen as having positive connotations,[38] it is also associated with the devil and with a misogynistic view of women. In the *Estoire* the devil is depicted as being constantly on watch to trick Christians and to try to make them deviate from the straight road of faith.[39] The suggestion that some members of the implied audience might feel tricked if they did not know more about this thus associates the narrative voice with the devil. Indeed, this passage further augments the suggestions of skepticism on the part of the implied audience through the repetition of the word "*doutance*" ("doubt") and the insistence that this digression is being made in order to reveal the truth. The linking of truth with a detour from the straight road of the story uncovers the narrator-poet's tricky role: like the devil, he leads the public off a straight road; yet by turning off the road, he claims to reveal the truth and thus to be unlike the devil, for, thereby, the public is not tricked.

The enchased text recounting the origin of the colored spindles contains a number of narrative interventions as well. In the context of this paper it is not possible to examine them; we will therefore turn to Nascien, as does "*li contes*" at the end of the digression. The formulaic return to Nascien's adventures reminds the public of what has just been recounted and announces the new section. This version of the formula emphasizes the long silence about Nascien during the digression:

Si retourne a conter de Nascien dont il est grant pieche [teüs].

(Hucher 2: 484)

(The story returns to Nascien, about whom it has been silent for a long time.)

Nascien remains on Solomon's ship only a short time. Because he doubts the natural colors of the three spindles, the ship opens up, and he finds himself in the water. He swims back to the Turning Isle, where he stays until his son Celidoine arrives on Solomon's ship, and they depart together. What happens to Nascien is suggestive of what might happen to the implied audience if it doubts the veracity of the story. The narrator-poet's persuasive voice seems to carry a threat.[40]

We will end our own critical voyage here by attempting to draw a conclusion from this sample of narrative interventions. The passage devoted to the Turning Isle is of particular interest because of the large number of intrusions and because the island's nature is suggestive of the narrative itself. The instability of the island, anchored only by magnetic force, resembles the instability of the narrative voice, which shifts between "*li contes,*" the "I" narrator, and a third entity, the narrator-poet, who can be seen as speaking through the other two instances. The use of "*li contes,*" like that of impersonal statements, can be considered as a distancing technique which makes the resulting text seem authoritative. The "I" narrator interjects on a more personal level, much less frequently than "*li contes.*"[41] While the "I" narrator seems to be largely responsible for communicating with the public, on occasion "*li contes*" can take on this function; similarly, though "*li contes*" usually organizes the narration, the "I" narrator sometimes shares this function. All three instances guarantee the truth of the text, an indication of the importance placed on veracity. All three also seem to share the functions of narration and even of ideology. For the emphasis on the truthful nature of the text corresponds to ideological concerns with the nature of reality and the ability of language to reflect it.

The depiction of the implied audience as skeptical or doubtful and even wary of being tricked is the correlate of this insistence on truth. Like Nascien, however, the public that doubts such things as the natural colors in the spindles may regret its skepticism. Another analogy can be found in the hermit's doubts about the Trinity, which are cleared up through divine intervention. The public's doubts will be effaced by the text itself, which is likened to an article of faith.

The assertions of veracity are associated with straightness or propriety and opposed to doubt, lies, and interlaced words. (Paradoxically, the term "interlace," which literary critics use to describe the structure of this romance, is employed in the text to denote unreliability.) However, these affirmations take the form of a kind of narrative pirouette in which the story is seen to guarantee its own truth. Like the Turning Isle, the narrative thus turns, uncovering its own fictionality. Further, the ambiguous narrator even seems associated with the devil, when it is suggested that the audience might feel tricked if he did not make a detour from the *"droite estoire."* The devil's attempts to trick humankind are depicted on several occasions as attempts to make him *"desvoier"*—step off the path of faith. The narrator, therefore, somehow seems to be tempting the implied audience as he steps off the main narrative track, the *"droite voie."*

The *Estoire* as a whole is a surprising mixture of sacred and secular "history." The framework of sacred material is used to develop a story that constantly reworks and makes additions to it—an enterprise fraught with danger.[42] The assertions of truth, of following a *"droite voie,"* and of telling the story the right way thus cover up the heretical nature of the adventure.[43]

Notes

I wish to thank Steve Fineberg for his helpful comments on an earlier version of this paper.

1. The Lancelot-Grail cycle was probably written during the first third of the thirteenth century. Michelle Szkilnik outlines the scholarship on the dates of the *Estoire* in *L'Archipel du Graal: Etude de "L'Estoire del Saint Graal"* (Geneva: Droz, 1991): 1 n. 1. Three editions of the romance exist: Eugène Hucher, ed., *Le Saint Graal ou le Joseph d'Arimathie, première branche des romans de la Table Ronde, publié d'après des textes et des documents inédits*, 3 vols. (Le Mans: E. Monnoyer, 1875–1878), the *Estoire* is contained in vols. 2 and 3; H. Oskar Sommer, ed., *The Vulgate Version of the Arthurian Romances, Edited from Manuscripts in the British Museum*, vol. 1 (Washington: Carnegie Institution, 1909); Jean-Paul Ponceau, ed., *L'Estoire del Saint Graal, texte de la version longue d'après le ms. du Mans B.M. 354* (thèse de doctorat, 1989). Ponceau's edition uses the same manuscript as Hucher; it presents a longer version than that published by Sommer. Neither Sommer's nor Hucher's edition is entirely satisfactory; Ponceau's is not available. On the differences between Hucher's and Sommer's editions, see Szkilnik 10–12. I have chosen to use Hucher's text because it presents a more complete version of some episodes. All citations are from

this edition. Punctuation and diacritical marks have been inserted following modern conventions. Material in brackets has been corrected, following Sommer and/or Ponceau.

2. On this aspect, see Emmanuèle Baumgartner, "Géants et chevaliers," *Spirit of the Court*, edited by Glyn S. Burgess and Robert A. Taylor (Cambridge, Eng.: D. S. Brewer, 1985): 12; and Szkilnik 113–114.

3. Szkilnik 19–28, 137–138.

4. For a detailed study of the series of "initialités" that introduce the *Estoire*, see Alexandre Leupin, *Le Graal et la littérature* (Lausanne: L'Age d'Homme, 1982): 24–35. E. Jane Burns studies the "textual genealogy" of the cycle as a whole in *Arthurian Fictions: Rereading the Vulgate Cycle* (Columbus: Ohio State University Press, 1985): 8–34.

5. References to Robert de Boron as translator occur at Hucher 3: 102, 194, and 269. Robert de Boron is the author of the verse *Roman du Graal* or *Joseph d'Arimathie;* the attribution of the translation to him is undoubtedly intended to lend authority to the *Estoire*.

6. Leupin 21–34; quoted material is on p. 34 (my translation).

7. There is even an occasional "*on*." See E. Jane Burns, "The Teller in the Tale: the Anonymous *Estoire del Saint Graal,*" *Assays* 3 (1985): 73–84; this material is developed more fully in chapters 1 and 2 of *Arthurian Fictions*. Burns suggests that "*nous*" sometimes refers to the narrator and the implied audience; that at other times, it represents the "*je*" narrator plus "*li contes*" (*Arthurian Fictions* 50–51).

8. The term "implied public" is adapted from concepts developed in reader-response criticism. See Wolfgang Iser, *The Implied Reader* (Baltimore: Johns Hopkins University Press, 1974), and Gerald Prince, "Introduction à l'étude du narrataire," *Poétique* 14 (1973): 177–197. A number of interesting studies have been done on the implied audience in Chrétien de Troyes; for an overview, see Roberta Krueger, "The Author's Voice: Narrators, Audiences, and the Problem of Interpretation," in *The Legacy of Chrétien de Troyes*, edited by Norris J. Lacy, Douglas Kelly, and Keith Busby (Amsterdam: Rodopi, 1987) 1: 115–140. References to other articles in this volume will be cited as *Legacy*, vol. 1.

9. See Burns, *Arthurian Fictions*, 40.

10. Burns (works cited in note 7) and Leupin 24–35. Douglas Kelly investigates narrative interventions related to the concepts of "conjointure" and "disjointure" in "L'Invention dans les romans en prose," in *The Craft of Fiction: Essays in Medieval Poetics*, edited by Leigh A. Arrathoon (Rochester, Mich., 1984): 119–142.

11. In *Figures III* (Paris: Seuil, 1972): 261–263, Genette sets forth five functions: *fonction narrative, fonction de régie, fonction de communication, fonction testimoniale ou d'attestation*, and *fonction idéologique* (narrative, organizational, communicative, testimonial, and ideological).

12. Elspeth Kennedy has analyzed in detail these transitions, or "formal switches," in the *Prose Lancelot;* see *Lancelot and the Grail: A Study of the Prose Lancelot* (Oxford: Clarendon, 1986): 156–201.

13. "At this point the story becomes silent about Mordrain and speaks of

Nascien. Here the story says . . .''; "But now the story leaves off speaking about him and returns to Duke Ganor."

14. See Frank Brandsma, "Interlace and the Implied Audience of the *Préparation à la Queste*," *Arturus Rex: Acta Conventus Lovaniensis 1987*, edited by Willy Van Hoecke, Gilbert Tournoy, and Werner Verbeke (Leuven: Leuven University Press, 1991) 2: 273–277.

15. That is, the producer of the speech act; linguistic theory distinguishes it from the *"sujet de l'énoncé,"* or the subject in the resulting linguistic object. See Genette, *Figures III* 226, and Dominique Maingueneau, *Eléments de linguistique pour le texte littéraire* (Paris: Bordas, 1986): 1–9. Perhaps the first to suggest that the story itself is the *"sujet de l'énonciation"* was Tzvetan Todorov in "La Quête du récit," *Poétique de la prose* (Paris: Seuil, 1971): 149–150. See also Michèle Perret, "De l'Espace romanesque à la Matérialité du Livre: L'Espace énonciatif des premiers romans en prose," *Poétique* 50 (1982): 173–182; Burns, *Arthurian Fictions*, 10–15; Emmanuèle Baumgartner, *L'Arbre et le pain: Essai sur "La Queste del Saint Graal"* (Paris: Société d'Edition d'Enseignement Supérieur, 1981): 23–31. A more complete bibliography on this question is provided by Colette-Anne Van Coolput, *Aventures querant et le Sens du Monde: Aspects de la réception productive des premiers romans du Graal cycliques dans le Tristan en prose* (Leuven: Leuven University Press, 1986): 191 n. 1.

16. Hucher 3: 73.

17. All translations are my own. See Carol Chase, *The History of the Holy Grail*, in *Lancelot-Grail: The Old French Arthurian Vulgate and Post-Vulgate in Translation*, edited by Norris J. Lacy, vol. 1 (New York: Garland, 1992).

18. Pointing out the presence of a first-person narrator in a passage in the *Prose Lancelot*, Emmanuèle Baumgartner suggests that the *"je"* narrator retains certain narrative functions ("Les Techniques narratives dans le roman en prose," *Legacy* 1: 176). In her study of the *Prose Tristan*, Colette-Anne Van Coolput states that despite numerous references to *"li contes,"* the first-person narrator takes an active role (Van Coolput 208–219). On the *Prose Tristan*, see also Lyn Pemberton, "Authorial Interventions in the *Tristan en prose*," *Neophilologus* 68 (1984): 481–497.

19. The term "narrator-poet" is adapted from a distinction made between the "author" and the "writer" by Maingueneau, *Eléments*, 71.

20. Szkilnik 22–28.

21. *Ibid.*, 138.

22. ". . . in the way you will hear . . . "; "and you have heard above that the story says that . . . "; "When the mass I spoke to you about came floating up to the place where the magnet was, it stopped, for the power of the magnet held it, since it was ferrous, just as you have heard . . . "

23. Sommer's edition presents a shorter version of this complex passage.

24. This is a simplification of a complex question. On medieval views of language, see R. Howard Bloch, *Etymologies and Genealogies: A Literary Anthropology of the French Middle Ages* (Chicago: University of Chicago Press, 1983): 44–58, 149–158; R. H. Robbins, *Ancient and Mediaeval Grammatical Theory in Europe* (London: Bell, 1951): 69–90; E. R. Curtius, *European Literature and the Latin Middle Ages*, translated by Willard Trask (Princeton, N.J.: Princeton Uni-

versity Press, 1973): 42–45; Marcia Colish, *The Mirror of Language: A Study in the Medieval Theory of Knowledge*, rev. ed. (Lincoln: University of Nebraska Press, 1983). A debate over the natural or conventional origins of language animated antiquity and the Middle Ages; according to Bloch, medieval thinkers accepted that words were imposed, but resisted "breaking entirely with the wish for continuity between language and matter" (Bloch 46). The growing importance of logic in the thirteenth century changed this view by considering meaning within the syntactical context.

25. Szkilnik 65–69.

26. Michelle Szkilnik points out that one of the procedures the *Estoire* uses to prove its authenticity is to "root" itself in the Bible (Szkilnik 70–73).

27. See Burns, *Arthurian Fictions*, 39.

28. See John 20: 30 and 21: 25: "Now Jesus did many other signs in the presence of his disciples, which are not mentioned in this book"; "But there are also many other things that Jesus did; if every one of them were written down I suppose that the world itself could not contain the books that would be written." I wish to thank Emmanuèle Baumgartner for suggesting this connection.

29. In the article "L'Ecriture romanesque et son modèle scripturaire: écriture et réécriture du Graal," Emmanuèle Baumgartner suggests that Arthurian romance in general is in rivalry with the Bible; in *L'Imitation: Colloque de l'Ecole du Louvre* (Paris: Documentation française, 1985): 140.

30. Leupin 30–31.

31. Among the many other examples of this view of the narrative, the following might be cited: "Or s'en vait Josephés et sa compaignie par le plaisir et par le coumandement de nostre segnour, mais de toutes leur journees ne de toutes lour aventures, ne de cascun liu u il hierbiergierent, ne parole mie li contes ichi endroit, ansçois retourne la droite voie del estoire sour le roy Mourdrains et sour sa compaignie . . ." (Hucher 2: 321, "Josephus and his followers left, through Our Lord's pleasure and commandment, but the story does not speak here of all their days of traveling, all their adventures, or each place where they were lodged. Rather, the straight way of the chronicle returns to King Mordrain and his retinue . . . ").

32. Bloch 52.

33. *Ibid.*, 53.

34. "The Aesthetics of Indirection in the Vulgate Cycle," *The Legacy of Chrétien de Troyes*, 154.

35. Burns suggests that this is part of the tradition of *auctoritas*: "reference to another tale is more important than whether that tale really exists or what it might actually say" (*Arthurian Fictions* 41–42).

36. On this formula, see Baumgartner, "Les Techniques narratives," 177.

37. Burns points out that the early Church Fathers were wary of the seductive powers of language, but that the Lancelot-Grail cycle was written at a point when rhetorical treatises began to "instruct medieval authors how to cultivate beauty of expression in order to induce pleasure in the reader" (*Arthurian Fictions* 21–27).

38. See Kelly, "L'Invention dans les romans en prose."

39. See for example Hucher 2: 453, at the beginning of the story of the Tree of Life.

40. Michelle Szkilnik points out that one of the characteristics of the *récit* of the *Estoire* is the alliance between threat and persuasion in the Christians' attitude toward the pagans they wish to convert (Szkilnik 73).

41. See Burns, *Arthurian Fictions*, 15.

42. See Szkilnik 138.

43. In the discussion following the oral presentation of this paper, the problem of heresy was raised. Since the Church seems never to have condemned this text, one should perhaps speak of heterodoxy rather than heresy. The way the *Estoire* uses the biblical tradition should be considered in the context of popular stories about Christ that were widely accepted in the Middle Ages, such as the Veronica story, which the *Estoire* uses. I wish to thank Douglas Kelly for his comments on the problem of heresy.

8. *Cité* or *Vile*? A Lexical Problem in the Lancelot-Grail Cycle

Carleton W. Carroll

The Lancelot-Grail cycle contains a large number of references to towns, cities, and other named localities.[1] The usual label for such places is *cité*: it occurs much more frequently than *vile* (see table). Indeed, some places never seem to be called anything else. Thus Benoic, which is usually the name of a kingdom, refers in four cases to a town or city, and in all four it is *cité* that is used. Likewise Norgales, usually a kingdom, is a *cité* on at least three occasions and receives no other label. Similarly, Boorges (Bourges), Constantinople, Corente/ Coranges, Sorhaut/Sorhan, and Zelegebres are apparently always labeled *cité*. On the other hand, Carlion seems always to be labeled *vile*. And Carduel, although it is one of Arthur's favorite places, where he often holds court at Christmas and for other important feast-days such as Saint John's Day and All Saints' Day, never seems to be called a *cité*, but is rather a *vile*.

Some places, on the other hand, are sometimes called *cité* and at other times *vile*. This apparent inconsistency can seem puzzling to the modern reader, as in the following examples.[2]

As a result of an oath he has sworn, Lancelot is obliged to do battle with a knight defending a causeway. Following his victory, he rides along the causeway, accompanied by a maiden, "tant qu'il aprochent d'une *chité* que l'en clamoit le Pui de Malohaut" (Micha 7: 456, my emphasis, "until they drew near to a city that was called Malehaut Bluff"). The same place is referred to as la *chité* a few lines later (Micha 7: 456). When he arrives there, Lancelot is attacked by more than forty knights and men-at-arms; he defends himself as well as he can, until "la dame de la *vile*" (Micha 7: 456, "the lady of the city") comes along. She tells him to surrender to her because he has killed her seneschal's son; he complies, and she holds him prisoner.

The scene then shifts (chapter division) to King Arthur, who gets word of Galehaut's incursion and sets out against him. Two pages

Occurrences of "*Cité*" and "*Vile*" in the *Estoire de Merlin, Lancelot Proper,* and *Mort Artu*

	cité	*vile*
Merlin[a]	117	84
Lancelot		
1	17	17
2	9	22
3	10	26
4	7	4
5	8	10
6	64	5
7	50	34
8	13	23
Mort Artu	63	13
Totals	358	238

Note: An attempt was made to note all occurrences of both *cité* and *vile* within the indicated corpus; no such effort was made for either *chastel* or *borc*. Since electronic searches of the various texts were not possible, the figures should be considered as minima; we can be sure there are at least the indicated number of occurrences of each term. They may nevertheless be taken as indicative of the relative frequency of the two terms.

[a]These figures are for the first half of the *Merlin,* pages 1–233.

into the chapter the author sets the scene, reiterating the name of the place:

> Pres del castel ou li rois est avoit une *cité* qui avoit non li Puis de Malohaut. . . . Entre le roi Artu et la *chité* avoit .I. haut tertre et plus pres de l'ost que de la *chité* . . .
>
> (Micha 8: 2–3)

> (Near the castle where the king was there was a fortified town named Malehaut Bluff. . . . Between King Arthur and the town there was a high hill, nearer to the camp than to the town . . .)

Four pages later the place is again referred to as a *cité;* it is again identified by name, but this time without the words "li Pui": "Pres d'iluec estoit la *chités* de Malohaut. La *chité* tenoit une dame . . ." (Micha 8: 6, "Near there was the town of Malehaut. It was held by a lady . . ."). This is followed by a summary of the situation; there is no doubt that this is the same lady who was first introduced as "la dame de la vile" in the preceding chapter.

Following the first battle between Galehaut's forces and Arthur's, "s'en vinrent li chevalier del païs en la *chité* a la dame et conterent les noveles de cele assamblee a la dame" (Micha 8: 7, "the knights of the land came to the lady and told her news of the battle"). As preparations begin for the next battle, "Li chevalier du païs furent tout venu en l'ost et chil de la *vile* del Pui de Malahaut et des autres terres entor" (Micha 8: 9, "The knights of the land had all come into camp, those from the town of Malehaut Bluff and from the other lands around")—where the "Pui de Malahaut" is now called a *vile*. But in the very next sentence we again find *cité*: "La dame de la *chité* ot au chevalier que ele tenoit en prison douné .I. cheval et .I. escu vermeil . . ." (Micha 8: 9, "The lady of the town had given a horse and a red shield to the knight she held prisoner [Lancelot, unnamed at this point] . . ."). The next morning he leaves the "*chité*" (Micha 8: 10) to ride toward Arthur's army. Beyond this point, although the Lady of Malehaut figures prominently in the story, the place from which she comes does not: it is only mentioned twice, and both times as "Malohaut", without benefit of either label.[3]

In the course of about a dozen pages, then, we find this one place referred to as *cité* ten times and as *vile* twice.[4] While *cité* predominates, we must conclude that *vile* is not deemed entirely unsuitable in referring to this locality.

The same is true in the case of Logres, a place of much greater stature and importance. Most of the time it is a *cité*, as when "Lyoniax trova la roine sejornant a Logres, la maistre *cité* le roi Artu car che estoit li chiés de son regne" (Micha 8: 407, "Lionel found the queen staying at Logres, King Arthur's principal city because it was the capital of his kingdom"). And, to cite an example which occurs in dialogue, Arthur's chaplain, speaking to the king, refers to "la *cité* de Logres, qui est chiés de ton roialme" (Micha 1: 22, "the city of Logres, the head city of your realm"). Yet we also find *vile* used to refer to it, although the label never seems to be closely linked to the name in the way that *cité* is in the previous examples. Thus Merlin tells Arthur:

[Je] vous commans que vous facies pourtendre toutes les rues de logres de pailes & de samis la ou il doiuent passer . si faites caroler toutes les puceles & les damoiseles de ceste *ville* & aler encontre aus chantant hors de la *uille*.

(*Merlin* 101.40–42)

(I recommend that you have all the streets of Logres overhung with damask and samite wherever they [the two kings] are to go, and have the maidens and young ladies of this town go out to meet them dancing and singing.)

Most of the time, when *vile* refers to Logres, we must infer that fact from the context: the name "Logres" is mentioned, and then, separately, something is said of the *vile*, as when Doon de Carduel finds:

quil estoient issu hors de la *ville* iusqua .vij.m. hommes . lors vint a els si lor dist biau signor il ne seroit mie boin que la *ville* remansist desgarnie de gent.

(*Merlin* 138.17–19)

(that up to seven thousand men had gone out of the town. Then he came to them and said to them, "Dear sirs, it would not be well for the town to be left stripped of all fighting men.")

Thus the *vile* connotation appears to be more oblique and perhaps somewhat more generic, less directly and intimately linked to the specific identity of the particular place it refers to.

There are, of course, a number of ways in which the name of the place can be linked to the label *cité* or *vile*. The formula "qui avoit a non" or "qu'on apeloit" ("that was named" or "that people called"), with minor variations, is used primarily for the lesser-known places. Most of the time it is then associated with *cité*. Similarly, a place mentioned only in passing, which is likely to be preceded by the indefinite article and either "avoir a non," "apeler" or "clamer" (all meaning "to be named" or "called"), is labeled *cité* in the majority of cases. Thus we find such formulae as "vne sieue *cite* qui ot anon belande" (*Merlin* 131.14, "Belande, one of his cities"); "une *cité* que on apeloit Nordelone" (*Mort* 154.2–3, "a city called Nordelone"); "la *chité* qui avoit non Orkenise" (Micha 7: 387, "the city of Orkney"). These three places are mentioned nowhere else, according to West.

On the other hand, one finds phrasing such as "la *cite* de garles qui ne fait mie a oublier" (*Merlin* 126.2–3, "the city of Garles, which was not to be forgotten"), which suggests that is a place of some importance, and yet this too is a unique occurrence, according to West.

We also find this type of formula for the first mention of a setting of greater importance to the story: "une riche *vile* et moult bele, si estoit apelee Cambenync" (Micha 8: 218, "a rich and beautiful city; it was called Cambenic") or the first occurrence of "le Pui de Malohaut" (Micha 7: 456 mentioned above).

Sometimes this initial mention is amplified by further identifying details, bridging the gap between the Arthurian world and the known geography of the world of the audience, as in "li rois Artus . . . tint court a logres sa *cite* qui ore est apelee londres en engleterre" (*Merlin* 96.6–7, "King Arthur . . . held court in the city of Logres, which is now called London in England") and "vne *cite* que on apeloit benoyc que on apele ore borges en berri" (*Merlin* 98.10–11, "a city named Benoic, which is now called Bourges in Berry").

This general type of formula is also used with place-names which, though objectively important in themselves, do not figure prominently in the narrative, as in "une soe *cité* molt riche qui estoit chiés de son regne et avoit non Caellus" (Micha 3: 11, "a splendid city of his, which was the head city of his [Galehaut's] realm and was called Caellus"; this place is named only twice in *Lancelot*) and "une soe *cité* qui estoit chief de son roialme et avoit non Zelegebres" (Micha 1: 109, "Zelegebre, the head city of the kingdom"; the possessives refer to the false Guenevere).

Passages of this type, in which a locality is first named, generally use *cité*. Indeed, of the examples given above, only one, Cambenync, links the name to the noun *vile* (Micha 8: 218).[5]

Similarly, whereas the phrase "la cité de" is very commonly used to link the name with a label, the parallel phrase with *vile* is very rare: just four such occurrences have come to light, referring once each to Camelot (*Merlin* 180.15), Carlion (*Merlin* 89.2), "la riche *uile* del gaut destroit" (*Merlin* 164.34–35, "the wealthy town of the Narrow Wood"), and, as we have already seen, "la vile del Pui de Malahaut" (Micha 8: 9). It may be significant that three of these are found in the *Merlin*. While the first two places are very frequent names in the Lancelot-Grail cycle and in Arthurian texts in general, the latter two are not. According to West, "Gaut Destroit" is mentioned but once in the *Merlin*, and all other occurrences are limited to the *Livre d'Artus* (Sommer 7). Moreover, the latter two names, involving the definite article and what is basically a common noun ("wood" and "mount") are not in the same semantic and syntactic category as the proper names Camelot and Carlion.

The name of a place can be coupled to *cité* or *vile* in a number of ways, some of them more telling than others. Some of these tell us that the place, N, *was* a *cité*, etc., using the verb *estre*, "to be," in which case it is *cité* that is used in almost all instances, as in "Clarance estoit une *cité* moult boine . . ." (Micha 8: 468, "Clarence was a very fine city . . ."). Here, too, the rare exceptions—and I can cite only two of them—involve Camelot:

> A cel jor tenoit le [*sic*] rois Artus sa cort a Camaalot qui estoit la plus aventurose *vile* qu'il eust et une des plus delitables.

> (Micha 2: 2)

> (On that day, King Arthur held his court at Camelot, which was the city most full of adventures that there ever was and one of the most delightful.)

Also:

> [Lyoniaus] trueve lo roi a Camahalot ou il sejornoit volantiers por ce que c'estoit la plus aeisiee *vile* de son regne.

> (Micha 3: 14)

> ([Lionel] found the king at Camelot, where he liked to stay because it was the most comfortable city of his kingdom.)

We might note in passing that, as a special form of exception, two or more places can be grouped together in a series of examples of *viles*: "Quant li rois ot esté a Logres et a Camaalot et a Carlion et a maintes autres boines *villes* . . ." (Micha 8: 133, "When the king had visited Logres and Camelot and Carlion and many other good cities . . ."). These examples seem to indicate that *vile* is not deemed an altogether unworthy name for Camelot, at least in some contexts, even though it is much more often called a *cité*.

On the other hand, the frequently contrasting use of *cité* and *vile* suggests that these were not always two interchangeable words used to refer to the same place. A close examination of a passage in the *Merlin* concerning Camelot illustrates this point: "Al matin se leua si sen parti de lui & sen uint deuant la *uille* de camaalot" (*Merlin* 180.14–15, "[Merlin] got up in the morning and departed [from Blaise], and he came straight to the city of Camelot"). His approach is gradual: he is first outside the *vile*, and then, a few lines later, he is before the *cité*:

> Et quant il fu deuant la *cyte* si commencha a faire moult grant duel & a crier si fort que cil des murs loirent moult clerement.

> (*Merlin* 180.19–21)

(And when he was before the city, he began to moan and wail so loudly that all the people atop the walls heard him clearly.)

Merlin's lamentations are quoted directly in the following lines (*Merlin* 180.21–29), followed by the commentary

Ceste parole dist merlins si lentendi bien gauaines & si frere car il estoient sour le mur de la *uile* monte . . .

(*Merlin* 180.30–31)

(Merlin uttered these words, and Gawainet and his brothers heard them. They had gone up on the wall of the town . . .)

It is the *vile* that is defended by walls and moats: "car il estoient uenu a camaalot pour la *uile* garder" (*Merlin* 180.32–33, "for they [Gawainet and his brothers] had come to Camelot to protect the town"). Gawain calls to Merlin, "& cil saproce tant quil uint desous les murs sor les fosses dehors la *uile*" (*Merlin* 181.11–12, "And he drew nearer, until he came to the edge of the moat, at the foot of the wall, outside the city"). When Merlin informs Gawain that Sagremor needs help, Gawain and his brothers "sen issent de la *cite*" (*Merlin* 181.34, "they rode out of the city"). Later, after the battle, "li troi compaignon voent que lor gent ont tant erre quil sont en la *cyte*" (*Merlin* 185.5–6, "the three companions saw that their army had made its way into the city"). The companions are reunited. They search for Merlin, but when they cannot find him, they come back into the *vile*, which is defended by bridges and gates:

Et quant li enfant uirent quil ne le porent trouer si sen repairent vers camaalot ou il troeuent lor compaignons qui encore les atendoient al chief del pont. . . . Lors sen entrent en la *vile* si lieue on les pons & freme on les portes si montent en haut sor les murs por sauoir se li sesne venroient assaillir la *uile* mais il nen auoient nul talent car il ne baoient mie aseiourner.

(*Merlin* 186.19–24)

(And when the young men saw that they could not find him, they went back to Camelot, where they found their companions still waiting for them at the head of the bridge. . . . Then they all went into the city. After the bridges were raised and the gates shut, they climbed high on the walls to see whether or not the Saxons were coming to storm the city, but the Saxons did not have the will, and they were not eager to tarry there.)

Thus it is the *vile* that the Saxons would attack, if they attacked. For it is now fairly clear that the two expressions, "la cité de Camaalot" and "la vile de Camaalot" are not precisely parallel. The former may be said to designate on the one hand the place as a whole (its essence, as it were: Camelot *is* a *cité*), and on the other, the central, most important portion, which the *vile* surrounds. And when the author, just a few lines after the previous quotation, announces a change of subject, he uses the label *cité*: "Si se taist ore li contes a parler des enfans qui sont en la *cite* de camaalot . . ." (*Merlin* 186.31–32, "So the story now stops talking about the young men who were in the city of Camelot")—confirming the basic identity of Camelot as a *cité*.

Other passages similarly indicate that the *vile* is outside the *cité*, and that an enemy would first have to attack the former:

> Et pour ce que la *cité* de Gaunes estoit forz et riche et ainsi come forteresce des .II. reaumes, fist il leanz son estage. . . . Et . . . garni il la tor et les creniaux d'archiers . . . si mervilleusement que a celui tens n'avoit home el monde qui bien ne deust douter a asaillir la *vile*.
>
> (Micha 6: 48)

> (And because the city of Gaunes was strong and rich, being the fortress of the two kingdoms, he [King Claudas] made his headquarters there. . . . And . . . he [Claudas] supplied the keep and the battlements with archers . . . in such profusion that every man alive at that time should have feared to attack the city.)

Or that one would first arrive at the *vile*:

> et dist Galehoz qu'il iroit a une soe *cité* molt riche qui estoit chiés de son regne et avoit non Caellus. Si envoia Galehoz avant et fist savoir a la *vile* con il vandroit [*var.*, qu'il i vandroit].
>
> (Micha 3: 11)

> (and Galehaut said he would go to a splendid city of his, which was the head city of his realm and was called Caellus. And Galehaut sent messengers ahead to let [the people of] the city know how he was coming [variant, that he was coming].)

Some of the apparent inconsistency discussed earlier, with respect to the "Pui de Malohaut" and Logres, may in fact be resolved in the light of these observations.

Pres, meaning "meadows" or "fields," seem always to be localized with respect to the *vile* or the *chastel*, and not with respect to the *cité*, as in this sentence (the action occurs in Camelot):

Lors commence li palés a vuidier de genz; si descendent li grant et li petit et vont es prez dehors la *vile*, la ou il fesoient acoustumee-ment les batailles en une place moult bele.

(*Mort* 84. 1–4)

(Then the palace began to empty out; and all the people, the great and small, went down into the meadow outside the town, in a beautiful open space where battles were customarily held.)

There are at least eight co-occurrences of *pres* and *vile*,[6] but none of *pres* and *cité*.

Similarly, the noun *gent*, or its plural form *genz*, seems to be part of a set expression, "la gent de la vile" ("the people of the town," "townsfolk," or "townspeople"), linking the notion of *vile* to that of relatively lower social position:

Et a cele hore meismes entrerent en la *cité* les genz Galehot ; si leva si granz li bruiz que molt an furent esbahi les genz de la *vile*.

(Micha 3: 49)

(Just at that time Galehaut's people [probably his troops] entered the city [Carmelide], and such a great noise arose that the towns-folk were quite aghast.)

On at least one occasion we find the variant expression *li communs de la vile* (literally, "the commoners of the town"), as in this passage which contrasts the two groups, those of the *vile* and those of the *cité*:

. . . au matin firent une biere . . . et chevauchierent tant qu'il vin-drent a Kamaalot; et quant cil de la *cité* sorent que c'estoit li cors de monseigneur Gauvain, il furent de sa mort moult tristre et moult amati. . . . Quant li communs de la *vile* sot que li cors mon-seigneur Gauvain estoit aportez, si i vint tant de gent que nus ne les porroit nombrer.

(*Mort* 175. 3–13)

(. . . the next morning, they prepared a litter . . . They rode until they came to Camelot, and when the people of Camelot learned that the body they were bringing was that of Sir Gawain, they were very distressed and downcast. . . . When the masses learned that the body of Sir Gawain had been brought there [to the main church], so many people came to the church that they could not be counted.)

It seems clear, then, that the two terms, *cité* and *vile*, connote a difference in status. This reveals itself in various ways, among them passages dealing with travelers' lodgings. Housing is almost always found in a *vile* or just outside one, and the word *vile* is often linked to the noun *ostel* or the verb *herbergier*: "Atant s'em part Guidan de la cort et vait en la *vile* herbergier" (Micha 4: 80, "With these words Guidan left court and went to take lodging in the town"). Similarly, it seems always to be the word *vile* that appears in the oaths people swear when setting out. We find numerous examples similar to the following:

Et Galahos vient au roi et prist congié et dist que jamés ne geroit que une nuit ensemble en une *vile* devant que il avra oïes de son compaignon vraies noveles.

(Micha 3: 226)

(And Galehaut came to the king to take his leave, saying that he would never sleep more than one night in any town until he had learned reliable news of his companion.)

The relative status of *cité* and *vile* is particularly clear in the following passage:

Al matin se partirent de Cardueil et vindrent a Camaalot et furent tuit li pre portendu de loges et de paveillons, kar li haut home herbergierent en la *cité* tuit et cil qui avec els ne porent chevir furent tuit espandu es pres defors la *vile*.

(Micha 1: 89–90)

(In the morning, they left Carduel and went to Camelot, where all the fields were covered with tents and pavilions, for the great vassals were all lodged in the castle, and the men who could not be accommodated with them were all scattered through the fields outside the walls.)

The prestige of the *cité* is manifested in other ways as well. The principal town of a region or realm, characterized as either *chief* or *maistre* ("main," "chief" or "principal"), is regularly called a *cité*. We have already seen examples of this in connection with Logres (Micha 8: 407), Caellus (Micha 3: 11), and Zelegebres (Micha 1: 109). The first of these, concerning Logres, uses both of these "prestigious" terms: "Lyoniax trova la roine sejornant a Logres, la maistre *cité* le roi Artu car che estoit li chiés de son regne" (Micha 8: 407, "Lionel found the queen staying at Logres, King Arthur's principal city because it was the capital of his kingdom"). Similarly in reference to Carmelide: "'Et ge voil,' fait li rois, 'que li jugemenz soit faiz d'ui en tierz jor en la *cité* de Tamelide qui est li chiés de cest regne . . .'" (Micha 3: 45–46, "'And I want the trial held two days from now,' said the king, 'in the city of Carmelide, which is the capital of this realm . . .'").

As in various contexts already examined, here, too, the noun *vile* seems to be extremely rare, but there is at least one such occurrence, referring to Carmelide, just five pages after the previous example: "si sera trainee par mi ceste *vile* qui est li chiés del reiaume" (Micha 3: 51, "and she will be dragged through this city, which is the capital of the kingdom").

The relative ranking of *cité* and *vile*, extending to other terms as well, seems obvious in Pharien's apostrophe to Gaunes:

Hai, boine *chités*, honeree d'anchiserie, hantee de preudommes et de loiax, maisons et sieges de roi et ostex a droit jugeor, repairs a joie et a lieche, cors pleniere de boins chevaliers, *vile* onoree de vaillans borgois, *païs* plains de loiax vavasors et de boins gaaigneors,[7] *terre* plentiveuse et raemplie de tous biens, ha, Diex.

(Micha 7: 219)

(Ah, good city, honored by our forefathers, home of worthy men and true, seat and dwelling of kings and house of upright judges, place of joy and gladness, court of fine knights, honored town of valiant householders, countryside full of loyal vavasors and good laborers, fruitful land filled with every good—ah, God!)

Here we have a veritable inventory, listing, in order, the various divisions of the realm: first the *cité*, most central and highest in status; then the *vile*, residence of the *borgois*; this is followed by the *païs*, home of *vavasors* and *gaaigneors*; and finally the *terre*, home, by implication, of the peasants.

Much more could be said concerning the use of the terms *cité* and *vile*. There are other instances of co-occurrence to explore, for example that of *cort* with *cité* or *vile*, and the use of various adjectives, some of which we have seen in the preceding examples, to describe one or the other of these terms—or both of them.

Nevertheless, there seems to be considerable evidence indicating that *vile*, at the time these texts were composed, was in the process of extending its range of connotation into the sphere of *cité*. The relative hierarchy of the two terms was apparently still felt, but the limit between them was by no means absolute. The use of *vile* for such preeminent places as Carduel and Camelot, its occasional use in place-naming formulae, and its association with at least one capital city may be seen as a sign of its rising status and its eventual displacement of *cité* in the language.

Notes

1. Much of the basic research and many of the examples for this paper were contributed by Samuel N. Rosenberg of Indiana University, who also made a number of helpful suggestions for its final form. I also wish to express my thanks to Lois Hawley Wilson, who contributed additional examples, and to my wife, Paulette Carroll, for her invaluable close reading and editorial advice.

2. References to the various texts are given parenthetically, using the following editions and formats: *Lancelot*, edited by Micha, volume number, page number; *Merlin*, edited by Sommer, page number, line number; *Mort Artu*, edited by Frappier, paragraph, line number. The translations are those prepared for *Lancelot-Grail: The Old French Arthurian Vulgate and Post-Vulgate in Translation*, edited by Norris J. Lacy. I thank my co-translators for supplying me with their translations of passages from forthcoming volumes: Samuel N. Rosenberg (Micha 1 and 7); Roberta L. Krueger (Micha 2); William W. Kibler (Micha 4); Norris J. Lacy (*The Death of Arthur*). Translations of examples from *Merlin* are by Rupert T. Pickens (*Lancelot-Grail*, vol. 1, *The Story of Merlin*); those from Micha 6 and 8 are my own, as are those from Micha 3, containing shorter versions of the text which are not to be included in the *Lancelot-Grail* collection.

3. There are in addition two occurrences of *la cite(i) de Malahaut* in *Merlin*, 131.16–17 and 364.26 (listed by G. D. West, *An Index of Proper Names in French Arthurian Prose Romances* (Toronto: University of Toronto Press, 1978): 206.

4. In Kennedy, *Lancelot do Lac*, 274.31–281.14, the count is 11 occurrences of *cité* and one of *vile*. If we consider only the places where one of these words is used in conjunction with the *name* of the place, "Malahaut" or "Pui de Malahaut," the count is 3–to–1 in Micha in favor of *cité*; in Kennedy it is *cité* in every case (281.7–8 has "la cité do Pui de Malohaut," corresponding to *vile* in Micha 8: 9.24).

5. There is also one instance of the naming of a *borc*, the one below the *castel* of Dolorouse Garde: "si avoit non li *bors* Chanevinche" (Micha 7: 314.11,

"The town was called Chanviere"; Kennedy 184.4, "Chaneviere"). According to West, this place is named just twice, the other occurrence being in the *Livre d'Artus* (Sommer 7).

6. *Merlin* 143.32–34 (Aneblayse); Micha 1: 89–90 (Camelot), 1: 90 (Camelot), 2: 219 (Floego), 4: 267 (Corbenic), 4: 268 (Corbenic), 7: 158–159 (Gaunes); *Mort* 84.1–4 (Camelot).

7. Micha's text has "seignors" ("lords"); this reading is taken from his variants.

9. Ladies Don't Wear *Braies*: Underwear and Outerwear in the French *Prose Lancelot*

E. Jane Burns

As the translators of the Lancelot-Grail cycle worked together over the past few years, hammering out solutions to some of the more difficult transitions from Old French to modern English, we struggled over many problematic terms.[1] One of the most troublesome translation snags, for which we never found a satisfactory solution, involved the terminology for medieval undergarments, most specifically, the words *chemise* and *braies*. Although these terms do not occur frequently in the Lancelot-Grail corpus, their occasional appearance did send us on a hunt for adequate English equivalents. How were we to describe, for example, the temptress who is said to be dressed only in a *chemise* when trying to seduce the wayward Lancelot?[2] The word "shirt" bears connotations that are obviously too masculine. To say that the seductress was wearing a "shift" suggests outer clothing rather than the garment often described in medieval French texts as lying next to the skin.[3] The word "slip," which readers would readily recognize as underwear, describes a tight-fitting sleeveless garment, whereas the medieval *chemise* was loose-fitting and had long sleeves.[4] What about the word "chemise" itself, defined in the *American Heritage Dictionary* as "a woman's loose, shirt-like undergarment?"[5] It seemed a perfect solution. And yet how many speakers of English would in fact know what the English term "chemise" meant?

The case of the Old French *braies* was even more problematic. When Lancelot, who is eventually forced into bed by the temptress, coyly resists her advances by undressing without removing his *braies*, what are we to say?[6] "Lancelot got into bed as the damsel ordered, but did not take off his shorts?" Certainly "Lancelot refused to remove his 'briefs'" is inadequate. And more colloquial expressions which might suggest that Lancelot retained "his skivvies" or "his BVDs" are even less viable. To translate the passage as "Lancelot refused to remove his underpants" sounds infantile. "He refused to remove his underwear" is too general. "Drawers" smacks of the nineteenth rather than the thirteenth century. "Breeches," as it appears in the *American Heritage Dictionary* and indeed as it is taken by most American readers today, designates an outer garment defined as "trousers extending to or just below the knee" (p. 163) rather than the undergarment that Lancelot retains.

Unmentionables

It was because of these difficulties in translation that I became interested in medieval underwear and found, as I read more and more, that I learned less and less. Indeed, the very characteristic that defines underwear—its being worn beneath another garment—makes it literally invisible and historically elusive. Many histories of medieval costume list no category for underwear at all, partly because information regarding medieval clothing in general derives so often from art historical materials which treat only the outer, visible layers or from literary references which for the early centuries are, as one source cogently put it, "extremely scanty."[7] References to clothing in medieval theatrical productions prove equally problematic because they tend to be generic, indicating that a character is wearing a *chaperon*, *bonnet*, or *robe* but providing no more descriptive detail for these items of clothing than for the occasional mention of *chausses* or *chemise*.[8] And it is of course not clear that medieval theatrical costume would, in any event, provide a representational equivalent of everyday dress.

As for actual wardrobes, when historians look at inventories of aristocratic clothing from the thirteenth through fifteenth centuries, undergarments are strikingly absent. Among the evidence of gowns, robes, opulent silk and woolen garments, and many dresses and furs, the linen items mentioned in these inventories include very few *chemises* or none at all.[9] Even the richest inventories, belonging to people who owned lots of linen tablecovers, for example, counted linen for the body in single figures.[10] Wealth tended to be invested in visible clothing, according to the historian Vigarello, who explains further that "the existence of the skin and the concrete conception of the body were largely forgotten in the presence of coverings of wool and fur. It was as if everything should relate to the visible, as if material and form exhausted the potential qualities and the envelope assumed the role of the body" (Vigarello 53). As the outer garments and the body beneath were collapsed into this single envelope or body substitute, the unseen garments, aptly characterized in one history of Western costume as a *terra incognita*,[11] simply disappeared. What were to become "unmentionables" in the modesty of the Victorian era were, for very different reasons, most often simply "unmentioned" in thirteenth-century France.[12]

This leads C. Willett Cunnington and Phyllis Cunnington to conclude: "Throughout the Middle Ages the underclothing of both sexes possessed a characteristic inherited from earlier times. By tradition it was a part of costume entirely lacking in significance" (Cunnington and Cunnington 19). Elizabeth Ewing concurs: "Underwear existed in some form before fashion began, but it did not acquire any significance or any history until the dawn of fashion. . . . Fashion was born as the Middle Ages ended."[13]

Yet if these assessments are correct, why are underclothes mentioned at all in medieval literary texts? If, as the Cunningtons contend, medieval underwear "is *not* used to express class distinction and only very indirectly to enhance sex attraction" (Cunnington and Cunnington 19, my emphasis), what is its function in those rare literary moments when we hear of *braies* and *chemise*?

The Politics of Outerwear

It is well known that medieval outer clothing was widely used to express social status and at times sexual attraction. In addition to clearly marking religious orders, military orders, and chivalric orders in the later Middle Ages, costume was used to single out pilgrims, Jews, heretics, lepers, prostitutes, the insane, and individuals condemned to death.[14] Beginning in the second half of the thirteenth century in Mediterranean Europe, sumptuary laws—designed perhaps to restrain competition among the families of young women of marriageable age—simultaneously restricted female adornment in the form of jewelry, ornament, and lavish clothing and limited the amount of flesh that could be exposed.[15] Both restrictions were designed to curtail seduction.

Before the fourteenth and fifteenth centuries (when sumptuary laws were most in evidence), however, medieval outerwear, while often used to distinguish social position or rank, bore little evidence of sexual differentiation. For the upper classes in particular, the standard indoor costume in the twelfth and thirteenth centuries (apart from garments worn by men on horseback, either during the hunt or on the battlefield) was strikingly similar for males and females.[16] It was composed of a *chemise*, an ankle-length undergarment with rounded neck and long sleeves, covered by a *cotte* or *bliaut* (the outer robe) and a cloak or mantle fastened at the neck.[17]

The Unisex Chemise

The *chemise* was most often linen, sometimes pleated, commonly referred to in literary texts as a "chemise ridee et blanche" whether worn by men or women. A well-known passage from Chrétien de Troyes's *Erec et Enide* describes the heroine as wearing a *chemise* with wide, pleated tails:

> d'une chemise par panz lee,
> delïee, blanche et ridee.
>
> (vv. 403–404)

Yet in Chrétien's *Yvain* the châtelain's daughter welcomes the hero by removing his armor and offering to dress him in a *chemise risdee* pulled from a chest where clothing is stored: "Chemise risdee li tret / fors de son cofre . . ."[18]

That the *chemise* was typically worn next to the skin is seen in the *Chevalier de la Charrette* when Lancelot holds the queen's golden hairs to his chest: "An son sain pres del cuer les fiche / entre sa chemise et sa char"[19] ("He tucks them between his *chemise* and his skin"). The only garment worn beneath the *chemise* was the hairshirt. Queen Elaine of Benoic is said to wear a stiff and prickly hairshirt under her white *chemise* in the noncyclic *Prose Lancelot*: "ele avoit totes hores vestue la haire aspre et poignant par desouz la chemise qui mout estoit blanche et deliee."[20] Though romance characters generally sleep naked, the *chemise* sometimes serves as a nightshirt for men and women alike. In Chrétien's *Chevalier de la Charrette*, the temptress gets into bed without removing her *chemise*:

> Et la dameisele s'i couche,
> mes n'oste mie sa chemise.
>
> (vv. 1202–1203)[21]

A few lines later, Lancelot too beds down in his *chemise*:

> Et il se couche tot a tret,
> mes sa chemise pas ne tret.
>
> (vv. 1213–1214)

If the *chemise* was thus worn by both sexes in the courtly milieu, it differed at times only in length: the man's *chemise* seems to have been somewhat shorter than the woman's (Goddard 94).

Yet the man's *chemise* was typically accompanied by a second undergarment, the *braies*. The two words often appear together as a linguistic pair in the medieval male wardrobe. In fact, when Lancelot faces off against the temptress in the passage from the *Prose Lancelot* with which we began (see note 6), he actually refuses to remove both *braies* and *chemise*: "il n'oste ne braies ne chemise."[22] In Chrétien's *Yvain* the hero dons *chemise* and *braies* and *chausses noires*:

> et avoec ce i met del suen
> chemise et braies deliees,
> et chauces noires et dougiees.
>
> (vv. 2982–2984)

(And from her own belongings she added a *chemise* and soft *braies*, and black, fine-spun stockings.)

Even the dress of peasants often follows the same model in the *Dit de l'Eschacier*, where we learn that the workingman's clothing was layered from the outermost *chape* and *mantel* to the "cote sur gonele." Beneath all of this were the "braies et chemise" (Evans 9).

It is, then, precisely at the invisible level of underwear that a most significant difference in the dress of aristocratic men and women can be discerned in the High Middle Ages, a difference marking one of the most striking absences in the whole underwear story: the general absence of *braies*—or any equivalent form of drawers—from the woman's costume. Indeed, in literary texts from the twelfth and thirteenth centuries, when aristocratic women take off the *mantel* and *cotte*, they are left most often with the *chemise* alone.[23] The Seductive Damsel in Chrétien's *Charrette* is naked to the navel beneath her *chemise*:

> Cil voit que molt vileinnemant
> tenoit la dameisele cil
> descoverte jusqu'au nonbril.
>
> (vv. 1080–1082)

(He saw that the other villainously held down the girl, uncovered to the waist.)

The fairy in Marie de France's "Lanval" lies on a beautiful bed wearing nothing but her *chemise*:

> Ele jut sur un lit mut bel—
> Li drap valeient un chastel—
> En sa chemise senglement.
>
> (vv. 97–99)[24]

(She was lying in a most beautiful bed, whose covers were worth a castle, clad only in her *chemise*.)

Her flank—from lower rib to hip—is nude: "Tut ot descovert le costé" (v. 104).

In the later and less courtly genre of Old French fabliau, the tale entitled "Berengier au lonc cul" records an extreme example of unfettered flesh beneath the female *robe*. The unnamed wife in this fabliau, disguised as a knight, challenges her unsuspecting husband to a joust or, failing that, requires that he kiss her naked ass:

> Comment que uos iostoiz a'moi
> . . .
> Ou ie descendrai ius a'pie,
> Deuant vos m'ire abaissier
> Si me pranrai a estuper,
> Vos me uandroiz o'cu baissier
> Tres o mileu o par delez.[25]

(Either you joust with me or I will dismount and I will bow before you. As I bend over, you will kiss my ass, square in the center or off to the side.)

When the befuddled husband chooses the second option, "La dame n'i uolt respit qerre / Tot maintenant descent a'terre / La robe prant a'soleuer / Deuant lui prant a'estuper" ("The lady doesn't delay. She dismounts at once, raises her gown and bends over in front of him"). What the shocked knight sees is the naked female anatomy, puzzling to his untrained eye, but clearly naked nonetheless. We are told in no uncertain terms, "Et cil esgarde la creuace; / Du cul et del con ce li sanble / Que trestot se tienent ensanble" (v. 264, "He sees the crack [between her buttocks]; where it appeared to him that the asshole and the cunt were one").

The woman's costume in texts ranging from Old French romance to fabliau is thus marked by a significant lack: the lack of linen breeches that often accompany the man's *chemise*. Historically, no drawers existed for women in England until the turn of the eighteenth century when, sometime between 1791 and 1820, women's fashion changed drastically in response to the introduction of the thin and transparent dress. Drawers were then imported from men's wear, marking a major innovation in women's fashion. Pantaloons, also pirated from male dress where they had served as an outergarment, were longer and frillier than the original women's drawers and remained popular only until the 1830s.[26] Bloomers were not invented until 1850 and appeared first in the American Midwest as an outergarment when Amelia Jenks Bloomer sought to make women's attire more practical by inventing ankle-length trousers to accompany a short skirt and jacket.[27] Cunnington and Cunnington report finding no evidence of drawers being worn by Englishwomen of any class before 1800, except for a solitary reference in Samuel Pepys's diary of 1663. Pepys, who suspected his wife of infidelity, watched her dressing and recorded the following:

> I am ashamed to think what a course I did take by lying to see whether my wife did wear drawers today as she did use to, and other things to raise my suspicions of her.
>
> (Cunnington and Cunnington 46)

There is some evidence reported by the historian Leloir that French ladies wore "caleçons" from the middle of the sixteenth century.[28] Maureen Mazzaoui's study of the linen trade in medieval Italy finds evidence that Italian women wore drawers from the mid-twelfth century.[29] But such is not the case for medieval Frenchwomen, at least not the ones depicted in literary genres ranging from romance to fabliau. With rare exceptions, these ladies wear no *braies*.

Braies

The history of medieval *braies* is fascinating in its own right as a particularly apt illustration of the fluidity between categories of underwear and outerwear in the history of clothing. Cunnington and Cunnington remind us how women's stockings, once concealed as an undergarment, subsequently became visible, how the waistcoat was originally an undervest for both men and women, and how

Saxon breeches shifted from an outergarment (trousers) to underwear (drawers) as they were concealed beneath the Norman tunic in
the mid-twelfth century (*History of Underclothes* 12). Long breeches
emerged again at the end of the eighteenth century as tight-fitting
long trousers (an outer garment and alternative to the breeches and
stockings which were the dominant style in England and France at
the time). These new, long pants were called pantaloons and were
the forerunner of modern men's pants.[30]

Even before the Saxons, Roman troops wore knee-length drawers,
fastened at the waist beneath their outer breeches, as did the Carolin-
gians.[31] However, from the ninth to the eleventh centuries, the Norman *"braies"* referred to an outer garment: relatively loose pajama
trousers with cross garterings or leather thongs tied over them from
knee to ankle.[32] Shorter *braies* also existed at this time, ending above
the knee. Both styles were worn by all classes.[33] By the mid-twelfth
century, when *braies* became linen drawers for the nobility, they grew
progressively fuller and shorter and were eventually tucked into hose
(*chausses*). Over the course of the thirteenth and fourteenth centuries,
the hose grew longer as the *braies* diminished in length, becoming in
the fifteenth century little more than a loincloth.[34] Whatever their
length, shape, or visibility, *braies* remained, throughout the Middle
Ages, a distinctly male garment.

Braies as Outer Clothes?

What is the significance of this disparity in male and female underwear during an era when outer clothing revealed little differentiation
between the sexes? What, we might ask, are the sexual politics of
chemise and *braies*, and what do they have to do with our reading of
the French *Prose Lancelot*?

In many instances, the man's *braies* become a visual locus for that
margin of safety between social acceptability and social disgrace. In
the *Queste del Saint Graal*, for example, when Perceval finds himself in
bed with a naked temptress, he wounds himself in the thigh and then
sees that he is "toz nuz fors de ses braies"[35] ("completely naked except for his braies"). The undergarment alone stands between him
and the nudity that would signal moral perdition.

In Béroul's *Roman de Tristan*, similarly, it is when King Marc sees
the undergarments that clothe the adulterous lovers who sleep side
by side in the forest bower that he becomes convinced of their fleshly
purity. If the sword lying between them is "naked" (*"nue espee,"*
v. 1998), Tristan is not:

> Vit les braies que Tristran out
> "Dex!" dit le rois "ce que puet estre?
> . . .
> Se il s'amasent folement,
> Ja n'i eusent vestement,
> Entre eus deus n'eust espee,
> Autrement fust cest'asemblee." [36]

(The king sees the *braies* that Tristan is wearing. "God," he says, "What can this mean? If they were madly in love, they would not have clothing between them, nor a sword.")

However faulty King Marc's interpretation of the scene may be, for him the sight of Tristan's *braies* marks the male body as socially acceptable, protected from the adulterous deviance that would relegate the king's favorite nephew to exile. Underwear is significant in these scenes to the extent that it temporarily becomes outerwear—that it constitutes a visible sign of spiritual or social status. [37]

Yet male underwear in the *Prose Lancelot* can function in the opposite sense as well, to indicate social or chivalric nakedness. At one point in his travels Lancelot comes upon a mounted knight who pulls behind him a man hung by the neck from his horse's tail:

> Li hons estoit en chemise et en braies, tous descaus, si avoit les iex bendés et les mains liies deriere le dos et chou estoit .I. des plus biax hommes que on peust trover.
>
> (Micha 7: 374)

(The man was wearing *chemise* and *braies*, barefoot, blindfolded, his hands tied behind his back. He was one of the most handsome men you could ever find.)

Indeed, as he explains to Lancelot, the victim was one of the queen's knights, here made to suffer a ritual humiliation as a punishment for "treason and disloyalty" ("puis qu'il est traîtres et desloiaus," Micha 7: 375). The victimizer asserts that the hanged man had been caught *in flagrante delicto*, committing adultery with the mounted knight's wife (whose head he now wears slung around his neck). Stripping him down to underwear alone amounts to stripping him of social rank, making him vulnerable and defenseless for all to see. This man's status differs little from that of medieval prisoners condemned to death who were paraded through the streets "en che-

- - Ladies Don't Wear Braies   161

mise."[38] Indeed, in this case, underwear offers no protection from nudity. This knight may as well be wearing no clothes at all.[39]

When King Arthur allows himself to be duped by the wiles of the enchantress Camille, he finds himself similarly humiliated in his *braies* alone. Shortly after arriving at the nighttime rendezvous, a young maiden takes off the king's armor so that he can make love with Camille in a sumptuous bed. When forty armed knights break into the room, their swords drawn:

> Li rois saut sus si com il puet, car il n'avoit que ses braies et cort a s'espee, qu'il se voloit desfendre. . . . Et il dient qu'il ne se desfende mie et il non fait, car il est desarmés, si voit bien que desfense n'i a mestier.
>
> (Micha 8: 443)

> (The king leaps up, as well as he can, because he is wearing only his *braies*, and runs for his sword to defend himself. . . . They warn the king not to put up the least resistance; unarmed, he realizes that defending himself is pointless.)

Here Arthur finds himself in a situation opposite to that of the knights in *L'Escoufle*, of whom it is said, "Nus n'i a le cuer en le braie/ Ains sont hardi come lion"[40] ("No one had his heart in his *braies*; rather they were as bold as lions"). Arthur, caught unawares and without defense (whether arms or armor), cannot be *hardi* at all. He is presented as socially nude, though still wearing his *braies*.

Indeed Arthur's plight in this scene echoes Gawain's dilemma when he secretly meets the daughter of the King of Norgales in her bedchamber at night. At her request Gawain takes off his steely cold armor and slips into bed. They make love and fall asleep only to be awakened the next morning by two attackers sent by the enraged king:

> Et mesire Gauvain . . . se lanche hors del lit tout nu et errache l'espiel del mur et en fiert par mi les costés chelui qui apoié l'avoit sur lui, si le jete mort.
>
> (Micha 8: 384)

> (Sir Gawain . . . jumps out of bed completely naked, pulls the sword out of the wall [where it had lodged] and strikes the attacker in the thigh, killing him.)

He kills the second assailant with equal dispatch and then "jeté hors le premier que il avoit ochis et ot bien l'uis fremé, puis vient a ses armes, si s'arme" (Micha 8: 384, "threw the first man he killed out the window, firmly closes the door and puts on his armor"). Whether Gawain dons *braies* under the armor is not clear, but we know he was not wearing them at the time of the attack.

Is Gawain's situation significantly different from that of King Arthur or the unnamed knight accused of adultery? The knight charged with adultery is publicly humiliated: denuded of all marks of chivalric identity. Arthur and Gawain, like most knights in bed with women, are similarly disarmed. Whether literally stripped bare or close to it, they become defenseless against the seductive tricks of an enchantress like Camille. But men in this situation are also defenseless against other armed men. Once they are wearing only *braies* or *braies* and *chemise* they are socially naked; no longer knights, but unspecified bodies.[41] In this case, underwear cannot function as outerwear. It seems rather to meld into the skin as if it weren't even there.[42]

However, Gawain promptly regains his knightly identity as he suitably recovers his armor, Arthur shortly regains his clothing and royal stature, and the knight wrongly accused of adultery is taken to a manor house where, apparently, he is properly outfitted before journeying to see the queen. Nudity for these men, as Danielle Régnier-Bohler has noted for a wide range of male characters in Old French literature, is a passing phase, indicating a temporary rupture with social convention.[43] The male nude is indeed not typically described corporeally as a naked body. This is as true for the infant Tristan or the baby Lancelot in the *Prose Lancelot* as for Bisclavret and other werewolves covered with fur. For a man to be "completely naked," as Gawain is in his lady's bedchamber, is not, therefore, an anatomical state but a mark of social disfunction.[44]

Underwear and Social Status

What unites the foregoing examples with the seemingly quite different instances of protective underclothes we discussed above from the *Queste del Saint Graal* and *Tristan* is the following: both types of partial denuding adhere to a dichotomous logic by which the male protagonist is either clothed in some way (whether fully or partially) or unclothed (despite the existence of an undergarment); that is to say, he is either properly socialized and visibly operative as a member of a specified cultural group, or he is desocialized and visibly marginalized from the locus of proper social activity.

The system is perhaps most cogently described in Jean de Meun's

Roman de la Rose, where the rise and fall of individual fortunes are reg-
istered interestingly in the way a female goddess, Fortune, changes
her clothes. Fortune's house, we are told, is divided into two parts,
the elegant and the lowly:

> Et quant el vuet estre honoree
> Si se trait en la part doree
> De la maison, et la sejorne.
> Lors pere son cors et atorne
> Et se vest cum une roïne
> De grant robe qui li traïne
> De toutes diverses olors.[45]

(When she wants to be honored, she withdraws into the golden
portion of the house, adorns her body, dresses like a queen in a
grand trailing gown that emits perfumed odors.)

When she enters the sordid part of the house, in contrast:

> Sa chiere et son habit remue,
> Et si se desnue et desrobe
> Qu'ele est orfenine de robe
>
> (vv. 6152–6154)

(She changes facial expression along with her clothing. She un-
dresses, takes off her garments until she is wearing nothing at all.)

It is this version of Fortune that dishonors, ruins, and disempowers
men (v. 6167).

Ladies Undressed

But if social identity for the aristocratic male protagonist resides in his
being suitably dressed, the opposite is true of his female partner. Indeed, most of the courtly women described as wearing a lone *chemise*
are temptresses who readily lift their hem to expose what lies beneath. Rather than a visual icon registering a distance and distinction
from nudity, as in the cases of Tristan and Perceval discussed above,
the woman's *chemise* often connotes just the opposite: seduction and
nudity itself. Many women are tellingly described as being "nue en
sa chemise"[46] ("naked in her *chemise*").

Indeed, even aristocratic women who are fully and lavishly clothed often appear, curiously, to be fundamentally naked. The literary portraits of twelfth-century women detailed by Alice Colby reveal not only the lovely face of the lady on display (her hair, forehead, eyebrows, eyes, nose, mouth, teeth, and chin), but also the seductively white skin of her throat and chest.[47] And the standard description continues, detailing parts of the body that are actually hidden from view: the round breasts, elegant waist, delicate hips, and what is euphemistically termed "le sorplus"[48] ("all the rest"). Even at court, among throngs of onlookers, queens and ladies cast in the role of the dazzlingly beautiful object of desire are desired first and foremost as bodies. Their social identity resides less in being covered than in being uncovered, much as they are often naked beneath their *chemise*, unprotected by the *braies* that their male counterparts typically wear.[49]

Indeed, if we take the famous *costume de Logres* as an indicator of female social status and function in the Arthurian world, we find that the lovely and alluring lady is in fact distinctly vulnerable to attack, not only when naked but also when elegantly clothed. Chrétien's text and the *Prose Lancelot* both explain that when a knight comes upon a lady traveling in the company of another knight, the men may rightfully fight over possession of the damsel: whoever wins the battle may do with the lady as he pleases.[50] In this reading, Arthurian ladies wearing no *braies* have no social status or leverage independent of the knights who commodify and trade them as objects of exchange.

How Women Can Wear *Braies*

Are there other ways that women can wear the pants in the social arena? One thinks immediately not of romance but of the fabliaux, where henpecked husbands typically kowtow to domineering wives. The unnamed wife of the "Quatre Sohais Saint Martin," for example, is said to "chaucer les braies" (Noomen and Van den Boogaard 4: 196). For a long time I took this to mean that the wife "wore the pants" in the family, since peasants throughout the High Middle Ages wore knee-length breeches called *braies*, as did workmen of later centuries.[51] But in light of what we have been discussing here, could this sentence carry a second meaning? Could we be meant to understand that this sexually aggressive wife wears the underpants in the family as well—having stripped her mate of the "shorts," "briefs," or "skivvies" that are rightfully his?[52] When the wife in the "Quatre Sohais Saint Martin" sweet-talks her gullible (and sexually negligent) husband into giving her one of his precious wishes, she requests that his body be covered with what the fabliau inelegantly calls "pricks." When the additional members appear on the husband's nose, mouth, knees, forehead, and all the way down to his feet, the narrator remarks how this man covered with pricks, "Molt par fu bien de vis vestuz" (Noomen and Van den Boogaard 4: 182, "was very well dressed in pricks"). But he's not wearing pants of any kind.

One of the riddles from the *Adivineaux amoureux* of the 1470s casts the relative social influence and power between men and women specifically in terms of *braies*.

> Demande:
> A quelle heure du jour est tout homme trouvé moins aidable?
> Response:
> C'est en chaussant ses braies, car se garde lors d'estre sourpris.[53]

(Question: At what time of day is a man most helpless [least able to defend himself]?

Answer: In putting on his pants [underpants?] because he takes care not to be surprised [because he's preoccupied with not getting caught].)

The companion riddle, found a few pages later, states the following:

> Demande:
> En quel temps de l'an sont les femmes plus deffensables?
> Response:
> C'est quant elles chausent les brayes.[54]

(Question: When are women most well-defended [protected]?
Answer: When they're wearing pants [underpants].)

What we learn from these examples and from a particularly striking and very funny scene in the *Prose Lancelot* that I will discuss below, is that if male protagonists wear their *braies* literally as a sign of social status, women can "chaucer les braies" metaphorically. If men alone can wear *braies* visibly, women can be dressed in *braies* without wearing them at all. The unnamed wife in "Berengier au lonc cul" is a particularly apt example of how the female buttocks, naked under a long robe, can nonetheless "wear the pants in the family." This "lady," as she is called repeatedly, cross-dresses as a knight to reveal the cowardice of her unchivalric husband and, as the fabliau tells us, puts him in his proper place (literally, "shames him": "Ce est mes sires berangier / Al lomc cul qui uos feroit honte," Noomen and Van den Boogaard 4: 268).

About midway through the *Prose Lancelot*, Lancelot encounters a similarly aggressive "rival" female who, though she is not dressed in arms and armor, takes on the function of chivalric foe that Berengier plays out more literally. At issue here, as in "Berengier au lonc cul," is the knight's sexual, rather than chivalric, prowess. After Morgan le Fay temporarily frees Lancelot from her prison and sends him off in the company of a skillful young female guide, the damsel turns seductress along the route:

> Et quant ele voit un bel lieu plaisant, si li mostre et dist: "Veez, sire chevaliers, dont ne seroit il bien honis qui tel lieu passeroit avec bele dame ne avec bele damoisele sans fere plus?"
>
> (Micha 1: 317–318)

> (Showing him a lovely place by the roadside she said, "Look sir knight, don't you think that anyone who passed such a place, while traveling in the company of a beautiful lady or maiden, and didn't act further, would be dishonored?")

Though couched in courtly rhetoric, the damsel's request is wholly unladylike, and Lancelot rejects it out of hand. But when they take lodging for the night, the damsel instructs Lancelot to undress and lie down in a sumptuous bed (this is the passage with which we began):

> Lancelos s'est cochies par le commandement a la damoisele et samble bien qu'il ait de lui garde al samblant que il fet, kar il n'oste ne braies ne chemise.
>
> (Micha 1: 322)

> (Lancelot follows the lady's command to get into bed, but shows his hesitation by taking the following precautions: he does not remove his *braies* or his *chemise*.)

The damsel soon takes off her gown, but not her *chemise* (Micha 1: 323) and slips into bed next to the knight clad in underwear, to which Lancelot responds, much as Arthur and Gawain did when attacked by armed knights. Castigating the damsel for trying to "prendre chevalier par force" (Micha 1: 323, "take a knight by force"), Lancelot leaps out of bed. But unlike Arthur and Gawain, he has no one to fight—no one except the damsel, who accuses him pointedly of cowardice and disloyalty.[55] How can Lancelot boast of planning to liberate

Gawain, this damsel asks, when he, Lancelot "deserts his bed because of a lone maiden?" (Micha 1: 323)? The helpless Lancelot explains that he could easily defend himself against eight knights leveling such accusations, but, reminiscent of King Arthur in his *braies*, the accomplished knight is here thoroughly defenseless: unprotected, in this instance, against an unexpected female rival.

The verbal struggle between Lancelot and his lady guide then escalates, uncharacteristically, to actual physical combat, creating one of the most comical moments in the entire *Prose Lancelot*. When she lunges for the knight's nose and misses, the lady's bold attack focusses on the knight's underwear. She grabs his *chemise* and unwittingly rips it open, provoking Lancelot to hold her to the floor and force her to promise "qu'ele ne se cochera en lit ou il gise ne nel requerra de chose qui encontre lui soit" (Micha 1: 323, "that she will not sleep in his bed or ask him for anything else against his wishes").

The now seemingly cooperative lady agrees to promise one thing (Micha 1: 323), but she insists on whispering it in Lancelot's ear. When Lancelot bends low to hear the lady's whispered words, she falls to the floor in an apparent faint. As the stunned knight leans in, cartoonlike, to take a closer look, the damsel "gete la boche, sel baisse" (Micha 1: 324, "throws her mouth forward and kisses him"). The enraged Lancelot recoils from her body and literally spits out the unwanted kiss. When she runs after him, he threatens her with a sword, but she calls his bluff, knowing "qu'il ne ferroit por nule rien" (Micha 1: 324, "that he won't strike her"). Lancelot finally throws down his sword and runs out of the tent, the damsel close on his heels. If Lancelot is literally dressed in *braies* during this exchange, the damsel is clearly the one wearing the pants, whether we choose to characterize them as underwear or outerwear.[56]

Cross-dressed Knights

What has happened here to the neat dichotomy between dress and undress that was signaled in Jean de Meun's description of Fortune, a dichotomy between clothing and nudity that structures the way both underwear and outerwear function for male protagonists in the *Prose Lancelot*? This hybrid lady/knight tellingly unsettles, along with the pat categories of male and female, the text's more subtle distinctions between clothed and unclothed bodies and between visible and invisible garments. This problematic damsel plays the roles of both seductress "en chemise" and the rival *chevalier* who would, under normal circumstances, be fully armed and dressed. Her metaphorical cross dressing, along with the more literal transvestism of the lady-turned-knight in the fabliau "Berengier au lonc cul," heralds in fact the coming of another cross-dressed knight, one who was put on trial by the Inquisition, not only for heresy, but also for transvestism: Joan of Arc.

Marina Warner points out that Joan, throughout the trial, never tried to pass as a man. "She was usurping a man's function but shaking off the trammels of his sex altogether to occupy a different, third order, neither male nor female."[57] Wearing the visible signs of maleness and the political power that accrues thereto, Joan identified herself throughout the trial as a woman in man's clothes. It was the very indeterminacy of her position, according to Marjorie Garber, the fact that she insisted on being both a woman and a man visibly and publicly that so disturbed her accusers.[58] The trial record bears this out on nearly every page. The affront is often recorded in terms of dress and more specifically in terms of underwear. To take but one example, we read in the entry from Wednesday, March 28, 1431:

> The said Jeanne put off and entirely abandoned woman's clothes, with her hair cropped short and round in the fashion of young men, she wore shirt, breeches, doublet, with hose joined together [*chemise, braies, gippon, chausses*]. . . . And in general, having cast aside all womanly decency not only to the scorn of feminine modesty, but also of well instructed men, she had worn the apparel and garments of most dissolute men, and, in addition, had some weapons of offense.[59]

That Joan of Arc could never literally be a man was of course clear, much as the women in the *Prose Lancelot* could never literally be dressed in *braies*. But Lancelot, like the fifteenth-century inquisitors, is troubled by the unexpected mixing of gender roles in his metaphorically cross-dressed rival. "How could she, a lady, take a knight by force?" he asks. Ladies don't do these things.[60] Ladies don't speak this way (Micha 1: 318). Recasting Lancelot's words into the register of underwear, we might say that "Ladies don't wear *braies*." But the very lady Lancelot addresses in this remarkably funny and telling scene is wearing the pants, if not also, possibly, the underpants.

Notes

1. Members of the translation team, under the direction of Norris J. Lacy, included Carleton Carroll, Carol Chase, William W. Kibler, Roberta L. Krueger, Rupert T. Pickens, Samuel N. Rosenberg, and Martha Asher.

2. "Si voit qu'ele a tote sa robe ostee fors sa chemise," in Alexandre Micha, ed., *Lancelot: Roman en Prose du XIIIe siècle*, 9 vols. (Geneva: Droz, 1978) 1: 323. All subsequent references to the *Prose Lancelot* are from this edition.

3. The definition becomes codified in later centuries. Lacurne de Sainte-Palaye, for example, offers a primary definition of *chemise* as "la première chose qu'une dame met en s'habillant." He cites, among many examples, the following phrase from the *Lettres de Louis XII*, "plus pres est la chemise que la robe," and from the *Histoire de France* by Godefroy de Paris, "Plus pres m'est char que m'est chemise," in *Dictionnaire historique de l'ancien langage françois* (Paris: Champion, 1877) 3: 444–445. The word *chemise* derives from the Latin *camisa*, meaning "a long (male) linen undergarment worn next to the skin (e.g. by priests and soldiers)," according to Alexander Souter, *A Glossary of Later Latin to 600 A.D.* (Oxford: Clarendon Press, 1957): 36. See also Alfred Ernout and A. Meillet, *Dictionnaire éytmologique de la langue latine* (Paris: Klincksieck, 1959): 90.

4. Joan Evans, *Dress in Medieval France* (Oxford: Clarendon Press, 1952): 5; Eunice Rathbone Goddard, *Women's Costume in French Texts of the Eleventh and Twelfth Centuries* (Baltimore: Johns Hopkins University Press, 1927): 91–97; C. Willett Cunnington and Phyllis Cunnington, *The History of Underclothes* (London: Faber and Faber, 1981): 21, 25.

5. William Morris, ed. (Boston: Houghton Mifflin, 1969): 230.

6. "Lancelot s'est cochiés par le commandement a la damoisele et samble bien qu'il ait de lui garde al samblant que il fet, kar il n'oste ne braies ne chemise" (Micha 1: 322).

7. Cunnington and Cunnington, *The History of Underclothes*, 11. Odile Le Blanc provides a concise account of the historiography of clothing from classic works by Quicherat, Viollet-le-Duc, and Enlart to more recent studies by Barthes and Lemoine-Luccioni, "Historiographie du vêtement: un bilan," in *Le Vêtement: Histoire, archaeologie et symbolique vestimentaires au moyen âge*, edited by Michel Pastoureau (Paris: Le Léopard d'Or, 1989): 7–33.

8. See, for example, Andre Tissier, "Le Rôle du costume dans les farces médiévales," *Fifteenth Century Studies* 13 (1988): 371–386.

9. Georges Vigarello, *Concepts of Cleanliness: Changing Attitudes in France Since the Middle Ages*, translated by Jean Birrell (Cambridge: Cambridge University Press, 1988): 51.

10. Vigarello 51. Françoise Piponnier reports that inventories of peasant dress from Burgundy in the fourteenth and fifteenth centuries show that many peasants had only one *robe*, one *chaperon* and "quelques rares pièces de linges." ("Le Costume dans l'Occident médiéval," forthcoming in *L'Encyclopédie Treccani*, cited by Perrine Mane, "Emergence du Vêtement de travail à travers l'iconographie médiévale," *Le Vêtement*, 105 n. 2.)

11. Cunnington and Cunnington, *The History of Underclothes*, 20.

12. Before the second half of the nineteenth century when the term "lingerie" entered the English language, a host of euphemisms were used to designate underwear in addition to "unmentionables," among them: "underpinnings, indescribables, unwhisperables" (Doreen Yarwood, *Encyclopedia of World Costume* [New York: Charles Scribner and Sons, 1978]: 423).

13. Elizabeth Ewing, *Dress and Undress: A History of Women's Underwear* (New York: Drama Book Specialists, 1978): 11, 19.

14. Michel Beaulieu, "Le Costume: Miroir des mentalités de la France (1350–1500)," in *Le Vêtement*, pp. 255–276.

15. James Brundage, "Sumptuary Laws and Prostitution in Late Medieval Italy," *Journal of Medieval History* 13 (1987): 352; and more generally, Diane Owen Hughes, "Sumptuary Law and Social Relations in Renaissance Italy," *Disputes and Settlements: Law and Human Relations in the West*, edited by John Bossy (Cambridge, England: Cambridge University Press, 1983); Pierre Kremer, *Le Luxe et les lois somptuaires au Moyen Age* (Paris, 1920).

16. Goddard 7, 96; Evans 14; François Boucher, *20,000 Years of Fashion: History of Costume and Personal Adornment* (New York: Abrams, 1987): 180–182. See also, Yarwood, *Encyclopedia of World Costume*; Margaret Scott, *History of Dress Series: Late Gothic Europe 1400–1500* (London: Mills and Boon, 1980); Wolfgang Bruhn and Max Tilke, *Pictorial History of Costume* (London: A. Zwemmer, 1955); James R. Planche, *A Cyclopedia of Costume and A Dictionary of Dress*, 2 vols. (London: Chatto and Windus, 1876); Iris Brooke, *English Costume of the Early Middle Ages: The Tenth to the Thirteenth Centuries* (London: Adam and Charles Black, 1977); Cunnington and Cunnington, *Handbook of English Medieval Costume* (Boston: Plays, Inc., 1969).

17. Goddard 14; Evans 14. By the end of the twelfth century, the *bliaut* was often replaced by a *cotte* and *surcot*. Stockings, worn in both centuries, were called *chausses*. Literary characters are often described wearing these garments in varying combinations. In the *Prose Lancelot*, Lancelot sees Guenevere at the window in a *chemise* and *surcot* alone (Micha 7: 442). Nobles in *Erec et Enide* are described as wearing "mantiax et chauces et bliax" (Carleton Carroll, ed., [New York: Garland, 1987]: v. 1928, "cloak, hose and robe"). The Old French term "robe" in thirteenth-century texts often refers to a three-piece ensemble: *cotte, surcot*, and *mantel* (Boucher 180). By the fourteenth and fifteenth centuries, "robe" for the nobility commonly includes six garments: "*cotte, surcot, cloche, surcot ouvert, chape* and *mantel fermé*." (F. Pipionnier, *Costume et vie sociale, la cour d'Anjou, XIVe–XVe s.* [Paris: Mouton, 1970], cited by Frédérique Lachaud, "Les Livrées de textiles et de fourrures à la fin du Moyen Age: l'Exemple de la cour du roi Edouard 1er Plantagenêt (1272–1307)," in *Le Vêtement*, 179.) Children wore a *cotte* over a *chemise de linge blanc* and in summer a *chemise* alone. See Daniele Alexandre-Bidon, "Du Drapeau à la cotte: Vêtir l'enfant au Moyen Age, 13e–15e siècle," in *Le Vêtement*, 123–168. Based on a study of iconographic images, Perrine Mane reports that workmen wore a simplified version of aristocratic dress up to the fourteenth century: *braies* and *chemise* and a *robe* or *cotte*, belted at the waist, and later a *pourpoint* and *chausses* ("Emergence du Vêtement," *Le Vêtement*, 93–122).

18. Edited by William W. Kibler (New York: Garland, 1985): vv. 5424–5425. In the *Lai de l'ombre* as well, we read that "Autretel avoit chascuns d'eus/ Et chemise ridee et blanche." (Jean Renart, *Le Lai de l'ombre*, edited by Joseph Bédier [Paris: Firmin-Didot, 1913]: vv. 280–281.)

19. Edited by William W. Kibler (New York: Garland, 1981): vv. 1468–1469.

20. *Lancelot do Lac: The Non-Cyclic Old French Prose Romance*, edited by Elspeth Kennedy, 2 vols. (Oxford: Clarendon, 1980) 1: 132. A. Tobler and E. Lommatzsch cite the example of a *chemise* being worn beneath other garments in place of a hairshirt: "N'ot pas desoz haire vestue, / Mais blanche chemise ridee." (*Joufrois, roman français du XIIIᵉ siècle*, v. 1945, *Altfranzösisches Wörterbuch* [Berlin: Weidmannsche Buchandburg, 1925] 2: 344.)

21. See, in contrast, v. 1267, when the temptress returns to her room after leaving Lancelot: "si est an sa chanbre venue/ et si se couche tote nue" (vv. 1267–1268, "she went to her room and got into bed naked").

22. Micha 1: 322.

23. A significant exception to this rule can be found in the discussion of rape in the *Roman de Renart* analyzed by Kathryn Gravdal. Here the female character Hersent, a woman not a lady, has been raped by Renart, who insists he engaged only in adultery, not forced sex. His defense is that he allegedly did not remove the woman's *braies*, "breakdown her door," or "split apart her gates" ("et puis qu'i n'i ot braies traites/ ne huis brisiez, ne portes fraites . . . ," Branch I, v. 1287–1288; and *Ravishing Maidens: Writing Rape in Medieval French Literature and Law* [Philadelphia: University of Pennsylvania Press, 1991]: 98). The passage suggests that women's *braies*, if and when they wear them, can provide at least symbolic protection against sexual violation, whereas the absence of *braies* signals sexual availability or vulnerability to attack.

24. *Lanval*, Jean Rychner, ed. (Paris: Champion, 1973): vv. 97–99.

25. *Nouveau recueil complet des fabliaux*, edited by Willem Noomen and Nico Van den Boogaard (Maastricht, Netherlands: Van Gorcum, Assen, 1988) 4: 264. For a more detailed reading of the complex sexual politics at play in this fabliau see E. Jane Burns, "Knowing Women: Female Orifices in Old French Farce and Fabliau," *Exemplaria* 4, 1 (1992): 81–104.

26. Cunnington and Cunnington, *History of Underclothes*, 70 ff.; Ewing, 56–57; Yarwood 135, 314. The earliest known example of female drawers is provided by a Babylonian figurine from about 3000 B.C., wearing what today would be described as briefs, though Ewing believes them to be outerwear (Ewing 13).

27. Yarwood 37–38; Ewing 63.

28. Cunnington and Cunnington, *History of Underclothes*, 46.

29. Maureen Fennell Mazzaoui, *The Italian Cotton Industry in the Later Middle Ages (1100–1600)* (Cambridge: Cambridge University Press, 1981): 202 n. 45.

30. In the early nineteenth century pantaloons became women's underwear or drawers worn first by children and then women (Yarwood 314), though children in the Middle Ages are said not to have worn breeches before the age of seven (Alexandre-Bidon 139).

31. The Carolingian garment was termed *femoralia* because of its proximity to the thigh/femur and alternately (and intriguingly) *feminalia* (Yarwood 135; and Ernout and Meillet 1: 224). The equivalent garment worn by the lower classes was termed *subligaculum*, a type of loincloth that wound around the

waist and through the legs (Yarwood 338). Charlemagne is said to have worn linen *femoralia* beneath gaiters (*tibiales*), and the monk Abbon of St. Gall describes Frankish workmen of the ninth century who wear trousers over linen underpants (Boucher 157).

32. *Braccae* for the Gaulish Bretons and other Celts were an outergarment: trousers gathered at the ankle (Planche 56).

33. Cunnington and Cunnington, *Handbook*, 13.

34. By the fourteenth century in England, a distinction is drawn, at least for the king, between inner and outer *braies*. Mary Stella Newton gives one account of the wardrobe of Edward III that lists six pairs of linen *robarum*, frounced and lined in the new fashion—i.e., to be worn with the short tunic—and six pairs of linen *robarum* made in the old way, for wearing under the tunic (*Fashion in the Age of the Black Prince* [Suffolk, England: Boydell Press, 1980]: 17). Those not lucky enough to have such properly fashioned "outer" braies risked being punished for indecent dress, at least acccording to the anonymous author of the *Grandes Chroniques de France* (1344–1350), who attributes the defeat of the French army at Crecy (1346) to the fact that some of the soldiers wore short clothing that barely covered their rump; when they bent down to serve their lords, they showed their braies as well as what was inside them! (Cited by Newton, p. 10.) Françoise Piponnier discusses in detail the major shift in men's costume to *pourpoint* and *chausses* in fourteenth-century France in "Une révolution dans le costume masculin au 14ᵉ siècle," in *Le Vêtement*, 225–242. Ewing discusses general changes in women's dress from the twelfth through the fourteenth centuries (Ewing 18–20). On the evolution of *braies* generally, see Cunnington and Cunnington, *Handbook of English Costume*, 24; and Boucher 195. Boucher also explains that the codpiece does not develop until after the fifteenth century, growing out of the *braye*, a small triangle added between the two front parts of the *chausses* to meet the criticism of immodesty (ca. 1371) (Boucher 195). It should be remembered that the foregoing changes in attire apply only to aristocratic costume. The dress of workmen and the poor remained relatively constant throughout the Middle Ages, consisting only of outer breeches and a *cottelle* or *gonelle* (long overshirt) (Boucher 180).

35. *La Queste del Saint Graal*, edited by Albert Pauphilet (Paris: Champion, 1923): 111.

36. Béroul, *Le Roman de Tristan*, edited by A. Ewert (Oxford: Basil Blackwell, 1971): vv. 2000–2001, 2007–2010.

37. Philippe Ariès and Georges Duby cite an amusing passage from the *Moniage Guillaume* that substantiates this point. A monk who seeks advice about protecting himself against bandits is told that, as a monk, he cannot of course defend himself; not, that is, unless it is a question of defending his *braies* (*A History of Private Life*, translated by Arthur Goldhammer, vol. 2 [Cambridge, Mass.: Harvard University Press, 1988]: 373). The man's *braies* function here, as in the case of Perceval and Tristan, as a last line of social defense. In Béroul's text, the *chemise* that Iseut retains in the forest scene serves a protective function similar to that provided by Tristan's *chemise*, though women are not generally protected by their undergarment in this way.

38. Beaulieu 270.

39. Such also is the state of King Arthur when he confesses his sins in the noncyclic *Prose Lancelot*. His dilemma is rendered literally as being "touz nuz an braies" (Kennedy 284, "completely naked in his *braies*").

40. Jean Renart, *L'Escoufle* (Paris: Firmin Didot, 1894): v. 1128.

41. The condition is epitomized by the literal nakedness of Chrétien de Troyes's hero, Yvain (in *Le Chevalier au Lion*), who lives for a time as a wild man, running naked through the forest. Cut off from the civilized world at court, he loses his chivalric identity as he loses his clothes and becomes, temporarily, a male body like any other. See Jacques Le Goff, "Lévi-Strauss in Broceliande: A Brief Analysis of a Courtly Romance," *The Medieval Imagination*, translated by Arthur Goldhammer (Chicago: University of Chicago Press, 1985): 107–131.

42. Ariès and Duby provide a range of literary examples of male and female nudity and their varying significations (Ariès and Duby 361–373).

43. Régnier-Bohler, "Le Corps mis à nu: perception et valeur symbolique de la nudité dans les récits du Moyen Age," *Europe* (October 1983): 51–62.

44. It is not only that clothes provide a social envelope for the wearer, but also, as Ariès and Duby point out, that social status itself functions as a garment protecting the individual from harm. They offer the example of Baudouin de Conde's *Li Contes dou wardecors* in which a lord's loyal vassals, those he can count on for physical protection, are compared to a *garde-corps*, a life-saving garment (Ariès and Duby 370).

45. Jean de Meun, *Roman de la Rose*, edited by Daniel Poirion (Paris: Garnier-Flammarion, 1974): vv. 6119–6125.

46. See, for one example among many, the lady in Marie de France's "Yonec," "Ele esteit nue en sa chemise," Jean Rychner, ed., *Les Lais de Marie de France* (Paris: Champion, 1966): v. 341.

47. Alice Colby, *The Portrait in Twelfth-Century French Literature* (Geneva: Droz, 1965). For a more recent and avowedly feminist reading of the complex relation between medieval women's clothing and their bodies and voices, see E. Jane Burns, *Bodytalk: When Women Speak in Old French Literature* (Philadelphia: University of Pennsylvania Press, 1993).

48. For one particularly striking example among many, see the Old French *Philomena*, edited by C. de Boer (Paris: Paul Guethner, 1909): v. 165.

49. For an analysis of the social and semiotic differences between male and female clothing in the late Middle Ages see Odile Blanc, "Vêtement féminin, vêtement masculin à la fin du Moyen Age," *Le Vêtement*, 243–251.

50. *Charrette* vv. 1302–1316, and Micha 2: 24.

51. See Mane, "L'Emergence," *Le Vêtement*, 94.

52. Sainte-Palaye cites a definition of domineering wives wearing *braies* that links the garment specifically not to pants but to underpants: "comme on dit aujourd'hui qu'elles portent la culotte" (*Dictionnaire* 105).

53. *Amorous Games: A Critical Edition of Les Adevineaux Amoureux*, edited by James Woodrow Hassell, Jr. (Austin: University of Texas Press, 1974): #615, p. 148.

54. *Amorous Games*, #619, p. 149. One thinks here of the intriguing lexical

doubling that characterized the early Roman and later the Carolingian equivalent of *braies*. See above, note 31.

55. This, we will recall, is the same charge leveled against the supposed adulterer in the example cited earlier from Micha 7: 374.

56. For an interesting account of how pious women's dress might have constituted a covert act of rebellion against their husbands, see Dyan Elliott, "Dress as Mediator Between Inner and Outer Self: The Pious Matron of the High and Later Middle Ages," *Mediaeval Studies* 53 (1991): 279–308.

57. Marina Warner, *Joan of Arc: The Image of Female Heroism* (New York: Vintage Books, 1982): 146.

58. Marjorie Garber, *Vested Interests: Cross-Dressing and Cultural Anxiety* (London: Routledge, 1992): 216–217.

59. *The Trial of Jeanne d'Arc*, translated by W. P. Barrett (New York: Gotham House Inc., 1932): 160, 163. For the original Latin text and modern French translation, see Pierre Champion, *Procès de condamnation de Jeanne d'Arc* (Paris: Champion, 1921), "Ladite Jeanne rejeta et abandonna entièrement le costume féminin: les cheveux taillés en rond à la façon des pages, elle prit chemise, braies, gippon, chausses. . . ." (vol. 2, pp. 131 and 134).

60. Lancelot says literally, "Avoi, damoisele, certes bien avés tote honte perdue, kar onques mes n'oi parler de dame ne de damoisele qui volsist prendre chevalier par force" (Micha 1: 323, "Truly lady, you have abandoned all shame. I have never heard of a lady or young lady who tried to take a knight by force").

10. The Acclimatization of the Lancelot-Grail Cycle in Spain and Portugal

Harvey L. Sharrer

Arthurian romance is generally considered a late phenomenon south of the Pyrenees. The notion exists because the principal texts—translations and adaptations of the Arthurian cyclical prose romances—all survive in manuscript copies and imprints dating from the fourteenth to the sixteenth centuries. The lateness of these texts has led historians and literary critics to underestimate the early arrival and enduring reception of the Arthurian legend in the Iberian Peninsula. Scholars have ascribed the earliest Hispanic Arthurian allusion to the Catalan viscount Gerau (or Guiraut) de Cabrera. In an *ensenyament* (*ensenhamen* in Provençal), written ca. 1170, Gerau attacks a jongleur for not being familiar with such names as Erec, Cardueil, Tristan, and Iseut.[1] But we now know that the Arthurian legend evidently reached the northern Iberian Peninsula well before Gerau's time and perhaps even before that of Geoffrey of Monmouth (fl. 1129–1154). David Hook has uncovered the early, primarily patronymic use of three Arthurian names—Artus (Arthur), Galvan (Gauvain or Gawain), and Merlin, with Artus and Galvan cropping up in Latin documents across northern Spain by the 1130s.[2] And in separate research, Serafín Moralejo has produced iconographic evidence suggesting that the Tristan legend was present in the peninsula by the early twelfth century. He finds the sculpted image of a wounded knight and his horse on an open boat decorating a column that once formed part of the *Porta Francigena* at the cathedral of Santiago de Compostela. The telling feature of the image is that the knight carries in one of his hands a nicked sword, the missing piece, according to the well-known story, having been left in Morholt's skull.[3] As Hook points out, this new onomastic and iconographic evidence for an early twelfth-century Arthurian influence in various parts of the peninsula "is consistent with the spread of the Arthurian legends throughout Europe around this time."[4] In northern Italy, for example, we have the famous Modena archivolt with its identifiable Arthurian figures, dated by Jacques Stiennon between 1120 and 1140.[5]

The entry point or points for the Matter of Britain in the Iberian Peninsula are uncertain, but it is likely they were multiple. Early critics made much of Galician or Portuguese priority in the acceptance of Arthurian legends, attributing the popularity of such material to the region's Celtic past. William J. Entwistle discounts the Celtic theory but believes that Castile, like Catalonia, received Arthurian material at an early date. He proposes that Geoffrey of Monmouth's treatment of the legend may have become known in courtly circles through Alfonso VIII of Castile's marriage in 1170 to Eleanor, daughter of Henry II of England.[6] María Rosa Lida de Malkiel, on the other hand, expresses the opinion that Catalonia likely received the Arthurian legends first "because of its closer linguistic and literary ties with France and Provence."[7] Hook's onomastic research, as we have seen, now offers us Arthurian names in twelfth-century documents across northern Spain, thus complicating the question of priority. We should also remember that the roads to Santiago de Compostela brought not only pilgrims but also artisans and permanent settlers whose cultural heritage left significant imprints on northern Spain. It is conceivable, for example, that a French sculptor produced the image of the wounded knight on the column at Santiago de Compostela. Atlantic ports, in the north of Spain and in Portugal, as Hook reminds us, could also have served as entry points for Arthurian material. Lisbon, for example, was conquered from the Arabs in 1147 with the participation of English crusaders.[8] Hook now provides the earliest known Arthurian reference from Portugal: the apparent patronymic Merlim, in a document dated 1186.[9] Scholars have yet to sift countless medieval documents in search of even earlier Arthurian nomenclature in the west.

Regarding the cyclical romances, the surviving Hispanic texts point to two principal geographical areas of initial reception: Aragon and Catalonia in the east and Galicia and Portugal in the west.[10] Independent translations of the *Prose Tristan* and the Lancelot-Grail cycle, or at least some branches of it, were apparently made in the northwest of the peninsula and in the eastern part of Spain. Subsequently the eastern *Tristan*, originally in Aragonese or Catalan, was translated into Castilian; and a western *Prose Lancelot*, in a seemingly mixed Galician-Portuguese and Asturo-Leonese language, was also rendered into Castilian. On the other hand, none of the branches of the Post-Vulgate *Roman du Graal* come down to us in Catalan or Aragonese, and surviving versions in Castilian give all appearance of deriving from a Galician-Portuguese translation.[11] Our knowledge of the Hispanic translations of the Lancelot-Grail cycle is limited to parts of the *Lancelot Proper*, the *Queste del Saint Graal* and the *Mort Artu*. Extant in Catalan are two small fragments of the *Lancelot* and the full text of the *Queste del Saint Graal*, all in fourteenth-century manuscripts; and an incunabulum fragment, dated ca. 1496, of a heavily reworked *Mort Artu*. In Spanish, we have a lengthy sixteenth-century manuscript copy (Madrid, Biblioteca Nacional, MS. 9611) of an earlier translation of the *Lancelot Proper*, the *Lanzarote del Lago*, containing the very end of Book 2, a long version of Book 3, and a condensation of Book 4. My unpublished linguistic analysis of the text provides strong evidence of a Galician-Portuguese and Asturo-Leonese substratum. The colophon speaks of a 1414 date for the work; yet many western features in the language of the text point to a pre-1414 date for the original translation.[12] Other, more complete versions of the *Prose Lancelot* may have once circulated. We also have allusions and references to manuscripts and imprints under a variety of titles that seem to refer to branches of the Lancelot-Grail cycle. These texts were apparently written in Portuguese, Navarrese, and Castilian.[13] For a study of the influence and development of the Lancelot-Grail cycle in Spain and Portugal one must look not only to the handful of surviving texts and fragments but also to a variety of other attestations: for example, courtly lyrics and traditional Spanish ballads, allusions and references in numerous medieval Hispanic texts, and the important influence of the cycle on other romances, like *Tablante de Ricamonte* (the Spanish prose adaptation of the Provençal romance *Jaufre*), the Catalan romance *Curial y Güelfa*, the Valencian chivalric novel *Tirant lo Blanc*, and indigenous Spanish romances such as *Amadís de Gaula*, as well as the recasting of cyclical Arthurian material in Hispanic sentimental romances in the fifteenth century.

Archaisms and other linguistic features in the Spanish *Prose Lancelot* manuscript may point to a thirteenth-century translation produced in the western or northwestern regions of the peninsula. In any event, the *Lancelot Proper*, be it in French or in a western Hispano-Romance translation, was well-known and appreciated at the Portuguese court from the mid-thirteenth century to the early fourteenth. Indeed, the romance inspired several court poets to produce lyric treatments of specific episodes.

Already in the thirteenth century we have a Portuguese court poet using to comic effect an episode from the *Prose Lancelot*. The poet, Martin Soares, flourished between 1230 and 1270 and was a troubadour at the court of Afonso III of Portugal. It is significant that Afonso, before becoming king, spent some twenty years in exile in France. He was a resident at the court of Blanche of Castile and, through his first marriage, to Mahaud II or Mathilde of Boulogne, he assumed the title of count of Boulogne.[14] Scholars of Old Portuguese literature, beginning with Carolina Michaëlis de Vasconcelos, have surmised that Afonso III and members of his entourage brought to Portugal in 1245 chivalric romances then in vogue in northern France.[15] Among these romances was the Post-Vulgate *Roman du Graal,* which Fanni Bogdanow dates between 1230 and 1240.[16] All three branches of this romance, as Ivo Castro has posited, are likely to have been translated into Portuguese soon after their original date of compilation.[17] I believe we should also consider the earlier Lancelot-Grail cycle, or at least the *Lancelot Proper,* among the texts presumably accompanying the new king to Portugal. The Spanish *Prose Lancelot* manuscript, as I mentioned above, was apparently translated from a western Hispano-Romance language. As Elspeth Kennedy has helped me discover, it corresponds in part to a very long version of the cyclical *Prose Lancelot.*[18] The translation could, in terms of its French exemplar, represent a text circulating in northern France close to the time of Afonso's return to Portugal. Just when Martin Soares composed his poem making use of the *Prose Lancelot* is not clear. However, given the circumstantial evidence, we may presume it was sometime after 1245, when the count of Boulogne returned to Portugal as the new king. Martin Soares's poem is a *cantiga d'escarnho,* of the burlesque or satirical genre of Galician-Portuguese lyrics. According to a rubric in the *Cancioneiro da Vaticana,* one of two songbooks that preserve the text, Martin Soares sent the poem to a sister of his who had complained about her sexual relationship with a *clérigo,* a priest or clerk, who hurt her while they were engaged in sexual intercourse. The *clérigo,* the rubric continues, refused to return to the poet's sister until she agreed to visit him and then take him back to her house.[19] Analogies between this personal situation and the content of Martin Soares's song are not completely clear; but the poem tells of a woman who refuses to relinquish her sexual hold on a man named Don Caralhote. Here we have an apparent parody of a long adventure, recounted in Books 2 and 3 of the cyclical *Prose Lancelot,* involving Caradoc le Gran's taking Gawain prisoner and holding him at the Dolorous Tower. Within the episode Lancelot tries to rescue Gawain, as do other knights. However, Morgan le Fay temporarily thwarts the attempt by imprisoning Lancelot as part of her scheme to keep Lancelot away from Guenevere. As Jean-Marie d'Heur has suggested, Martin Soares seems to make special jest of the adventure by playing with the names Caradoc and Lancelot.[20] Caralhote, according to d'Heur's reasoning, is a composite name made up of *cara-* from Caradoc, or the variant Carados, as we find in the Spanish *Prose Lan-*

celot, and *-ote* from Lançarote, the usual rendering of the name Lancelot in Portuguese. The truncated Spanish *Prose Lancelot* romance lacks the story of Caradoc carrying off Gawain but does contain the episode of Morgan's imprisonment of Lancelot and Lancelot's ultimate rescue of Gawain. We can assume that a more complete version of the cyclical romance was known at the court of Afonso III of Portugal. At any rate, the *-ote* ending in the bit of humorous parody in the name Caralhote suggests that Lançarote was already the accepted Portuguese equivalent of Lancelot at the time Martin Soares composed his poem.

Interest at the Portuguese court in the Lancelot story manifests itself again poetically some years later, in the so-called *Lais de Bretanha* ("Lays of Brittany"), a set of anonymous lyrics that may have been composed during the reign of Afonso III's son, Dom Dinis (1279–1325).[21] In the fifth and last of the *Lais*—all accompanied by prose epigraphs containing various Arthurian references and allusions—a group of maidens sings a song in praise of Lancelot. The poem is a *bailada* ("dance song"), a subgenre of the Galician-Portuguese *cantigas d'amigo* ("women's songs"), which was in vogue in the early fourteenth century. Characteristically, the *bailada* includes a refrain at the end of each stanza. In the refrain of this *bailada,* the maidens call Lancelot's shield that of the "melhor omen que fez Nostro Senhor" (Vasconcelos 1: 636, "best man made by Our Lord"). The song has no known French poetic source, and it is possible there never was one. Lyrics do not commonly appear in Arthurian prose romances, excepting the *Prose Tristan* and the *Perceforest.*[22] The Galician-Portuguese poet had evidently read or knew of the story of Lancelot's madness and his stay on the Isle of Joy, and this material inspired him to compose the song of the maidens and the prose introduction to it.[23]

The episode is found in the *Prose Lancelot* and expanded upon in the *Suite du Merlin* branch of the Post-Vulgate *Roman du Graal,* in the section Fanni Bogdanow has called *La Folie Lancelot.*[24] According to the story, Lancelot in his madness fights a shield. Later, when the Grail cures him of his *folie,* Lancelot goes with the daughter of King Pellés and twenty maidens to the Isle of Joy. In some French manuscripts of the cyclical *Prose Lancelot,* the episode contains a passage in which Lancelot is described as the "best knight in the world," followed by an allusion to a song of joy that the maidens sing every day around a pine tree. The immediate object of the maidens' attention is the shield that Lancelot hung from the tree, a shield which he had decorated to serve as a personal reminder of his having wronged Guenevere:

si an fu la renommee si grant par le païs qu'il ne parloient se de lui non et disoient que voirement estoit il le millor chevalier dou monde. En tel manniere demora Lanceloz en l'ille de Joie; mais l'ille n'iert pas ainsi apelee fors seulement por les demoiseles qui estoient avec la fille au roi Pellés qui faisoient la gregnour joie que nus hom veist onques fere a damoiseles ne ja ne fist yver si grant que eles ne venissent chacun jor queroler entor le pin ou li escuz pendoit, por quoi cil del païs l'apelerent l'ille de Joie.[25]

(his fame was so great throughout the land that they talked only about him, and they said that truly he was the best knight in the world. In this manner Lancelot remained on the Isle of Joy; but the island would not be called this if it were not for the damsels who were with King Pellés's daughter, who made the greatest rejoicing one ever saw damsels make; nor was the winter ever so bad that they would not come every day to dance around the pine tree where the shield was hanging, which is why those of the land called it the Isle of Joy.)

In *La Folie de Lancelot*, the episode is reworked to include a citation of the words the maidens sang as they danced around the tree, words which closely match those of the Galician-Portuguese refrain:

Et quant les damoyselles orent veue la jouste, elles viennent a l'escu et ly enclinent toutes, et puis commencent a karoler et a chanter et disoient en leur chanson: "Voirement est ce ly escus au meilleur chevalier du monde."[26]

(And after the damsels had seen the joust, they come to the shield and all kneel before it; and then they begin to dance and to sing, and they said in their song: "Truly this is the shield of the best knight in the world.")

References and allusions to the Lancelot-Grail cycle, as well as to other Arthurian romances, appear in a variety of Castilian poems and prose texts of the late medieval period. Three traditional Castilian ballads collected at the end of the Middle Ages and in the sixteenth century also reveal clear Arthurian romance connections. One concerns the tragic love of Tristan and Iseut, and the other two focus on Lancelot's adventures in the service of women. Yet other Spanish ballads refer to figures named Ginebra (Guenevere) and Galván (Gawain), but their narrative content is not particularly Arthurian.[27]

Both Lancelot ballads present features in common with the cyclical

Prose Lancelot romance. The ballad "Nunca fuera caballero" ("Never was a gallant knight") opens by speaking of the maidens and ladies who served Lancelot so attentively on his arrival from Brittany. Among them was a lady named Quintañona, who served Lancelot wine, after which Queen Guenevere took him to her bed. The remainder of the ballad narrates an adventure the queen gave to Lancelot concerning "el orgulloso," a haughty knight who verbally mistreated Guenevere. According to the queen, this knight would probably sleep with her, to Lancelot's sorrow. Lancelot arms himself and sets out to find "el orgulloso," eventually coming upon him below a pine tree. The two combat one another with lances and axes; the haughty knight faints and falls to the ground. Lancelot cuts off his head and returns to court, where the queen receives him warmly.

The story reminds us of many a typical Arthurian or chivalric adventure; but the few details provided in the ballad do not correspond to any particular episode of the *Prose Lancelot* or other Lancelot romances. The name of the lady servant, Quintañona, has no immediately recognizable parallel in Arthurian romance. However, the name implies in Spanish an old go-between, one who is fivescore, or one hundred, years old. There is such an old go-between in the cyclical *Prose Lancelot*, but her name is Brisane, a character who in name and deeds reminds us of Brangain, Iseut's young maid in the Tristan romances. Some French manuscripts say that Brisane is perhaps one hundred years old, and the Spanish *Prose Lancelot* says she is more than one hundred. In the episode of King Pellés's daughter's seduction of Lancelot, Brisane purposely serves Lancelot a wine that causes him to think that he is sleeping with the queen when it is really the daughter of King Pellés. As for "el orgulloso," we find haughty knights, including those called such, in various French Arthurian verse romances and in several prose romances.[28] In this case, however, there may be a conflation with an episode in the *Prose Lancelot*, retold from Chrétien de Troyes's *Lancelot* or *Le Chevalier de la Charrete*: the story of Lancelot's killing of the evil Meleagant who abducted Queen Guenevere.

"Nunca fuera caballero" achieved considerable popularity beyond the Middle Ages. Four sixteenth-century printed and manuscript versions of the ballad survive; two court poets of that period wrote glosses on it; and Cervantes cites the ballad's first four lines in part 1, chapter 13, of *Don Quixote* (published in 1605). Cervantes has Don Quixote mention Quintañona's role as a go-between in Lancelot and Guenevere's love affair; he also refers to the ballad's popularity and to the frequent singing of it in Spain.

The second Lancelot ballad, "Tres hijuelos había el rey" ("Three small sons had the king") is more enigmatic. It too seems to conflate diverse material, from the *Prose Lancelot* and other sources. That the poem was probably once much longer appears evident from its three changes in assonant rhyme. In the first eight lines (rhymed in -*á*), we learn that the King cursed his three sons and that they were meta-morphosed into a stag, a dog, and a Moor who sailed the seas. Trans-formations of this type are frequent of course in classical and medi-eval literature, but a direct parallel here with Arthurian romance is lacking. However, in the next set of lines, 9–22 (with *á-o* assonance), Lancelot is said to have been having pleasure with the ladies; one of them (confusingly identified as Quintañones at the end of the ballad) asks Lancelot to be hers and give her the white-footed stag as dowry. Without accepting the marriage offer, Lancelot agrees to look for the stag. In the last and longest set of verses, 23–54 (rhymed in *í-o*), Lan-celot sets out on his horse with his hunting dogs on a lead. He comes across a hermit and asks him where the stag has its lair. The hermit, as we know, is a common interpreter of mysteries in the Lancelot-Grail cycle. Here the hermit informs Lancelot that early that day, be-fore dawn, the white-footed stag had passed by with seven lions and a lioness with newly born cubs. In a warning to Lancelot, the hermit explains that the stag has killed seven counts and many knights and that Lancelot's life is also in mortal danger. The narrator concludes the ballad, telling the lady of Quintañones that she deserves to be burned for having caused so many knights to lose their lives.

Regarding the white-footed stag, critics have pointed out its occur-rence elsewhere in Arthurian literature, notably in the second part of the anonymous Old French lay *Tyolet* from the late twelfth century and in the thirteenth-century Dutch verse romance *Lancelot en het hert met de witte voiet* ("*Lancelot and the White-footed Stag*"), interpolated within a verse translation of the last three branches of the Lancelot-Grail cycle. We find it also in the Second Continuation of the *Prose Perceval*, the *Didot Perceval*, and the Welsh *Peredur*; but there is no evidence to show that any of these northern texts circulated in medi-eval Spain. The ballad is cited in Antonio de Nebrija's *Gramática cas-tellana* (Salamanca, 1492), in the early sixteenth-century *Comedia The-bayda*, and in a court lyric by Jerónimo Pinar in the *Cancionero general* (Valencia, 1511); various other court lyrics of the period also include echoes of the ballad. "Tres hijuelos había el rey" survived across the centuries, as we know from twentieth-century oral tradition in much altered versions collected in Andalusia and the Canary Islands. But the hero in these texts no longer bears an Arthurian name; he has become Baltasar.

One of the most original Hispanic treatments of Lancelot-Grail material is in the narrative poem *La Faula* (*"The Tale"*), by the fourteenth-century Mallorcan author Guillem de Torroella. Written primarily in Catalan with some dialogue in French, *La Faula* presents the poet's feigned autobiographical vision. He travels on the back of a whale to the *Illa Encantada* ("Enchanted Island"); there King Arthur and his sister Morgan le Fay await Arthur's return to Britain as a messianic savior.[29] The poet takes material for his tale from diverse sources, including the *Mort Artu* branch of the Lancelot-Grail cycle and the southern European legend of Arthur's passing to an island in the Mediterranean. This island may correspond to Sicily, which is previously identified with Arthur's passing in Gervase of Tilbury's *Otia imperalia* (ca. 1212) and *Floriant et Florete* (ca. 1250). Of the *Mort Artu* branch of the Lancelot-Grail cycle in Catalan we have, as mentioned above, only a fragment of an apparently much reworked incunabulum text; but Guillem de Torroella may have been familiar with a French-language version of the *Mort Artu*. *La Faula* includes dialogue in French, albeit a Catalanized French, to judge from the extant manuscript copies.

Guillem de Torroella's vision of adventure begins the morning of St. John's Day, a feast day much associated with Catalan and Iberian Christian culture in general. The first spatial reference is also localized, on the northern coast of Mallorca: Guillem tells us that he rode to the Port of Santa Caterina, in the Valley of Sóller. From there a large whalelike fish, led by a parrot, takes him rapidly across the sea. In the evening they reach land. A snake appears with a beautiful carbuncle illuminating everything before it and informs the poet that he has arrived at the *Illa Encantada*, where Arthur lives with his sister Morgan. After a night of rest, an enchanted horse takes Guillem to a palace; there Morgan receives him and takes him inside to King Arthur. Guillem describes the palace with much detail, including its stained-glass windows decorated with the feats of the principal knights of the Round Table. Descriptions of such palace paintings appear in the Lancelot-Grail cycle and were common in medieval courtly houses. But here all remains invisible to Guillem until Morgan passes in front of his eyes a magic sapphire ring, a common device in Arthurian romance. Then Guillem can see a young Arthur, about thirty years old, apparently ill on a bed, and kneeling before the king are the latter's sisters Amor and Valor. A lament for Arthur follows, after which Morgan explains to Guillem that there is a reason for his journey to the *Illa Encantada*: when he returns to Mallorca he can explain the island's marvels and the reasons for King Arthur's sadness. At this point the poet gives a short summary of the climactic episode of the *Mort Artu*, recounting Arthur's last battle at Salisbury Plain and the lack of information about Arthur's fate. Arthur then informs Guillem that Morgan had collected him three days after the battle of Salisbury Plain; she took him by boat to his present location, where she bathed him in a fountain of healing waters. Once a year the Holy Grail gives Arthur nourishment, thus explaining his refound youth. Guillem then asks Arthur the reason for his sadness. Arthur points to his sword, decorated with a scene showing two groups of people: one group represents avaricious kings, the other those who esteem valor but lack the will to accomplish their desires. The poet is reminded to make details of his trip known to his countrymen when the whale and parrot return him to Mallorca. The didactic lesson, a usual feature of medieval vision literature, evidently had political implications for Guillem's contemporary Mallorcan audience.

The most striking difference between the Arthurian story contained in *La Faula* and the *Mort Artu* is Arthur's passing not to Avalon but to the *Illa Encantada*. Another added detail is the role of the Grail in the story of Arthur's survival. Properties long identified with the Grail, as revealed in the *Queste* branch of the Lancelot-Grail cycle, keep Arthur much younger than his years.[30]

La Faula is not the only Hispanic Arthurian text to alter the *Mort Artu* account of Arthur's passing. In the 1470s, writing while imprisoned at his house near the Vizcayan port city of Bilbao, Lope García de Salazar summarized in Spanish the three branches of the Post-Vulgate *Roman du Graal*, with a few narrative details seemingly closer to material in the Lancelot-Grail cycle.[31] He ends the summary dramatically with a much altered version of Arthur's passing.[32] Based on a story told by sailors out of Bristol, England, García de Salazar recounts that Morgan le Fay took Arthur to the Island of Brasil, off the west coast of Ireland.[33] Morgan supposedly enchanted the island to prevent sailors from finding it. García de Salazar's treatment of Arthur's passing lacks the stylistic elegance of Guillem de Torroella's *La Faula*. However, like Guillem, García de Salazar apparently felt the need to respond to more contemporary, localized legends then circulating about Arthur. He even brings into his account an allusion to brazilwood trade. More than one reader, so it seems, became dissatisfied with the earlier *Mort Artu* closure to the Lancelot-Grail or Post-Vulgate Arthuriad.[34]

The last Lancelot-Grail text I will discuss here is also a late reworking of the *Mort Artu*: the surviving fragments of an incunabulum reworking of the *Mort Artu* by Mossèn Gras, the title of which Martí de Riquer has conveniently shortened to *Tragèdia de Lançalot*.[35] Riquer has studied in some detail Gras's alterations to the thirteenth-century

French romance. I wish only to reemphasize a feature of Gras's ad-aptation, which we also observe in other late Hispanic Arthurian ro-mances: namely the influence of and borrowings from the sentimen-tal romance, a genre that evolved in Spain and Portugal between the late fourteenth century and the first half of the sixteenth. Sentiments, especially amorous feelings, are the central feature of this new genre. In telling the story of two lovers, usually ill-destined in their love, sentimental romance authors frequently resort to highly rhetorical language. Mossèn Gras makes use of such rhetoric in his reworking of the *Mort Artu* love theme. As Riquer points out, in the second chapter of the incunabulum fragment Gras drastically condenses sec-tion 12 (Frappier's numbering) of the *Mort Artu*, about a vavasor who gives one of his sons' swords to Lancelot for a tournament.[36] Gras shortens this type of chivalric material, but within the same chapter he goes on to expand section 13 of the *Mort Artu* concerning the va-vasor's daughter, who falls in love with Lancelot. The daughter is anonymous in the *Mort Artu*, but Gras calls her Ysabel. This name occasionally appears in Arthurian texts (e.g., some versions of the *Prose Tristan*[37]), but it is also one with contemporary Hispanic reso-nance. In retelling the passage, Gras provides us with descriptive de-tail concerning the beauty of the vavasor's daughter; and we also learn more about her fiery passion for Lancelot:

> vist Lançalot, presa e cativada da la singular figura e presència d'ell, per les venes començà a nodrir secretes flames; mas, de la sua celada fervor e benvolença fer algun semblant, donzellil ver-gonya e honesta temor la retenien; e luytant longament ab si e re-sistint a si mateixa, més de cech foch se consumava.[38]

> (after seeing Lancelot, held prisoner and captivated by his singular figure and his presence, secret flames began to stoke in her veins; but, for her concealed ardor and kindness to come out some, maidenly shame and chaste fear held her back; and struggling with herself for a long time and refusing herself, she became more consumed by blind fire.)

Gras then makes a rhetorical judgment about the repercussions of holding back the pangs of love:

> ¡O, quant és cosa fort contrestar a la cremor enclosa, la qual, quant és més cuberta e constreta, ab major esforç e brogit ella mateixa se descobre e manifesta![39]

(Oh, how difficult it is to resist the burning trapped inside, which, when it is most hidden and constrained, manifests and reveals itself with greater force and rage!)

Such rhetoric is absent in the *Mort Artu*. However, it abounds in the Hispanic sentimental romances, some of which also incorporated elements from Arthurian prose romances much in vogue in the fifteenth century. In this period we find a fusion of the Arthurian and sentimental romances, each genre manifesting narrative and stylistic features of the other.[40] Gras, following such literary tastes of his day, altered his *Mort Artu* exemplar, coloring the narrative and dialogue with language evidently borrowed from the sentimental romance genre.

The acclimatization of the Lancelot-Grail cycle in the Iberian Peninsula was not limited by any means to the few texts discussed here. An important use of the cycle is found, for example, in the indigenous romance *Amadís de Gaula*, originally composed, according to Juan Bautista Avalle-Arce, toward the end of the thirteenth century.[41] This "primitive" version underwent various transformations. It survives today, however, in a short fifteenth-century manuscript fragment and in Garci Rodríguez de Montalvo's much reworked, condensed version, which appeared in print in 1508. As Riquer has strongly urged, we need to take into fuller account the cyclical *Prose Lancelot* in studying the literary influences on the author of the "primitive" version of the *Amadís*.[42] As an example of such influence, Riquer points out that the character Bruneo de Bonamar in the *Amadís* carries a shield similar to that of Lancelot on the Isle of Joy, a subject we discussed above in connection with the Galician-Portuguese *Lais de Bretanha*.[43] For the study of the *Prose Lancelot*'s impact on the *Amadís*, Riquer encourages the use of Alexandre Micha's edition of several different versions of the French romance.[44] I would also recommend a close examination of the *Lanzarote del Lago*, the Spanish *Prose Lancelot* manuscript, the remote exemplar of which was a translation from the French into a western Hispano-Romance language.[45] It may have been this translation that was in circulation at the time the "primitive" *Amadís* was composed. But the testing of such a hypothesis is a complex study that I leave for another occasion.

Notes

    1. Martí de Riquer and A. Comas, *Història de la literatura catalana*, 2d ed., 4 vols. (Barcelona: Ariel, 1980–1981) 1: 56–66.

    2. David Hook, *The Earliest Arthurian Names in Spain and Portugal*, Fontaine

Notre Dame, 1 (St. Albans, 1991). Cf. Hook's earlier work, "*Domnus Artus*: Arthurian Nomenclature in 13th-c. Burgos," *Romance Philology* 44 (1990–1991): 162–164.

3. Moralejo's drawing of the image is reproduced in his article "Artes figurativas y artes literarias en la España medieval: románico, romance y *roman*," *Boletín de la Asociación Europea de Profesores de Español* 17 (1985): 61–70, fig. 6; and on the front cover of *Actas del I Congreso de la Asociación Hispánica de Literatura Medieval (Santiago de Compostela, 2 al 6 de Diciembre de 1985)*, edited by Vicente Beltrán (Barcelona: PUP, 1988). Muriel Whitaker describes the image as "unmistakably" that of Tristan and places it in the context of other secular themes used for didactic purposes in medieval church art in *The Legends of King Arthur in Art* (Woodbridge, Suffolk: D. S. Brewer, 1990): 90–93.

4. Hook, *The Earliest*, 12.

5. Jacques Stiennon and Rita Lejeune, "La Légende arthurienne dans la sculpture de la cathédrale de Modène," *Cahiers de civilisation médiévale* 6 (1963): 281–296.

6. William J. Entwistle, *The Arthurian Legend in the Literatures of the Spanish Peninsula* (London: J. M. Dent, 1925): 35–36, 47, 51–52.

7. María Rosa Lida de Malkiel, "Arthurian Literature in Spain and Portugal," *Arthurian Literature in the Middle Ages: A Collaborative History*, edited by Roger Sherman Loomis (Oxford: Clarendon Press, 1959): 406–418, especially p. 407.

8. Hook, *The Earliest*, 12.

9. Hook, *The Earliest*, 8.

10. See Harvey L. Sharrer, *A Critical Bibliography of Hispanic Arthurian Material, I: Texts: The Prose Romance Cycles* (London: Grant and Cutler, 1977).

11. See, for example, Manuel Rodrigues Lapa, *A "Demanda do Santo Graal": Prioridade do Texto Português* (Lisbon, 1930); Fanni Bogdanow, "Old Portuguese *seer em car teudo* and the Priority of the Portuguese *Demanda do Santo Graal*," *Romance Philology* 28 (1974–1975): 48–51.

12. See the summary of my unpublished paper, "The Provenance and Date of the Spanish Prose *Lancelot*," *Bibliographical Bulletin of the International Arthurian Society* 33 (1981): 311. My transcription of MS. 9611 exists in machine-readable format at the Seminary for Medieval Spanish Studies, University of Wisconsin-Madison. I am preparing a microfiche edition for the Hispanic Seminary for Medieval Studies (Midland, Wisc.) and, in the longer term, an annotated edition with corrections to the many garblings in the manuscript based on readings from various French versions of the romance.

13. Entwistle, *The Arthurian Legend*, 190–192.

14. Solange Corbin, "Notes sur le séjour et le mariage d'Alphonse III de Portugal à la Cour de France," *Bulletin des Études Portugaises*, n.s., 10 (1945): 159–166; Ivo Castro, "Sobre a data da introdução na Península Ibérica do ciclo arturiano da post-Vulgata," *Boletim de Filologia* [Lisbon] 28 (1983): 81–98, especially pp. 84–91.

15. Carolina Michaëlis de Vasconcelos, ed., *Cancioneiro da Ajuda*, 2 vols. (Halle: Max Niemeyer, 1904) 2: 512; Castro, "Sobre a data," 84.

16. Fanni Bogdanow, *The Romance of the Grail: A Study of the Structure and Genesis of a Thirteenth-Century Arthurian Prose Romance* (New York: Barnes and Noble, 1966): 13.

17. Castro, "Sobre a data," 81–98.

18. Sharrer, *A Critical Bibliography*, Item Aa3.

19. See Valeria Bertolucci, ed., *Le poesie di Martin Soares* (Bologna: Libreria Antiquaria Palmaverde, 1963): 137–140; M. Rodrigues Lapa, ed., *Cantigas d'escarnho e de mal dizer dos cancioneiros medievais galego-portugueses*, 2d ed. (Vigo: Galaxia, 1970): 446.

20. Jean-Marie d'Heur, "De Caradoc à Caralhote: sur une pièce obscure de Martin Soares et son origine française présumée (Arturiana 1)," *Marche Romane* 23–24 (1973–1974): 251–264.

21. Carolina Michaëlis de Vasconcelos, "*Lais de Bretanha*," *Revista Lusitana* 6 (1900–1901): 1–43; Vasconcelos, *Cancioneiro da Ajuda*, 2: 479–503; and Silvio Pellegrini, "I *lais* portoghesi del codice vaticano lat. 7182," *Studi su trove e trovatori della prima lirica ispano-portoghese*, 2d ed. (Bari: Adriatica, 1959): 184–199.

22. Jean Maillard, *Evolution & esthétique du lai lyrique, des origines à la fin du XIVᵉᵐᵉ siècle* (Paris: Centre de Documentation Universitaire, 1961); *Les lais du roman de Tristan en prose, d'après le manuscrit de Vienne 2542*, edited by Tatiana Fotich and Ruth Steiner (Munich: W. Fink, 1974); Jean Lods, ed., *Les pièces lyriques du "Roman de Perceforest"* (Geneva and Lille: Droz, 1953).

23. See Harvey L. Sharrer, "La materia de Bretaña en la poesía gallego-portuguesa," *Actas del I Congreso de la Asociación Hispánica de Literatura Medieval* (Barcelona, 1988): 561–569.

24. Fanni Bogdanow, ed., *La Folie Lancelot*, supplement to the Zeitschrift für romanische Philologie 109 (Tübingen: Max Niemeyer, 1965).

25. Alexandre Micha, ed., *Lancelot: Roman en prose du XIIIᵉ siècle*, 9 vols. (Paris and Geneva: Droz, 1978–1983), 6: 234.

26. Bogdanow, *La Folie Lancelot*, 70.

27. See Harvey L. Sharrer, "Two Lancelot Ballads," *The Romance of Arthur III*, edited by James J. Wilhelm (New York: Garland, 1988): 259–264, especially p. 259; for bibliography on the subject, see p. 261.

28. G. D. West, *An Index of Proper Names in French Arthurian Verse Romances, 1150–1300* (Toronto: University of Toronto Press, 1969): 126–127; *An Index of Proper Names in French Arthurian Prose Romances* (Toronto: University of Toronto Press, 1978): 239.

29. Much of the information that follows may be found in Pere Bohigas and Jaume Vidal Alcover's "Introducció" to their edition of the poem: Guillem de Torroella, *La Faula* (Tarragona: Tàrraco, 1984): vii–lii. See also recent articles by Lola Badia, "De la *Faula* al *Tirant lo Blanc*, passant, sobretot pel *Llibre de Fortuna e Prudència*," in *Quaderns Crema. Deu Anys: Miscel·lània* (Barcelona: Quaderns Crema, 1989): 17–57; and Isabel de Riquer, "El viaje al otro mundo de un mallorquín," *Revista de Lengua y Literatura Catalana, Gallega y Vasca* 1 (1991): 25–36.

30. We have a close translation of the *Queste* into Catalan, in a manuscript

dated 1380 (Sharrer, *A Critical Bibliography*, Item Ab1), but Catalan scholars tend to date *La Faula* before 1375. See Bohigas and Alcover, "Introducció," pp. xx–xxi.

31. Harvey L. Sharrer, ed., *The Legendary History of Britain in Lope García de Salazar's "Libro de las bienandanzas e fortunas"* (Philadelphia: University of Pennsylvania Press, 1979): 57–73, 106–129.

32. Sharrer, *The Legendary History*, 18, 72–73, 126–129; see also Harvey L. Sharrer, "The Passing of King Arthur to the Island of Brasil in a Fifteenth-Century Spanish Version of the Post-Vulgate *Roman du Graal*," *Romania* 92 (1971): 65–74.

33. On Atlantic voyages out of Bristol, see Ian Wilson, *The Columbus Myth: Did Men out of Bristol Reach America before Columbus?* (London: Simon and Schuster, 1991).

34. On the *Mort Artu* closure, see Norris J. Lacy's contribution to this volume.

35. Mossèn Gras, *Tragèdia de Lançalot*, edited by Martí de Riquer (Barcelona: Quaderns Crema, 1984); see also Riquer's earlier article "La *Tragèdia de Lançalot*, texto artúrico del siglo XV," *Filologia Romanza* 2 (1955): 113–139.

36. Riquer, *Tragèdia*, pp. xx–xxi.

37. Tristan's mother is named Ysabel in the *Libro del esforçado cauallero don Tristan de Leonis y de sus grandes fechos en armas* (Valladolid, 1501), edited by Adolfo Bonilla y San Martín, Sociedad de Bibliófilos Madrileños, 6 (Madrid, 1912): 3; cf. Malory's Elyzabeth in *The Works of Sir Thomas Malory*, edited by Eugène Vinaver, 2d ed., 3 vols. (Oxford: Clarendon Press, 1967) 1: 371–372, 379, 391.

38. Riquer, *Tragèdia*, 6–7.

39. Riquer, *Tragèdia*, 7.

40. See Harvey L. Sharrer, "La fusión de las novelas artúrica y sentimental a fines de la Edad Media," *El Crotalón: Anuario de Filología Española* 1 (1984): 147–157; and Alan Deyermond, "Las relaciones genéricas de la ficción sentimental española," *Symposium in honorem prof. M. de Riquer* (Barcelona: Universitat de Barcelona; Quaderns Crema, 1986): 75–92, especially pp. 79, 80–82.

41. Among Avalle-Arce's various studies of the romance, see the "Introducción" to his recently published edition, Garci Rodríguez de Montalvo, *Amadís de Gaula*, Colección Austral, A119–120, 2 vols. (Madrid: Espasa Calpe, 1991) 1: 9–119.

42. Riquer, "Proemio," in Daniel Eisenberg, *Romances of Chivalry in the Spanish Golden Age* (Newark, Del.: Juan de la Cuesta, 1982): ix. Avalle-Arce's edition of Montalvo's *Amadís* contains numerous notes regarding Arthurian influence on the "primitive" version of the romance, including references to material in the *Prose Lancelot* as edited by H. Oskar Sommer, *The Vulgate Version of the Arthurian Romances*, 8 vols. (Washington, D.C.: Carnegie Institution, 1908–1916): vols. 3–5.

43. Riquer, "Las armas en el *Amadís de Gaula*," *Boletín de la Real Academia Española* 60 (1980): 331–427, especially pp. 425–426; and Riquer, "Proemio," pp. viii–ix.

44. See above, n. 25.

45. Antonio M. Contreras Martín is currently preparing a doctoral thesis for the University of Barcelona on the concept of chivalry in the Spanish *Prose Lancelot*, based on my machine-readable transcription and concordance to MS. 9611.

11. An Italian Reaction to the French Prose Lancelot-Grail Cycle: Matteo Maria Boiardo and the Knight's Quest for Identity

Elizabeth H. D. Mazzocco

The popularity of the prose Lancelot-Grail cycle spread rapidly throughout the great courts of Italy in the thirteenth century, exerting an influence more profound than either the Chrétien or Provençal traditions.[1] From Venice to Florence to Rome and Naples, Italians were quick to embrace and make their own a chivalric world devoid of Italian roots. Discarding late medieval genealogies, which made powerful Italian families descendants of Aeneas, the early Renaissance aristocracy searched for connections with Arthur and Lancelot. So pervasive was the dissemination of French chivalric romance that even in the early 1300s when Dante wrote the celebrated episode of Paolo and Francesca (*Inferno* 5) and says, "Galeotto fu il libro e chi lo scrisse,"[2] no explanation was necessary for his audience to grasp the literary allusion and make the connection between the Malatesta lovers and the adulterous affair of Lancelot and Guenevere. This dissemination of the French tradition was accomplished in two ways: importation of French Lancelot-Grail texts and the translation/embellishment of those texts into Italian.

Both types of texts make their presence felt in extant codifications of manuscript holdings of early Renaissance families. The Este of Ferrara, for example, held numerous versions of the Italianized *Lancillotto, Merlino, Galeotto, Morte del Re Artù*, and *Il Santo Gradale*, as well as their French originals. While both the French originals and their Italianized counterparts played an important cultural/literary role in the society of the early Renaissance, the lasting influence of the prose Lancelot-Grail cycle in Italy is due to Italian incorporation of and reaction to that cycle. This chapter will address the popularity of the French tradition at one of the great literary courts of fifteenth-century Italy—the Este court in Ferrara[3]—and will focus on the way that one of their court poets, Matteo Maria Boiardo, imitated and interpolated the French ideal in his epic *Orlando Innamorato*.

One of the more interesting features of the *Orlando Innamorato* is that Boiardo's poetic work and the society for which he wrote and in which he lived perfectly juxtapose each other. The Este's historical re-creation of chivalric fiction on a level of everyday reality indicates an involvement in the chivalric myth so intense that it inspired a way of life, an absurd immersion in a fictional past seen only in works of romance.[4] What makes Boiardo all the more clever is that he takes traditional chivalric formulas and conventions and inverts them to illustrate the fallacy of trying to live the chivalric ideal. He manipulates the familiar quest-for-identity theme in an attempt to awaken the Este (and their courtiers) to the realities of the early Renaissance.

Over one hundred years ago, Pio Rajna described the Este court of the fifteenth century as "quasi più francese che italiana"[5] ("almost more French than Italian") because of their intense desire to collect French manuscripts. While the obsession with French chivalric tradition manifested itself not only on a literary level but also on visual and historical levels, the library of the Este family is a good barometer by which to begin to measure the profundity and implications of the French prose romance.

As one might expect, due to the blossoming of nascent Renaissance humanism, most of early fifteenth-century Italy saw the decline of medieval romance. Indeed, the Ferrarese humanist Guglielmo Capello writes at the beginning of the century that he knows nothing of the stories of Uther Pendragon because he has *seen* few French books, much less *read* them ("pochi libri francesi ho veduti non che lecti").[6] Niccolò III d'Este (ruled 1393–1441) quickly remedied that situation by inundating his personal library with manuscripts of French prose romance. When his son, Ercole, ordered a library inventory late in the fifteenth century, over one quarter of the 279 titles held were French romances. There is no doubt that many of these manuscripts were part of the prose Lancelot-Grail tradition; the codifier is explicit in his distinction between prose and verse, noting for example "libro uno chiamado el libro de più *novele* [my emphasis] de Lanciloto . . . in francexe."[7] It is noteworthy that the Este considered the French manuscripts to be the authoritative originals and those in Italian to be mere translations or copies. In fact, a note from Borso d'Este asks for "un lanzalotto in franzexe in carte de capretto . . . per corezer uno in taliano."[8] By 1474, the library had multiple manuscripts of the *Lance-lot*, the *Sangradale*, the *Merlin*, the *Meliaduse*, *Death of King Arthur*, *Guron*, *Godffrey di Buoione*, *Roman della Rosa*, and *Tristan*.[9] Thanks to the scrupulously compiled library lending records, we know that the

"materia di Francia/Bretagna," as it was called, had an enormous circulation within the court,[10] and among the Este courtiers who had
access to the library would have been, of course, Boiardo. The contents of the Este library and the large circulation of French romance
assert the popularity of the French prose tradition on a literary level.
It was equally influential in the field of visual arts.

The frescoes at the Palazzo Schifanoia, one of the Este palaces,
are part of the extant visual evidence of the diffusion of chivalry in
fifteenth-century Ferrara.[11] Usually attributed to Francesco del Cossa,
the famous cycle at one time represented the entire calendar year in
twelve three-tiered frescoes. The three tiers were composed of astro-
logical, mythological, and earthly representations; the earthly images,
which were supposedly realistic reproductions from the everyday life
of Duke Borso d'Este, show significant scenes of a chivalric court de-
picting both chivalric game in then present-day Ferrara and military
exercise in the form of jousts and tournaments.

The uppermost tier of the April configuration depicts the triumph
of Venus. She sits enthroned on a carriage pulled by swans. At her
feet is Mars, kneeling and chained to her chair in a position of complete submission. Mars is outfitted in a suit of armor characteristic of
the Quattrocento, and the surrounding characters also wear dress
typical of that period. Although the art historian Paolo D'Ancona
notes in his study of the cycle that this fresco "sembra uscire dalle
pagine di un roman di Cretien, fra quelli tanto letti e pregiati alla corte
di Ferrara,"[12] it would have been more accurate to assume that the
fresco was fashioned after part of the much-circulated French prose
cycle or, even more probable, from the first cantos of the *Orlando
Innamorato*. In his more recent study of the frescoes, Ranieri Varese
sees the Schifanoia cycle as the depiction of an ideal goal laid out for
the Ferrarese, who, featured on the lower tiers, should imitate the
knights of the upper tier: "Sulle pareti, la corte presenta e definisce
una immagine di sè corrispondente a quello che vuole essere."[13] In
fact, some of the frescoes at the various Este palaces went beyond a
depiction of a mythic ideal for which the Ferrarese should strive;
there were frescoes which commemorated actual chivalric enterprise
in historic Ferrara.[14] Here we move beyond the literary or ideal sphere
into a historical example of how deeply Este Ferrara was entrenched
in chivalry.

The Este organized elaborate chivalric spectacles for all occasions—
both state and personal. An example pertinent to the present argu-
ment is a festive joust that involved defending the God of Love who
had been accused of being a traitor.[15] Following the tradition illus-

trated in the *Charrette* episode whereby a knight's being placed in a cart makes him the subject of ridicule, the God of Love was dressed as a knight and paraded throughout the town in a cart so that the people could mock and deride him. As at all jousts and tourneys, the women of the court watched the proceedings from balconies, tower windows, or marble benches, mirroring the fair maidens and queens who watched Lancelot and Perceval from afar. Of course, this was an *occasion*, a festival, but the Este adherence to chivalric ideal went far beyond mere show. It is one thing to find a court that was deeply immersed in the joys of chivalric reading, depiction, and even festivities; it is quite another to encounter a family of rulers so obsessed with an anachronistic medieval lifestyle that they not only ignored the realities of the present but forced their people to live in a fiction-based microcosm of chivalric enterprise.

That is exactly what happened in Ferrara. Court chroniclers' accounts reveal that jousts and challenges took place in closed fields at the instigation of the duke to settle disputes among his citizens. Some of the jousts resulted in the death of one or both of the participants; others saw a winner declared.[16] Clearly, the Este truly enjoyed bringing these conventions to life, but a by-product of the rulers' involvement in the fiction of French prose romance was that the people found themselves subjugated to an anachronistic lord-vassal relationship with the Este, which proved to be a politically expedient way for the Este to reinforce control in government. Fostering a feudal mentality among those they governed strengthened the bond of loyalty shared by the parties, thus discouraging treachery and individual action. However, this chivalric enterprise was carried beyond the boundaries of common sense as the Este knights were trained to battle for honor and ideal in a fifteenth-century world replete with mercenary armies.

Matteo Maria Boiardo recognized this danger and disparity at least as early as the 1470s. I believe that he saw the peril of living literally in a world with no present reality, a world that was created from the fictional pages of romance. The objective of his great epic, therefore, was not only to alert society to the dangers of following conventions inappropriate to contemporary times but also to spur society to put the past in the past and accept the reality of the Renaissance.

Boiardo has previously been seen by scholars and literary critics as being significant simply because he joined the worlds of Arthurian romance and Carolingian legend; his work is too often remembered as the epic that Ariosto used to produce his sixteenth-century masterpiece. Boiardo's real merit has not yet been acknowledged. Boiardo's most serious contribution in the *Orlando Innamorato* is that he turned the chivalric conventions against the Este and argued subtly that the humanistic traits of individuality and free will could no longer be subjugated to a fictional ideal. Indeed, the *Orlando Innamorato* is a humanist tract in fictional clothing.

In order to accept this reading of the epic, we must explore the intellectual environment of fifteenth-century Ferrara and recognize the part that Boiardo played in it. Himself a courtier and governor for the Este family, Boiardo was involved in several Este skirmishes and brief wars (particularly the Ferrara-Venice war of 1482–1484). He witnessed the practical realities of war. As someone personally involved in these skirmishes, he must have been distressed that in Ferrara there was no clear distinction between chivalric enterprise for game and chivalric enterprise for military training. His repugnance for the custom of masking the horrors of the reality of war with the frivolity of game manifests itself in the *Orlando Innamorato*; here he includes incidents where friends begin by jousting and then get so carried away with the moment that they literally forget whether they are jousting for pleasure or war and end up killing one another.[17]

Boiardo was both a realist and a humanist; he was, after all, the cousin of Pico della Mirandola, whose treaty *De Dignitate Hominis* became the humanist manifesto. With his feet firmly planted in the humanist ideology, Boiardo was convinced of the importance of free will and individuality, as well as of the necessity of facing what Machiavelli would later call "la verità effettuale della cosa"[18]—the real truth of the matter. He was imbued with humanistic concepts and would not have taken lightly the collectivism that flowed from the ideology espoused by the Este. Yet he was also deeply conscious of the chivalric proclivities of the Este, having tried for years to interest Duke Ercole in the study of classical history only to see him return time after time to French romance. So instead of writing a humanistic treatise which would have been ignored at court, Boiardo cleverly and purposefully took the very conventions that formed the Este obsession with chivalry and wove them into a charming tale which, when read correctly, destroys the myth of chivalry. He tried to accomplish this change not overtly but covertly, between the lines of what on the surface appears to be a delightful chivalric myth replete with all the French conventions: knights pristine, ladies fair, evil abundant, magic unharnessed, quests mystical, and love overpowering.

Boiardo implicitly states his intention to blend the Arthurian and Carolingian strains to form one great epic where the valiant knights of France have been instilled with courtesy, gentility, and love:

Fo glorïosa Bertagna la grande
Una stagion per l'arme e per l'amore,
Onde ancora oggi il nome suo si spande,
Sì che al re Artuse fa portare onore,
Quando e bon cavallieri a quelle bande
Mostrarno in più battaglie il suo valore
Andando con lor dame in aventura;
Et or sua fama al nostro tempo dura.

Re Carlo in Franza poi tenne gran corte,
Ma a quella prima non fo sembïante,
Benché assai fosse ancor robusto e forte,
Et avesse Ranaldo e 'l sir d'Anglante.
Perché tenne ad Amor chiuse le porte
E sol se dette alle battaglie sante,
Non fo di quel valore e quella estima
Qual fo quell'altra che io contava in prima.[19]

Boiardo is careful to underline that the Arthurian characters of which
he speaks are the same ones familiar to the Este court; he knows that
the Este and their court will listen to a story which includes characters
drawn from the popular Lancelot-Grail cycle, and he is quick to point
out their superiority over those of the Carolingian cycle. But this is
all quite tongue-in-cheek, because what Boiardo really does is to utilize the conventions, characters, and themes found in the works of
French prose romance to illustrate the intolerable weaknesses of the
chivalric system. From the first canto when the temptress Angelica
enters the court and addresses the knights at the Round Table, chaos
reigns, and the feudal/chivalric system that bound men to their lord
by oath of allegiance collapses. The knights become so obsessed with
possessing Angelica that they completely forget their identities as
knights and vassals to the king. Indeed, Boiardo seems to enjoy playing with the familiar theme of identity crisis, and it is through an
examination of this theme that we can capture much of Boiardo's hidden agenda.

The theme of the knight's quest for identity is, of course, fundamental to French romance.[20] Typically, the young man who will be
the hero of the work does not know who he is or what knighthood
entails. For example, Perceval had been reared in ignorance of knighthood by his mother, who was afraid of his being killed in chivalric
enterprise as were her husband and other sons, whereas Lancelot
had grown up with the Lady of the Lake. A knight has no identity

when he arrives at Arthur's court; indeed, he is usually not yet even a knight. It is only through an exploit like the Dolorous Guard that he learns his name and what knighthood is all about. Inextricably interwoven with the knight's search for identity is love, because it is through the love of a lady that the knight is driven to perform more and more exploits which lead him to self-discovery.

An important difference between the hero-knights of French romance and those of Boiardo is that Boiardo's hero-knights know their identities when the epic begins. They identify themselves (or are identified by the narrator) with lengthy descriptive passages about conquests and past glories; indeed, they are already recognized as valiant knights. They lose their identities in the course of the epic only when they become obsessed with an unattainable ideal (be it love or perfect chivalry); acting thus without identity and self-recognition, the knights engage in repetitive adventures. They emerge from one adventure no better off than when the adventure began and hasten to begin yet another; unlike the *Prose Lancelot* tradition, where chivalric adventure usually brings the knight closer to self-discovery, for Boiardo's knights, the cyclic chivalric adventures lead nowhere. Boiardo's knights have to learn to break the cyclic pattern.

In order for the chivalric ideal to function properly, the three forces that rule a knight's life—his God, his terrestrial lord, and his lady—must work in conjunction with one another, and their system of control must be a balanced one. Boiardo's knights differ significantly from the chivalric ideal of a collective group united under the same insignia to fight for a just cause; they are characters in a state of crisis. Boiardo's knights are fragmented selves engaged in self-discovery.

Boiardo seems to indicate that the fragmentation of the self occurs when man subordinates his personality to the rule of the chivalric ideal. The chivalric ideal is contrary to any *individual* impulse in one's personality because one must subordinate one's will to the will of others; serving the code means serving either God, the lord, or the lady, and one cannot take into account individuality. Thus the individual is suppressed and the self is fragmented.

This fragmentation is represented in the *Orlando Innamorato* by individual heroes who are not allowed to be themselves; because they have to subjugate themselves to the ideal, they thus become enslaved by concepts. Ranaldo is obsessed with honor, Orlando with love, Astolfo with service and courtesy. If the obsessions of these characters were combined and balanced, the resulting whole would be the embodiment of the ideal knight. However, alone, each fragmented knight's obsession with a particular facet of the chivalric myth undermines the ideal itself. Furthermore, because of his state of obsession, the knight loses perspective about his identity (self) and his individuality, so the obsession causes twofold damage. These characters lack understanding of the ideal they strive to achieve, and they are unable to make the chivalric code work for them.

At the same time that the knights lack an understanding of the chivalric ideal, they also lack an understanding of themselves. Their personal identities have become inextricably entangled with the ideal they seek. They are often lost, without memory and without stability in time. Memory loss signifies loss of self because when a person is without memory, he has no past and thus no identity, and with no past to build upon, the present and future are unstable.

The idea of the nonexistent past and the difficulties that ensue could have been applied also to the world of Boiardo's audience; people in fifteenth-century Ferrara living according to an anachronistic chivalric ideal were in a sense living in a fictional past that obfuscated the present. The dangers of living in an artificial past are explicitly presented by Boiardo's characters who without the past (memory) become lost and obsessed and are incapable of dealing with the present. They represent the peril of failing to realize the new reality. They are incapable of looking toward the future as they continue their repetitive quest for an impossible ideal.

In the same way that Boiardo makes his knights who lose their identities mirror opposites of the French heroes who are seeking their identities, so too does he imitate inversely the structure of the situations in which identity loss/gain occurs. After Lancelot and Gawain separate in Chrétien's *Charrette*, Lancelot is so bedazzled with his thoughts of the queen that he rides directly into a ford despite the warnings of the guardian. The cold water immediately brings him back to reality and out of his trance. In contrast, instead of being snapped back into reality, Boiardo's knights *lose* their memories when they come into contact with water. Ranaldo, for example, having drunk from a river, immediately forgets who he is and what he is doing:

> . . . non fa lungo la stalla
> Che tutto è tramutato a quel che egli era;
> Né sa per che qui venne, o come, o quando,
> Né se egli è un altro, o se egli è pur Orlando. [21]

Orlando, too, forgets himself after jumping into a river and arriving at its bottom:

Ma dentro a l'acqua sì come era armato
Gettossi e presto gionse insino al fondo . . .
Che per letizia s'amentava poco
Perché fosse qua gionto e di qual loco. [22]

When Boiardo's knight comes to a river, he is usually invited by a temptress to peer in and, having done so, becomes enthralled with what he sees. He inevitably ends up in the water and loses his memory like a chivalric Narcissus.[23] It is also noteworthy that the Italian knights often have the opportunity to save themselves from the fate of forgetfulness; warnings appear along the way in either written or pictorial form. Unfortunately, the men are rarely capable of understanding what they see or read; a woman (either human or spirit) has to interpret the signs for them.

Boiardo intimates that this inability to read the signs comes from obsession; the knights are so obessed with chivalry or love that they are blind to all else. In fact, in an adventure modeled after the Dolorous Guard, when Orlando finds himself in Morgana's garden faced with a prison full of knights and ladies who need freeing, Orlando *misreads* the signs ("il conte le parole non intese")[24] and succeeds in freeing the prisoners only because he is miraculously given a second chance! I believe that it is not coincidental that Boiardo's knights are trapped in a never-ending cycle of lost identity and that they are not expert enough interpreters to correctly read the signs that would free them; the knights in his epic parallel the knights at the Este court who were also trapped in a chivalric system that was militarily ineffective. Just as the men in Boiardo's epic were too obsessed to read the signs, so too was Duke Ercole too caught up in the fun of chivalric fantasy to realize the dangers of ignoring reality. It is for this reason that I believe Boiardo makes the *women* the characters who can interpret for the men; it is almost as if he is hoping that the wise Duchess Eleonora will be able to snap her husband Ercole back into reality.[25] There is no doubt that the female characters in the *Orlando Innamorato* are able to exert positive influence on the males, especially in the realm of reading and interpreting. Of all the women, Fiordelisa (who is, in my reading, the ideal woman) is the best reader of signs, and in one of the final adventures, her husband, Brandimarte, finally realizes the wisdom of heeding her advice and retains his identity.

The setting for this climactic episode is a familiar one. Brandimarte, Fiordelisa, and company are riding in search of adventure when they encounter a body of water.[26] Earlier in the epic, Fiordelisa tried to warn the men of the dangerous effects of such a body of water, but they ignored her warnings and ended up mesmerized in an enchantress's clutches. Here again, two of the men immediately fall prey to the temptresses, who lure them near the water. Brandimarte, however, has learned to heed Fiordelisa's warnings; this time, he listens to her. Not only does he *not* become a victim of lost memory (thus lost self/identity), but he is also able to release the river's other victims from their state of forgetfulness.

Fiordelisa tells Brandimarte that his "virtù" will see him through this situation, saying, "la virtù fa fare la strada." [27] We remember that "virtù" here does not mean Christian virtue but rather refers to the humanistic pre-Machiavellian *virtù*, which embodies self-reliance, common sense, and intelligence. Fiordelisa weaves Brandimarte a wreath of flowers which he places on his head, and then he proceeds toward the encounter with the water nymphs (who symbolize temptation). He ends up in the water, but the wreath keeps him safe; the healing power in the flowers (symbolizing knowledge) immunizes him against the forgetfulness of the water. As each knight dons the wreath, he too is freed.

Boiardo's metaphor is clear. The knights are trapped in a water of forgetfulness; they are without memory, thus without present, thus without self/identity. They resemble Narcissus, who likewise forgot everything when he saw his reflection in water and became enthralled with himself. He lost his identity in his obsession with self-love. Our knights, too, are obsessed; they, too, have lost themselves in obsession for love or in obsession with an ideal. The ancient antidote for the effects of obsession (which in the *Orlando Innamorato* causes memory loss) was a flower—the *Narcissus poeticus*, commonly called the "Pheasant Eye." In modern folklore, the flower still has the power to remove the curse of the evil eye in Mediterranean countries.[28] It is the flower that Brandimarte uses to remove the curse of forgetfulness, associated throughout the *Orlando Innamorato* with mirrors and water. It is the power of the *fiori* ("flowers") that *Fior*delisa (her very name intimates her close association with the *fiori*) knows about and interprets for Brandimarte, appropriating that power to help him when he needs it.

At the beginning of the fifth canto of the third book, Boiardo finally makes the connections that he hints at throughout and employs a poetic conceit to link the *flower* to the *text*. The cantos that Boiardo writes are described as *flowers*:

> Còlti ho diversi fiori alla verdura,
> Azuri, gialli, candidi e vermigli;
> Fatto ho di vaghe erbette una mistura
> Garofili e vïole e rose e zigli:

> Traggasi avanti chi de odore ha cura,
> E ciò che più gli piace, quel se pigli;
> A cui diletta il ziglio, a cui la rosa,
> Et a cui questa, a cui quella altra cosa.[29]

Boiardo's text, the *Orlando Innamorato*, mirrors the powers of the *fiori* that heal. Brandimarte has learned to understand the power of the wreath of flowers that Fiordelisa has woven. Boiardo's reader must understand the power of Boiardo's flower, his text; it is through a careful reading of the text that the reader will find his way. The text will teach him to interpret, to make decisions, to judge events. It will bring him to reality and make him realize the fallacy of the chivalric tradition just as the flowers enable Brandimarte to keep his memory intact, thus allowing him to continue making positive progress in his search for identity.

Boiardo seems to imply that just as the individual must be allowed to change and grow, so too must a text be seen to be in continuous change. While the form of the text remains the constant—thus the same themes and conventions seen in the *Prose Lancelot* are adopted by Boiardo—the contents are fluid, and the text lends itself to various interpretations whose validity depends on the expertise that the new interpreter brings to the text. Therefore chivalric romance should not be interpreted by readers of the fifteenth century in the same way as it had been by those in the thirteenth. The times have changed, and the interpretation must change as well.

Boiardo's Este audience was personally familiar with the theme of the knight's quest for identity—they had read the stories, had seen the stories in fresco form in the palaces, and had even lived the stories as they were forced to incorporate chivalry into their everyday lives. But just as Boiardo's knights in the *Orlando Innamorato* have to learn to interpret texts and signs for themselves, so too must the Este court learn to reinterpret texts to give them pertinence in the fifteenth century. In the *Orlando Innamorato*, the only knights who survive are those who learn when to break the chivalric code and act independently using the common sense and individual perception (the pre-Machiavellian *virtù*) that Fiordelisa talks about. Because of the fluid nature of the text, the reader—be he a fictional knight or a fifteenth-century Ferrarese—must establish his own relationship with it, instead of allowing the narrator (be it Boiardo or Ercole d'Este) to take away his independence and manipulate his view of the text. If the reader can become his own interpreter of texts, he can determine how to best utilize them in his own life. Therefore, the stories of Lancelot are the same in the fifteenth as in the thirteenth century, but the interpretation must perforce be different because the time is different. Following the chivalric code in the time of Arthur led to finding one's identity as a knight; in the time of Ercole d'Este, it led to losing one's identity as an individual.

When Shakespeare's Hamlet bemoans, "The time is out of joint" (act 1, scene 5), he is echoing Boiardo's cry. And yet, as I've shown, to offer this kind of criticism to a ruling family like the Este was not easy, and Boiardo had to work cautiously. So, instead of writing a treatise, like his cousin Pico della Mirandola, which would have been ignored except in the academies, Boiardo took the very chivalric characters and themes that formed the base of the Este obsession and wove them into an epic meant to delight at the same time that it offered a warning of the disastrous outcome of trying to live in a fictional past. Indeed, Boiardo has appropriated the self-mocking, self-critical tone found in the French prose romance and interpolated it into a wake-up call for the fiction-obsessed Ferrarese. The Ferrarese needed to heed the fay Morgana, who mockingly chants in her garden, "il tempo passato più non ritorna e non se ariva mai . . ."[30] and thereby understand that the medieval world had ended and the Renaissance had begun.

Notes

1. Daniela Branca asserted the popularity and dissemination of the French prose cycle in early Duecento Italy in her *I romanzi italiani di Tristano e la tavola ritonda* (Florence: Olschki, 1968): 15–16; "è innegabile che la 'matiere di Brettagne', a partire dalla metà del Duecento, penetra e si diffonde in tutti gli ambienti italiani. Non giunge più sulle ali delle vaghe e tradizionali allusioni della lirica provenzale, o tramite i poemi di Thomas e di Chretien, forse conosciuti e apprezzati solo da ambienti circoscritti, ma si impone trionfalmente col successo dei romanzi francesi in prose" ("it is undeniable that from the middle of the 1200s, the 'matter of Britain' penetrated all Italian circles. It [the matter of Britain] no longer surfaced merely as an afterthought to traditional, vague allusions to Provençal lyric or through the poems of Thomas and Chrétien (perhaps known and appreciated by a limited group), but it [the matter of Britain] triumphantly imposed itself, quite successfully, with the advent of the French prose romance").

2. Dante Alighieri, *La Divina Commedia*, edited by Natalino Sapegno (Florence: La Nuova Italia, 1981): vol. 1, canto 5, l. 137; "Galeotto was the book and he who wrote it."

3. The Este were the powerful family who ruled Ferrara and made it one of the more important states in Renaissance Italy. The four male rulers of the fifteenth century were Niccolò III, who ruled 1393–1441, Leonello, who ruled 1441–1450, Borso, who ruled 1450–1471, and Ercole, who ruled 1471–1505.

In the case of Ercole, it is important to remember that his wife, Eleonora of Aragon, was frequently left in charge.

4. The chivalric, medieval, feudal state of existence in fifteenth-century Ferrara has been noted by several scholars, including Werner Gundersheimer, *Ferrara: The Style of a Renaissance Despotism* (Princeton, N.J.: Princeton University Press, 1973); and Lewis Lockwood, *Music in Renaissance Ferrara* (Cambridge, Mass.: Harvard University Press, 1984).

5. Pio Rajna, "Ricordi di codici francesi posseduti dagli Estensi nel secolo XV," *Romania* 2 (1873): 58.

6. Cited in A. Graf, *Miti, leggendi, e supersitzioni del Medio Evo* (Turin: Loescher, 1892) 2: 346.

7. Rajna, entry 21, p. 50, "a book entitled the book of more *stories* of Lancelot . . . in French."

8. "a Lancelot in French of vellum . . . to be used to correct an Italian version." This entry is contained in the court *Memoriale 1457–68* and cited by Giulio Bertoni, *La Biblioteca Estense e la coltura ferrarese* (Turin: Loescher, 1903): 55 n. 1.

9. A brief glance at the various Este inventories reveals a wealth of French chivalric material. Included in Rajna's list of French works (Rajna 50–52) are:

——Libro uno chiamado Gutifre de Buione . . . in francexe
——Libro uno in francexe, chiamado Merlino . . .
——Libro uno chiamado Lanciloto, de la ocision de Charados, in francexe . . .
——Libro uno chiamado Guion in francexe . . .
——Libro uno chiamado San Gradale . . . in francexe
——Libro uno chiamado mierio [*sic*] de Tristano . . . in francexe
——Libro uno chiamado la destrution de la Tavola redonda in francexe . . .
——Libro chiamado San Gradale, in francexe . . .
——Libro uno chiamado Merlino in francexe . . .
——Libro uno chiamado Tristano in francexe . . .
——Libro uno chiamado Lanzaloto in francexe . . .
——Libro uno chiamado la desfatione de la Tavola redonda . . .

10. The original lending records are now scattered, but several published accounts have made the book circulation lists available for cursory scrutiny. See, for example, Bertoni's "La libreria ducale e i cortigiani estensi."

11. The other Este palaces (Belfiore and Belriguardo) contained similar frescoes with chivalric themes. Although some narrative describing the frescoes remains, the frescoes themselves have been destroyed. Belfiore is gone and only the shell and a staircase of Belriguardo remains.

12. Paolo d'Ancona, *I mesi di Schifanoia in Ferrara* (Milan: Esperia, 1954): 36; "[the fresco cycle] seems to come straight from one of the pages of a Chrétien romance which were much read and appreciated at the Ferrara court."

13. Ranieri Varese, "Il ciclo Cosmologico di Schifanoia: un momento della

civiltà cortese in Europe" in *Il Rinascimento a Ferrara e i suoi orrizzonti europei*, edited by W. Moretti (Ravenna: Mario Lapucci, 1984): 315; "On the walls, the [Este] court presents and defines an image of itself as it would like to be."

14. Extant court chronicles and narratives describing castle frescoes make it possible to identify the historical persons and events which inspired the frescoes. The following chronicle entry by Bernardino Zambotti records a joust which took place on June 30, 1490: "A dì 30, il dì de la festa de San Petro. Dui homini d'arme forastieri, uno zovene, chiamato Michele e l'altro vechio chiamato messer Adriano, vèneno armati a tutte arme, a cavalo, in sbarra facta dintorna a la Plasa." (Bernardino Zambotti, *Diario ferrarese dall'anno 1476 sino a 1504*, in *Rerum Italicarum Scriptores*, edited by G. Pardi, vol. 24 (Bologna, 1933): 7; ("On June 30th, the feast day of Saint Peter. Two foreigners, one young man named Michele and the other an older man named Adriano, come completely armed and on horseback to a challenge joust in the piazza.") Compare that entry with the following fresco description of Giovanni degli Arienti Sabadino. "Se li vede anchora affigurato dento da uno stechato che in paiza facesti fare, il combatere che fecerono quilli duo cavalieri Andriano neapolitano et Michael francioso, ali quali el campo concedesti dove molte gente confinante e alienizane per vedere concorse si vedeno." ("The depiction is of an arena constructed in the piazza and the joust was between two knights, the Neopolitan Andriano and the French Michael, who had come to the sight to joust and be watched by many.") Giovanni degli Arienti Sabadino, quoted in W. Gundersheimer, ed., *Art and Life at the Court of Ercole I d'Este: The "De Triumphis religionis" of Giovanni degli Arienti* (Geneva: Droz, 1972): 22; clearly the fresco was commissioned to commemorate a historical joust in Ferrara.

15. Zambotti, entry dated June 16, 1478.

16. Descriptions of the numerous jousts and tourneys can be found not only in Zambotti's chronicle but also in the anonymously written *Rerum Italicarum Scriptores, Diario ferrarese dall'anno 1409–1502*, edited by G. Pardi (Bologna, 1933) 24: 7.

17. Matteo Maria Boiardo, *Orlando Innamorato*, edited by A. Scaglione (Turin: UTET, 1974); see Book 2, canto 17, hereafter referred to as Boiardo 2.17.

18. Niccolò Machiavelli, *Il Principe*, edited by E. Janni (Milan: Rizzoli, 1982), chapter 15, p. 147. "Ma sendo l'intento mio scrivere cosa utile a chi la intende, mi è parso più conveniente andare drieto alla verità effettuale della cosa, che alla imaginazione di essa." ("But my intent being to write something useful for whomever wishes to understand it, it seems to me more to the point to go straight to the actual truth of the matter instead of to abstract idealization of what it could be.")

19. Boiardo 2.18.1–2, "Once upon a time Britain the great was glorious and known for arms and for love; it is still known today; the legends of Arthur still bring glory to the king with stories of good knights who, going with their ladies in search of adventure, showed their valor in battles. King Charles held a great court in France, but it was not as magnificent as Arthur's, even though it was strong and robust and had Ranaldo and Orlando, because

they closed their doors to love and fought only holy wars. They had not the valor and esteem of Arthur's court which I described before."

20. See Elspeth Kennedy, "The Making of a Name or Quest for Identity," in her *Lancelot and the Grail* (Oxford: Clarendon Press, 1986), pp. 10–48.

21. Boiardo 1.6.45, "It was not long until he was completely transformed from what he was and knew neither how he had gotten there or why or when, nor if he was Orlando or someone else."

22. Boiardo 2.31.47, "Completely armed, he jumped into the water and immediately arrived at the bottom . . . he was so happy that he thought little about why he was there and where he had come from."

23. The imagery of Narcissus is conjured several times by Boiardo but see especially Book 2, canto 17.

24. Boiardo 2.8.40, "the count did not understand these words."

25. Eleonora's influence at court cannot be underestimated. A thorough reading of court documents and letters confirms that it was she who ruled wisely while her husband, Duke Ercole, was frequently absent or involved in leisure activities. The situation is reflected in the following manner by Ugo Caleffini, the court chronicler, at the time of Eleonora's death. "Et dà [Eleonora] audentia al populo et spaza supplicatione et è accepta al populo ferrarese. Et il Duca se attende a dare piacere et zugare et fare il barcho." (Ugo Caleffini, *Cronica facte et scripte per Ugo Caleffini notaro ferrarexe* . . . Unpublished manuscript in Biblioteca Apostolica Vaticcana, MS Chigiana I, I, 4, folio, 280; "And Eleonora gave audience to the people, listened to their petitions, and was accepted by the Ferrarese people. The Duke occupied himself with pleasurable things, playing and boating.")

26. Boiardo 3.7.

27. Boiardo 3.7.15.8, "[your] virtue will make you go far."

28. See especially "Narcissus" in Tobin Siebers, *Mirror of Medusa* (Berkeley: University of California Press, 1983).

29. Boiardo 3.5.1, "I have gathered various flowers from the fields, blue ones, yellow, white and red; I have made a mixture of them, carnations, violets, roses and lilies; he who so desires should come forward and choose the one which pleases him the most; the lily delights some, for others it is the rose, for this person one flower and for that person another."

30. Boiardo 2.8.58.6–7, "Time which has past will not return again and will never recur."

12. The Idea of a Cycle: Malory, the Lancelot-Grail, and the *Prose Tristan*

James I. Wimsatt

Much testifies to the medieval taste for encyclopedism. Among written texts, the *Mirrors* of Vincent of Beauvais, the *Summas* of Thomas Aquinas, and the *Etymologies* of Isidore of Seville find counterparts in a large number of fictional histories that are comparably inclusive. Medieval writers and audiences liked for their verbal structures to begin at the beginning and to reach to the end: chronologically, existentially, alphabetically. The fact that the story of Homer's *Iliad* covers less than a year in the history of the Trojan War and that Benoît de Sainte-Maure's *Roman de Troie* begins with the remote pre-history of the war, with Jason's search for the Golden Fleece, and ends only with the death of Ulysses is not *prima facie* evidence that medieval writers had a primitive notion of literary form. Their favored long form was differently conceived from that of the Greek and Latin epic, with its tight unification around a single action. Instead, discursive inclusiveness was to their taste, exemplified most notably in the Bible, which embodies the canonical myth of our culture.

As with the Bible, an elaborate agglutinative process, for which we may hypothesize several major stages, created the encyclopedic Lancelot-Grail or Vulgate Cycle. As with the other Arthurian prose cycles beginning with Chrétien's *Conte du Graal* or *Perceval*, in its formation there was an accretive growth from a large nucleus. Briefly, several stages may be posited in the building of the cycle, and each stage has its own claim to encyclopedic completeness. We identify as complete works three *Prose Lancelots*: one that ends with the death of Galehaut,[1] one twice as long that culminates with Arthur's conquest of Gaul, and one that continues even further to the death of Arthur. Two other works extend the front end of the narrative at great length and bring it to completion: the *Estoire del Saint Graal* and the *Estoire de Merlin*.

The two *Estoires* perfect the Lancelot-Grail cycle or Vulgate Cycle, as the arch-cycle, containing the essential parts of the whole Arthurian history; that is, in the author's terms, the basic *branches* of the *conte*.[2] Vinaver suggests that the accretion of the early Grail story and the *Merlin*, placed before the *Lancelot*, shows the French cycles to be "indefinitely extensible."[3] In the sense that one could always elevate a *branche*—like the story of *Tristan*—to canonical status, it is true that the work could be enlarged, but it is hard to figure how the Vulgate Cycle might have been further extended on either end. The final part, the *Mort Artu*, provides a definitive end point for the major themes of Arthur's kingship, the Round Table, the Grail, and the love of Lancelot and Guenevere. To the questions that had been left open of how Arthur and the Round Table began and where the Grail came from, definitive answers were provided by units added to the front of the cycle. There is thus a full presentation of the major Arthurian themes. With its defective joints and inconsistencies, as Fanni Bogdanow states, the Vulgate Cycle is far from being a harmonious whole.[4] But for all its imbalances and structural looseness, and in part even because of them, it earns the title Vulgate Cycle. Though it can hardly claim the authority of the archetypal vulgate text, the Bible, the Lancelot-Grail has a comprehensiveness, and attained a stature, that quite surpasses that of other sequences of Arthurian history.

The multiple inclusiveness and the presumed authenticity of the Lancelot-Grail led later assemblers of cycles to exploit more restricted ends. The cycle that Bogdanow identifies as the "Post-Vulgate *Roman du Graal*" omits the central *Lancelot* portion to construct a three-part work consisting of the Vulgate *Estoire del Saint Graal*, a counterpart to the Vulgate's *Merlin* called the *Suite du Merlin*, and a Grail *Queste* combined with an abbreviated *Mort Artu*. Like the Lancelot-Grail and the Vulgate *Merlin*, this new cycle grew by expansion. The central *Suite du Merlin*, according to Vinaver's analysis, results from a "consistent evolution from simpler patterns to more coherent and comprehensive ones,"[5] and similarly, as Bogdanow states, the new *Queste del Saint Graal* "was transformed and expanded by the addition of fresh material which has a definite purpose in the economy of the work as a whole," the purpose being "to create out of the several branches of the Arthurian Cycle a unified romance centering upon Arthur."[6] The Lancelot-Grail is the obvious model for the whole, but there is a new focus on the story of Arthur.

The Lancelot-Grail likewise inspired the immensely popular *Prose Tristan*. Vinaver describes this voluminous work as "a sequel to, and an elaboration of" the Vulgate, which had not told the story of Tristan.[7] While the author-compiler works from the story of the French Tristan poems, he was mainly inspirited by the Vulgate, using its materials and basing his inventions on it. The *Tristan* exists in various versions, which suggests the work was built up from a romance that centers, like the *Lancelot Proper*, on the career of its central hero to a cyclical version that includes the contents of the Vulgate Grail quest and, in some manuscripts, a version of the *Mort Artu*.[8] After the story of Tristan's boyhood, his adventures become mingled with, and increasingly part of, the adventures of the Round Table knights. In the last part of the longer version the treacherous King Marc kills Tristan at the same time that Galahad is pursuing the Grail quest. The end of the Grail adventures and the presentation of Tristan's spear and shield at Arthur's court consummate the expanded romance.

The cyclical *Tristan* does not have the thematic unity of the various incremental stages of the Lancelot-Grail. Its nucleus appropriately presents a life of Tristan from birth to death, just as the Vulgate contains a life of Lancelot. The extensive Arthurian material presented in this part entails basic changes in the ancient biography of Tristan and imparts to the work an encyclopedic fullness characteristic of the prose cycles. However, the additions to the *Tristan* of the Grail quest and the story of Arthur's death point up its disparateness and completes the dispersal of its narrative unity. The cyclical version of the *Prose Tristan* lacks both the unification of the Vulgate around the major Arthurian themes and the tighter unity of the *Lancelot* in which the fate of the hero and of the chivalric society that coalesces around him are intrinsically bound together. But the narrative of the cyclical *Tristan* does have a splendid heterogeneity in which another type of encyclopedism is nascent and which evidently attracted Thomas Malory to it. With its delineation of character types and sharp separation of episodes, the *Tristan* presented so various a gallery of personages and set of adventures that the effect went beyond analysis of the practices of individual knights or groups of knights to evoke contemplation of the very idea of knighthood.

We might look at Malory's complete work in the light of his French models. For what he styles his "hoole book," the three cycles that I have been discussing—the Lancelot-Grail, the *Roman du Graal*, and the *Prose Tristan*—provided the main exemplars. Malory was probably familiar with the whole of these cycles and understood their construction. Indeed, his completed work, whose parts have sufficient separate integrity for Vinaver to insist that they are separate works, may well have grown by an accretive process similar to that which produced the French cycles; however that may be, in its final form it constitutes a unified cycle that is a fitting successor to the French works. Malory shows his acquaintanceship with the whole of the Lancelot-Grail, his main structural exemplar, by making appreciable use in sequence of three of the five chief parts of the exemplar: the

Lancelot, the Grail *Queste,* and the *Mort Artu.* Moreover, the *Suite du Merlin,* the original for Malory's famous opening section, "The Tale of King Arthur," developed from a fourth main part, the Vulgate's *Merlin* with its early history of Arthur. The *Suite du Merlin* itself, furthermore, is the hub and core of the second French cycle, the *Roman du Graal,* making it probable that Malory was familiar with the complete contents of that cycle also. His conversance with the whole of the third cycle, the *Tristan,* is demonstrated by his extensive use of the work and by his rubrics commenting on the contents of the *Tristan.*[9] Malory's complete work, then, may be seen as a synthesis of the three cycles. With his unification of the Tristan story into a cycle of Arthur, we might even think he had in mind the grand synthesis outlined in the Hélie de Boron epilogue to the *Prose Tristan.* There the author proposes to compose a "crown" of Arthurian narrative, a great book that would supersede in authority the Lancelot-Grail, comprehending the Vulgate, the *Roman du Graal,* and the *Tristan.*[10] If Malory could not have had in mind to accomplish the narrative in the massive proportions that Hélie evidently envisages, nevertheless, the pattern of his cycle, his careful selection of representative event, and his compressed presentation of event suggest that his "hoole book" represents an epitome of such a narrative.

The parallel of the narrative pattern of Malory's whole work with the Lancelot-Grail and with the other two cycles is notable. We might summarize. Like the *Merlin* stories of the Vulgate and the *Roman du Graal,* his "Tale of King Arthur" anchors his narrative in Arthur's beginnings. As in the *Prose Lancelot* and the *Prose Tristan,* his *Book of Sir Tristram* narrates the birth, development, and exploits of a great Arthurian hero. And all three cycles provide immediate precedents for Malory's Grail quest and death of Arthur. His book, however, is thematically individualistic. Since he does not preface his cycle with the early Grail story, his is hardly a comprehensive Grail history like the Vulgate and the *Roman du Graal;* and since he chooses not to present the story of Lancelot's youth and early love of Guenevere or the end of the Tristan narrative, he provides no comprehensive biography from birth to death of a knight-hero such as the Lancelot-Grail and the *Prose Tristan* contain. At the same time, as a result of the suppression of much of the history of Lancelot and the Grail, the subordination of the *Tristan* material to the Round Table history, and the alterations that aggrandize Arthur, Malory's is the most unified Arthuriad among the cycles.

Malory, then, builds a comprehensive and relatively unified cycle of stories on the model of the great French cycles, particularly the Vulgate. His main change in the established pattern is in the service of establishing Arthur's regal status. He places Arthur's continental campaign near the beginning of his career, basing this section of his narrative on the English *Alliterative Morte Arthure* rather than on a French model. The culmination of the campaign in Malory's version, in which the pope crowns Arthur as emperor, has virtually no precedent, even in the English poem that Malory is relying on. The effect of the changes is to establish Arthur's stature early and place him and his Round Table society firmly at the very center of the secular universe. The realms of King Ban and Bors and of Galehaut, foci in the early *Lancelot*, and that of King Marc, important in the *Tristan*, are more peripheral. The spiritual world of the Grail and Galahad, which shares the thematic center in the other cycles, while it retains its absolute existential superiority in Malory, is thematically subordinate, as it had not been in the other cycles, to the history of the worldly knights.

Indeed, it seems that Malory's promotion of Arthur to a new and unrivaled glory is in the service of an overriding thematic purpose, which is to present a mirror and anatomy of worldly knighthood. He is composing a companion to fifteenth-century courtesy books, exemplifying a different sort of encyclopedism. Certainly, the aspect of the courtesy book, or "Mirror for Princes," had always been present in heroic narrative, with the central figures illustrating the qualities which the society of the time values most; the *Odyssey*, the *Aeneid*, and *Beowulf* are particularly notable examples. In the French cycles, Lancelot and Tristan represent embodiments of chivalric ideals, and it is clearly in the mind of the creators of these stories to show through their heroes the way knights and lovers ought to behave. The lecture on knighthood that the Lady of the Lake delivers to the young Lancelot in the French story is an explicit courtesy-book feature; but the contents of the lecture are not notably reflected by the story in which it is embodied. The overriding aims of the Lancelot-Grail were to tell complete histories and provide comprehensive characterizations of the Grail, of Lancelot, of Lancelot and Guenevere's love, and of Arthur and the Round Table.

Malory also was telling an inclusive history of Arthur and his Round Table. At the same time, he was writing when the prose treatise on the proper behavior of gentlefolk—often presented in dialogue, as in the most famous Renaissance example, Castiglione's *Book of the Courtier*—had come into vogue in England, making it natural that his Arthurian cycle should have the marks of a courtesy book for knights. Malory effects a marriage of encyclopedic forms: a narrative summa of the French cycles joins with a thematically inclusive mirror for knights. A courtesy-book intent for Malory's book is stated explicitly in Caxton's Preface, and Malory's ideal of knighthood finds direct formulation in Arthur's establishment of a rule for his knights and in Hector's final eulogy for Lancelot. This intent is implicit in much of the structure and contents of the whole work, especially of the long, undervalued Tristram section.

When William Caxton printed Malory's work in 1485, it was part of a publishing program that promoted the ideal of chivalry. Caxton had published his translation of Ramon Lull's popular thirteenth-century mirror for knights as *The Book of the Ordre of Chyualry* in 1484, and six years later he would translate and publish Christine de Pizan's treatment of the methods and rules of civilized war, calling it *The Book of Fayttes of Armes and of Chyualrye*.[11] In Lull's and Christine's works a knightly ideal is extensively formulated. Caxton found it expressed in action in Malory, as the familiar prologue clearly shows: "I, accordyng to my copye, have doon sette it in enprynte to the entente that noble men may see and lerne the noble actes of chyvalrye, and jentyl and vertuous dedes that knyghtes used in tho dayes, by whyche they came to honour, and how they that were vycious were punysshed and ofte put to shame and rebuke."[12] It is to be a lesson-book for all, men and women, high and low. He bids "al noble lordes and ladyes wyth al other estates, of what estate or degree they been of, that shal see and rede in this sayd book and werke, that they take the good and honest actes in their remembraunce, and to folowe the same. . . . For herein may be seen noble chyvalrye, curtosye, humanyté, frendlynesse, hardynesse, love, frendshyp, cowardyse, murdre, hate, vertue, and synne. Doo after the good and leve the evyl" (Malory, *Works*, 1: cxlv–cxlvi).

Much in Malory's complex work may be cited to show that he thought of his book as an inclusive *speculum*, teaching proper behavior, everywhere by positive and negative example and sometimes by explicit precept that he adds to the source. In the beginning of his reign, upon marrying Guenevere and acquiring the Round Table, Arthur establishes for his knights his well-known rule, renewed annually at Pentecost. The rule enjoins them not to commit outrage, murder, and treason, to give mercy to those that ask for it, to assist ladies and widows, and never to take up wrongful quarrels. Balancing this set of precepts at the end, the very last speech of the "hoole book," Ector's lament for his brother embodies a description of the ideal worldly knight: "the curtest knyght that ever bare shelde . . . the trewest lover, of a synful man, that ever loved woman . . . the kyndest man that ever strake with swerde . . . the mekest man and the jentyllest that ever ete in halle emonge ladyes, and . . . the sternest knyght to thy mortal foo that ever put spere in the reeste"; he was, says Ector, "never matched of erthely knyghtes hand" (Malory, *Works*, 3: 1259). Courtesy, truth in love, kindness—i.e., faithfulness to one's better nature—meekness, gentility, relentlessness in battle: such are the virtues of the best earthly knight. Malory's emphasis throughout, except in the quest of the Grail, is on the life and behavior of earthly knights, by definition "synful" men. Heavenly knighthood is possible only for a spiritual elite, like Perceval and Galahad. By knighthood's power the Maimed King could be cured. But earthly knighthood also has its power. By it, the sinful Lancelot could cure Sir Urry. He could also qualify for the death of a saint, as Kay Harris points out in her contribution to this collection.

Malory's Lancelot is the best knight and the best lover, but his deeds do not dominate the work as they do the *Prose Lancelot*. Malory enhances the reputation of Lancelot appreciably, but whereas Lancelot presides over the vast center of the Lancelot-Grail, the stories of heroes from the *Prose Tristan* occupy the middle of Malory's work. Gareth, Tristram, Lamorak, and Palamydes—all great heroes with substantial individuality—are present together with Lancelot to show the diversity of characteristics that can define the good knight: the youthful virtue and prowess of Gareth, the endless aspiration of Palamydes, the endurance of Lamorak, and the immense versatility of Tristram join with the magnetism and indomitability of Lancelot to compose Malory's picture of ideal knighthood. They converge on Logres from all points of the compass: the Orkneys, Saracen land, Wales, Scotland, Cornwall, and Gaul. They are all lovers, but with varying aims and success. The composite of their adventures lends to Malory's book a more various inclusiveness than characterizes the Lancelot-Grail or any of its parts individually. The main source, and the main model, for this kind of inclusiveness is the *Prose Tristan*.

Despite its late medieval popularity, the *Prose Tristan* has not been much admired. Bédier, for example, called it an "enormous *fatras* [hodgepodge] of knightly fabrications." [13] Similarly, Malory's *Sir Tristram* section—almost 40 percent of his whole book placed in the very center—has been evaluated as a failure even by Malory's admirers. [14] The modern reader indeed is quite likely to be confused and fatigued by the *Tristram* and left with the impression that it too is a mere hodgepodge of knightly adventure. Such reaction to both works is conditioned by the canons of modern fiction and results in an undervaluing of their anatomies of knighthood. Malory's anatomy centers on—or rather is dispersed over—the *Tristram* section. The *Tristram* is of the essence: without it the very heart of Malory's book is lacking. Its importance is only weakly explained by the parallel of the tragedy of Tristram to that of the Round Table, the explanation that Thomas

Rumble offers.[15] The deaths of Tristram and Isode are barely part of Malory's story. The elegant intricacies of narrative interlace brought to perfection in the *Prose Lancelot* also are not in question. Malory has aims for his *Tristram* that are different from the *Lancelot* author's for his work, and his style and form differ accordingly. Vinaver has noted that Malory unweaves much of the interlace he found. For this, one must further note, he substituted a narrative style that highlights rather than conceals variety. The effect of Malory's *Book of Sir Tristram*, in Larry Benson's words, "is less of a stately tapestry than of a dazzling kaleidoscope of the color, sounds, and emotion of the chivalric life."[16]

Much the same can be said of the *Prose Tristan* itself, important as a model for Malory's style as well as for his story. The writer of the *Tristan* did not labor to produce the tapestry-like interlace of the *Lancelot*. In its stead he presented a great variety that provided Malory with an agreeable model for his mirror of chivalric life. Benson notes that the *Prose Tristan* "is closer in spirit to [Malory's] own work than any of the Vulgate romances, and he seems to have found it more congenial to his tastes."[17] Not only to his tastes, we may emphasize, but also to his purposes.

While Malory derives from the *Tristan* a style which emphasizes variety, the narrative theme of Malory's "hoole book" is quite unlike the French work. Whereas in *Tristan* the role of the king, as Baumgartner says, is reduced almost to nothing,[18] Malory anchors his book in the stories of Arthur's rise and fall and produces an Arthuriad, even while he includes great stretches of narrative from the *Tristan* in which Round Table knights rather than the royal Arthur are central. But what Malory's book derives generically from the French work is not simply a random variety. In its variety he finds a plan. Its implicit plan shows up particularly in its spectrum of characterizations, both of the various knight-heroes that I have mentioned and of other types appropriate to romance. Baumgartner notes that the author of the *Prose Tristan*, in taking over characters from his models—the poems of *Tristan* and the Lancelot-Grail—has a strong tendency to schematize and caricature them.[19] This is the method of Theophrastan character writing and—more relevantly for Malory—of medieval Estates satire, a common English form and the main model for Chaucer's portraits in his "General Prologue" to the *Canterbury Tales*.

Malory's procedure in his *Tristram* reflects the French work's techniques of characterization: Marc, a complex figure in the *Tristan* poems, becomes a type of the treacherous coward in the prose works. Gawayn and his brothers, who are brave though flawed knights in the *Lancelot*, have few redeeming features in the *Prose Tristan* and Malory's *Tristram;* with the exception of Gareth, they are thugs faithful only to clan, not to knighthood. The figures of Mark and Gawayn, of course, grow out of the tradition of twelfth-century romance. Malory's schematizing is especially highlighted by characters for whom the *Prose Tristan* provided his chief models. Among such type-figures, who include Lamorak and Palamydes, Alexander the Orphan, dedicated to avenging his father, the fair unknown La Cote Male Tayle, the singularly vicious Breunys sans Pité, and the clown Dagonet, the most interesting of all is Dynadan. He is, as Malory says, a good knight and a japer, and he particularly exemplifies wise and moderate knighthood. Since an exhaustive inspection of Malory's mirror is hardly in order here, let me offer in its stead a succinct analysis of Dynadan's contribution to it.

Malory's Dynadan is not entirely the same as his counterpart in the *Prose Tristan.* As seems always the case with characters who speak ironically (and irony is the French Dinadan's chief mode), the critics do not entirely agree about how we should understand the French characterization: Vinaver finds in this Dinadan an unrelenting and unsympathetic critic of chivalry,[20] while Baumgartner sees him as "the perfect type of the moderate and wise knight, sufficiently wise to know and not go beyond his own limits."[21] In her view, he criticizes only the absurdities, not the practice. Both evaluations have validity: through his words, he offers a humorous but cogent critique of practices of chivalry that other good knights find quite normal, yet in his actions, he is brave but prudent, neither foolhardy nor full of bravado.

I will cite one from numerous examples of Dinadan's commentary on the practices of knight-errantry. As happens not seldom in the romances, he and Tristan one day arrive at a castle where they have to joust before being put up for the night. When inside, Dinadan is told complacently that such is the custom of the castle. If a knight-errant triumphs in his joust, he can stay; but if he loses, he has to go elsewhere. Dinadan says that this is not hospitality but rather "sorrow, and unhappiness, and wrath." He goes on to decry the custom, making a wordplay on *"oste"* ("host, guest"), *"osteler"* ("to lodge"), and *"oster"* ("to send off"). "Good host," he says, "your house is no proper lodging . . . for it suddenly and frequently throws out its guests. Now you may be sure that never in my life will I come back to your hostel, if God allows me to leave with honor." The host knights are deeply troubled by his words and declare that he is not courteous in thus criticizing the custom of the castle, but rather is guilty of very bad manners, *"vilonnie trop grant."*[22] Yet Dinadan persists, here as elsewhere, in decrying their practices. Tristan as observer is simply amused. Dinadan is both humorous and eloquent in speaking of these and similar practices of knights. Clearly, implicit in his extensive commentary is a Cervantes-like comic satire of the conventions of chivalric romance by which, for instance, knights are forever being required to fight before they can pass a ford, enter a castle, or proceed on their paths. He is equally biting and effective in talking about what seem absurd practices of knightly lovers.

But Tristan, a knight whose love brings him more grief than happiness and who insists to Dinadan's disgust on challenging twenty knights at one time, is no Don Quixote. And Dinadan's practices are those of a good knight; he is not as strong as Tristan or Lamorak, but his prowess fully matches that of Arthur's nephews from Orkney, and in character he is quite unlike those treacherous murderers. Consistent with the other thirteenth-century romances, the *Tristan* takes romance practices seriously, and the French Dinadan is a particular type of good knight, an important segment of the mirror of knighthood that the work provides. His ironic commentary on knightly practices provides a dialogical complexity, showing that this romance writer, and his characters themselves, recognize potential paradoxes and absurdities in their practices when ordinary reason is brought to bear. Such commentary is particularly useful in works that aim at the analysis appropriate to the courtesy book.

Malory's Dynadan differs from the Dinadan of the *Prose Tristan*, but not radically so. Pointing out Malory's severe reduction of Dinadan's ironic speeches, Vinaver claims that Malory fails to appreciate the French Dinadan's satirical commentary on chivalry because he had "no sympathy with anything that reveals a critical attitude toward his favorite ideal."[23] Nevertheless, though in the process of reducing the *Prose Tristan* to a sixth of its size Malory excises much of Dinadan's trenchant humor and the heart of his critique of chivalry, his Dynadan gets more than proportionate space and has a vital place in Malory's mirror. He is one who "loved all good knyghtes that were valyaunte and hated all tho that were destroyers of good knyghtes" (Malory, *Works*, 2: 614), and whom only murderers such as the Orkney brothers disliked. Particularly, he is one who can evaluate others and does not hide his opinion. Better than any other he knows good knights, and he knows bad ones. Of Lamorak, when Arthur is wondering at his feats, Dynadan states flatly: "merveyle ye nothynge thereof, for . . . there is nat a valyaunter knyght in the world lyvynge, for I know his myght." After riding with King Mark, he tells him, "I see . . . ye ar full of cowardyse, and ye ar also a murtherar, and that is the grettyst shame that ony knyght may have" (Malory, *Works*, 2: 585). At the same time, though he largely lacks the ironic wit of his

French predecessor, he is still a knight who says "fye on that crauffte" of love (Malory, *Works*, 2: 689), and on commonsense grounds declines a battle of two against twenty.

It is important too that, though Malory excises much of his irony, Dynadan is still funny; in Tristram's words he is "the beste bourder and japer that I know." What Malory retains of his humor, particularly, is his unsubtle practical joking and the revenge in kind that his victims take on him. Twice in response to Dynadan's tricks, an incognito Lancelot knocks him down and takes him to be derided before the king and queen. On one of these occasions, Lancelot is dressed in girl's clothes and Dynadan ends up in them. Dynadan's skill in clerkly humor is exemplified in a scurrilous lay he composes about Mark and has sung at Mark's court. Such matters lead Tristram to salute him as "the beste bourder and japer that I know," at the same time stating that he is "the beste felawe that I know, and all good knyghtes lovyth his felyship" (Malory, *Works*, 2: 692). Despite Dynadan's open opposition to lovers, both Guenevere and Isode enjoy his company. Repeatedly, he makes them, the king, Lancelot, and Tristram "laughe, that unnethe they myghte sytte" (Malory, *Works*, 2: 758). We can regret the loss of Dinadan's subtle irony, but Malory's story is not subtle, and what he retains of his character fills an essential role. Dynadan is representative of the good knight with *mesure*, a touchstone for judging other knights, and he provides a spark for laughter in Arthur's court, where humor is often lacking. The sport and good fun he supplies have an important function in romance and in the life of a knight.

Emmanuèle Baumgartner states that the French *Tristan* is not a manual of chivalry and that in it there is little trace of a didactic intention explicitly formulated. Nevertheless, she continues, one can sort out from it a detailed description of the different aspects of the knight's life, as well as the customs and principles which rule the conduct of the knight-errant and his relation with society.[24] Malory's narrative, too, is no systematic manual. However, it does reflect the literary tastes of its time and effectively supplements contemporary courtesy books; thereby it is nearer to being such a manual for knights than any of its predecessors in the French Arthurian romances, including the *Tristan*, its main model for this aspect.

The three prose cycles that Malory draws on extensively were built additively and almost obsessively to achieve a chroniclelike comprehensiveness, proceeding from remote beginnings to absolute endings. Their vast contents were likewise extended thematically to explore and exploit the lives, loves, and adventures of their chief figures and the characters associated with them: the progeny of Kings

Ban and Bors, the closely bound kin of Arthur and Lot of Orkney, the intertwined ancestry and family of the Grail and Pellinore. The French cycles create a mirror of Arthurian society, showing especially what it was like to be a knight in that milieu. Malory recognized and respected the chronological inclusiveness of the predecessor cycles; he created a chronicle of Arthur, following him from his conception to his death. Instead of finding an exhaustive inspection of the family groups in a well-woven fabric with few seams, however, he found nascent in the cycles, especially in the variety and unraveled loose ends of the *Tristan*, an encyclopedia that particularly suited the tastes of his time. An Arthuriad and an epitome of the most prominent thirteenth-century prose cycles, Malory's "hoole book" offers above all a mirror for knights, in turn representative of man in society. The long life of the work as a vivid lesson-book for boys was thoroughly in its spirit. In Caxton's words, all lords and ladies, and all people "of whatever estate or degre," may find in it an ethical model: "Doo after the good and leve the evyl" (Malory, *Works*, 1: cxlvi).

Notes

1. Elspeth Kennedy, ed., *Lancelot do Lac: The Non-Cyclic Old French Prose Romance*, 2 vols. (Oxford: Clarendon Press, 1980); *Lancelot and the Grail* (Oxford: Clarendon Press, 1986). Alexandre Micha, using extensive manuscript evidence, argues against the independence of the *Lancelot do Lac*: "Il nous faut abandonner l'hypothèse d'un *Lancelot* autonome, ne mentionnant que la quête du Graal" (*Essais sur le cycle du Lancelot-Graal* [Geneva: Droz, 1987]: 29; "We must abandon the hypothesis of an autonomous *Lancelot* that only mentions the quest of the Grail"). He presents his full argument in *Essais*, pp. 13–83. On internal evidence I am strongly inclined to accept that the text which Kennedy presents identifies in some fashion an original nuclear *Lancelot*.

2. See Micha, *Essais*, 301–302.

3. Eugène Vinaver, ed., *The Works of Thomas Malory*, 3d ed., revised by P. J. C. Field, 3 vols. (Oxford: Clarendon Press, 1990) 3: 1275. All quotations from Malory's text herein are to this edition.

4. Fanni Bogdanow, *The Romance of the Grail: A Study of the Structure and Genesis of a Thirteenth-Century Arthurian Prose Romance* (New York: Barnes and Noble, 1966): 198–199.

5. Malory, *Works*, 3: 1269.

6. Bogdanow 48 and 200.

7. Eugène Vinaver, "The Prose *Tristan*," in *Arthurian Literature in the Middle Ages*, edited by Roger Sherman Loomis (Oxford: Clarendon Press, 1959): 339.

8. See E. Löseth, *Le Roman en Prose de Tristan* (Paris: Bouillon, 1890): xii, xvi, 421–422.

9. See especially Malory's *Works* 2: 845: "Here endyth the secunde boke off Syr Trystram de Lyones. . . . But here ys no rehersall of the thirde booke." The third book of the *Prose Tristan* narrates the Grail quest.

10. The full Hélie epilogue is quoted in Emmanuèle Baumgartner, *Le "Tristan" en prose: Essai d'Interprétation d'un roman médiéval* (Geneva: Droz, 1975): 94.

11. Both of these publications of Caxton were edited by Alfred T. P. Byles for the Early English Text Society: *The Book of the Ordre of Chyualry*, EETS, OS, 168 (London: Oxford University Press, 1926); and *The Book of Fayttes of Armes and of Chyualrye*, EETS, OS, 189 (London: Oxford University Press, 1932).

12. Malory, *Works*, 1: cxlv.

13. Quoted in Baumgartner 173. Vinaver ("The Prose *Tristan*," pp. 339–347) analyzes the work as exemplifying the distintegration of interlace, with loose threads scattered everywhere (p. 345).

14. The comment of E. K. Chambers, that "Malory would have done better to have left *Tristan* alone" (*Sir Thomas Malory* [London: English Association, 1922]: 41), expresses the typical sentiment. Numerous similar, if less famous, comments could be adduced. Vinaver excuses Malory's "seemingly indiscriminate accumulation of adventures" by his being "at the mercy of his original and it was not in his power to alter its fundamental character" (Malory, *Works*, 3: 1444). I am arguing, of course, that Malory need not be excused for his *Tristram*.

15. Thomas C. Rumble, "'The Tale of Tristram': Development by Analogy," in *Malory's Originality*, edited by Robert M. Lumiansky (Baltimore: The Johns Hopkins Press, 1964): 118–183.

16. Larry D. Benson, *Malory's Morte Darthur* (Cambridge, Mass.: Harvard University Press, 1977): 109.

17. Benson 109–110.

18. Baumgartner 176.

19. Baumgartner 233–234.

20. Eugène Vinaver, *Malory* (Oxford: Clarendon, 1929): 66–69.

21. Baumgartner 187.

22. Philippe Ménard, ed., *Le Roman de Tristan en prose* (Geneva: Droz, 1987): 133–134.

23. Vinaver, *Malory*, 67.

24. Baumgartner 174.

13. Lancelot's Vocation: Traitor Saint

E. Kay Harris

Heroes of medieval romance, as many critics have pointed out, often undergo a "canonization" process. Supernatural phenomena often attend their deaths and their tombs become sites of pilgrimage.[1] Both the *Mort Artu* and Malory's *Morte Darthur* instantiate such a process for Lancelot. At the end of his life, for example, each work devises a religious vocation for him. Lancelot enters a hermitage, taking on the life of a disciplined religious and priest, and when he dies, angels bear his soul to heaven. Malory takes the canonization process one step further: As Lancelot lay "starke dede," Malory writes, there was the "swettest savour aboute hym that ever [was] felte" (Malory 1258).[2] Even before his death, however, both works prepare the groundwork for Lancelot's sanctification. People in the *Mort Artu* recognize his extraordinary inherent goodness; they swear to lay down their lives for him "com se ce fust Dex meismes" (*Mort* 97. 25,[3] "as if he were God himself"). Likewise in the *Morte Darthur*, Lancelot's deeds incite the same type of love and loyalty. Gareth and Gaheris, for instance, will "beare none harneyse of warre" (Malory 1177) against Lancelot when Arthur orders them to accompany the queen to the pyre.

From such textual evidence, the circumstances of Lancelot's death and his ability to inspire extraordinary love and loyalty in others, we can see that the *Mort Artu* and Malory's *Morte Darthur* project Lancelot as a type of cultic object worthy of veneration. Since Lancelot's adultery with the queen runs counter to such a projection, I want to examine in this paper how each text, but primarily the *Morte Darthur*, treats the adultery within such a hagiographized narrative. The emphasis on Malory's text is due in part to the fact that by his day, adultery with the king's wife was not only a sin but a crime of high treason.[4] Thus, the translation of Lancelot from traitor to saint appears blatantly incongruous with its time and runs counter to attempts to historicize the *Morte Darthur*. Yet this is my task, and in the process I attempt to do a bit of historicizing with the *Mort Artu*, despite Micha's warning that such an endeavor is risky business.[5] The examination that I will carry out reveals that each text constructs a type of sanctity for Lancelot that participates in a strain of political discourse peculiar to its respective era: the politicization of cultic piety. In order to demonstrate the peculiarity of each text's representation of Lancelot as a type of cultic object, I begin by situating the *Mort Artu* within a politics of holiness current in thirteenth-century France and then I move on to compare this thirteenth-century French context to a fifteenth-century English version of political sanctity. Such a comparison helps us to understand many of Malory's departures from the *Mort Artu*'s representation of Lancelot and forms the basis of my argument that Malory's text simultaneously exalts Lancelot as a hero-saint and punishes him as a traitor.

Contractual arrangements between knights and their lords, as between Lancelot and Arthur, were not unlike the informal relationships that bound particular saints to particular groups of people. Both types of arrangements were reciprocally binding. A patron saint of a community, for example, was expected to protect that community. In turn, the community's members "responded to this protection" by venerating the saint, and in fact through their veneration of the saint, they "earned the right" to that protection.[6] Although articulated in terms of punishment, the oath which the knights of the Round Table swear to Arthur in the *Morte Darthur* sets up a similar relationship between Arthur and his knights. By the terms of this oath, if a Round Table knight committed a crime such as treason or murder or if he failed to give mercy when he was asked, then the knight forfeited the "worship and lordship of kynge Arthure" (Malory 120). Here, Arthur is in the position of the community, as the one who is to be protected by his knights. It is his duty to reward them with his worship when they perform their obligations and to withhold it from knights who fail to uphold the oath. Analogous to the medieval concept of "honor," which denotes both property and moral prestige,[7] "worship" includes the giving of concrete gifts, such as land, as the manifestation of one's reverence or adoration for the virtue seen in another. Thus the knight, according to the oath of the Round Table, has the opportunity through his deeds to be the recipient of Arthur's worship and attain a status similar to that of a patron saint.

Lancelot occupies such a position of honor in both the *Mort Artu* and the *Morte Darthur*. After hearing that he is to be banished from Logres, Lancelot, in the *Mort Artu*, recalls for Arthur the time he saved the king and his kingdom from Galehaut. Had it not been for Lancelot, Arthur would have lost his land, his honor, and his crown. Arthur, Lancelot claims, ought to love him and be grateful, as a king should, for such deeds (*Mort* 119. 92–117). Earlier in the text when Guenevere is angry at Lancelot for wearing the red sleeve, Bors warns her that she risks bringing great damage to "cest roiaume et maint autre" (*Mort* 59. 81, "this realm and many others"). Not only does the security of Logres rest with Lancelot, but the well-being of other realms depends on him as well.

Whereas these types of statements depict Lancelot's exceptional prowess and document his capacity to act as a patron saint for both Arthur and his realm, the *Mort Artu* does not rely solely or primarily on a record of deeds to establish the grounds for Lancelot's veneration. Rather than emphasizing concrete deeds, the *Mort Artu* deploys abstract concepts to create a sense of the exceptional inherent worthiness in Lancelot, an inherent worthiness that nonetheless is self-evident to others. It is this worthiness which compels the Maid of Escalot to ask Lancelot to wear her sleeve, as she avers to him: "[V]os estes li premiers chevaliers a qui ge feïsse onques requeste de riens, ne encore nel feïsse ge pas, se ne fust la grant bonté qui est en vos" (*Mort* 14. 31–34, "You are the first knight of whom I have ever requested anything, and I would not have done that even now had it not been for the great goodnesss there is in you"). At this point the maiden does not know she is speaking to Lancelot; she makes her decision not based on what she has heard about him or on what she has seen him do but rather for "la grant bonté" in him. Over and over again the *Mort Artu* constructs Lancelot's virtue by having others speak of it. Like the Maid of Escalot, Bors attests to Lancelot's goodness when he tells Guenevere that all noble virtues exist more perfectly in Lancelot than in any other person (*Mort* 59). The presence of such goodness, such virtue, in Lancelot indicates that he has been especially blessed by God. This judgment is articulated by Lancelot himself when he tells Bors not to worry about him "car cil qui jusques ci m'a soufert a avoir victoire en touz les leus ou ge ai esté ne souferra pas par sa grace que il me meschiee en leu ou ge soie" (*Mort* 60. 81–84, "because the one who until now has permitted me to have victory in all the places where I have been will not allow by his grace things to turn out badly for me wherever I am"). Thus Lancelot has not only the physical prowess that enables him to act as the protector of Arthur and his realm but also the God-given virtue that makes him eminently suitable for such a role.

This integration of the physical and the spiritual within Lancelot creates an image of strength and holiness, an image that medieval monarchs endeavored to achieve. None perhaps were more successful in that effort than the kings of France. The success of Capetian kings, particularly Philip Augustus and his grandson Louis IX, in this area was due in part to their willingness to be seen as vassals of St. Denis, the protector of the realm of France and patron saint of the monarchy. In an article that analyzes the relationship between the cult of St. Denis and Capetian kings, Gabrielle Spiegel questions why Philip Augustus and Louis IX would actively promote the cult of St. Denis and perform obeisance to him, thereby acknowledging him as their lord and benefactor. Spiegel argues that Capetian devotion to the saint provided a means for the monarchs to transcend their "more limited identit[ies] as feudal overlord[s]" to become national leaders; what the "French kings sought in allying themselves with the cult of St. Denis was the enlargement of royal personality."[8] To do this, the kings, in a sense, made the cult of St. Denis into a cult of kingship. By working incessantly and effectively to stamp "a national character on the cult" by claiming that the saint was the protector of the realm and patron of the king, the monks of St. Denis had created "a ritual vehicle by means of which the kings of France could reach out and tap a significant reservoir of national feeling. By identifying themselves with a revered national saint, Capetian kings could hope to transfer to themselves the affections of their subjects already directed to the saint."[9]

While the connection between the cult of St. Denis and Capetian kings may seem to have little or no relevance to the *Mort Artu*'s representation of Lancelot, since the text does not make him a king, its relevance becomes clearer when one considers how the *Mort Artu* portrays the one king who figures prominently in the work, namely, Arthur. Subject to his emotions, dismissing sensible advice when it is given him, and indirectly accused of treason by his own people for sentencing Guenevere to death, Arthur does not emerge from this text as a king who can by virtue of his goodness inspire loyalty and love in others. In fact, while Arthur plans to pursue Lancelot, his knights are hesitant to follow his lead.[10] King Yon, for example, warns Arthur that anyone who cared about the realm would not declare war on King Ban's kinsmen since "Nostre Sires l'a eslevé par desus touz autres lingnajes" (*Mort* 104. 12–13, "Our Lord has raised them above all other families"). Conversely, Lancelot has no difficulty finding eager supporters in his conflict with the king; the *Mort Artu* reasons that "por ce qu'il estoit tant amez de toutes parz, en vint tant que, se Lancelos fust rois tenanz terre, ne cuidassent mie moult de genz qu'il assemblast si grant chevalerie comme il assembla adonc" (*Mort* 106. 12–16, "since he was so loved so much every where, so many came to him that had Lancelot been a king holding land, many people would not have believed at all that he could assemble such great chivalry as he assembled at that time"). Although not a king, Lancelot wields the power of a king, and that power finds its base in the affection and respect people hold for him. Moreover, despite the fact that he is not a king, Lancelot has the power to create them. Kneeling before Lancelot, his kinsmen receive their power as kings from him; on the feast day of All Saints, the day chosen by Lancelot, Bors and his kinsmen receive their crowns from him (*Mort* 124–126).[11] In doing this, Lancelot acts in an ecclesiastical capacity, and, given the historical relationship of St. Denis and the kings of France, we can say that he acts in a saintly capacity. Like the kings of France who held the realm by the authority of their lord St. Denis, Bors, Lionel, and Hector rule their territories by the authority given them by Lancelot.

In assessing the importance of the notion of a holy king, historians have suggested that the forging of such an identity contributed to the formation of national identity. By successfully portraying themselves as the embodiment of the religious ideals held by their subjects, monarchs created the conditions by which they could become the object of their subjects' religious fervor.[12] Thus both monarch and people shared in the work of God: they were a holy nation. The Capetians capitalized on such a strategy. Styled as the most Christian of nations, a type of Jerusalem, France was regarded by its people and king as being especially blessed by God. With such divine favor, France was preeminent among nations, and consequently it gave birth to saints,[13] not to mere kings as did other nations.[14] In thirteenth-century France, "royal" and "most holy" were virtual synonyms.[15] The importance, then, of "small acts of devotion and obedience which [the Capetians] performed at the altar of [St. Denis]" played a part in this process.[16] Such acts distilled an image or an identity of the king as an object worthy of loyalty and love.

I do not intend to suggest that the *Mort Artu* renders an image of a unified holy nation via Lancelot's sanctity. However, by making a clear distinction between King Ban's descendants and the knights who are subject to Arthur's rule, the *Mort Artu* sets a course in that direction. In the case of Lancelot and his family, Arthur holds no power over them. Bors and his relatives, for example, do not always come to court when Arthur summons them. Once when they chose not to, Arthur, we are told, "ne l'en osa plus proier" (*Mort* 44. 4, "did not dare to entreat them any longer"). As Guenevere points out to Arthur during the poisoned fruit episode, neither Bors nor any of his family is obliged to fight for her since they do not hold anything from Arthur, "einz sont d'une terre estrange" (*Mort* 79. 49, "rather they are from a foreign land"). As a group, then, these foreign knights, the descendants and relatives of King Ban, are set apart from the king and subjects of the Round Table. They are described as "li plus re-

nommé del monde et de greigneur proesce et de greigneur chevalerie" (*Mort* 37. 21–22, "the most renowned in the world and of the
greatest prowess and of the greatest chivalry"), and as having no
equals in the world (*Mort* 144. 10–12). In fact, God "l'a eslevé par
desus touz autres" (*Mort* 104. 12, "has raised them above all others").
Thus the *Mort Artu* not only invents a cult for Lancelot but also for
his family and, by extension, his country as well.

The *Mort Artu's* many references to Lancelot's exceptional virtue
together with those small acts of devotion he performs, such as giving
gifts to the Church, keeping a vigil before battle, going to mass and
confession, and his prayer and blessing for the kingdom of Logres at
the time of his exile, do their part to make Lancelot an object worthy
of loyalty and love and to demonstrate to us, and perhaps to the
readers of the day as well, the political potential contained in such an
integrated image of physical strength and holiness. Such an image
effectively erases Lancelot's adultery with the queen, for it is after he
has been accused of adultery and has taken the queen from Arthur
that the popular adulation of Lancelot occurs. When he rides to Joyous Guard, after rescuing the queen, the people from the castle
"vindrent a l'encontre ausi grant joie fesant com se ce fust Dex
meïsmes . . . li jurerent sur seinz qu'il li aideroient jusqu'a la mort"
(*Mort* 97. 24–29, "went to meet him carrying on with such great joy
as if he were God himself . . . they swore to him on the saints that
they would help him up to the moment of death"). There are other
instances of such veneration. Banished from England, Lancelot sends
his shield to St. Stephen's so that he will not be forgotten. The shield
was "meintenant pendre el milieu del moustier a une chaenne d'ar-
gent aussi richement com se ce fust uns cors sainz. Et quant cil del
païs le sorent, il le vindrent veoir espessement a grant feste" (*Mort*
121. 8–12, "immediately hung up in the middle of the church on a
chain of silver of such magnificence as if it [the shield] were a holy
relic. And when those in the country knew about it, they came to see
it in throngs, great in number"). Lancelot's adultery, then, disappears, literally written off by a written record that, with incessant
references to his virtue (comparable to a media blitz), transforms him
into something very like a cultic object.

Popular outpourings of devotion such as those just cited attest to
Lancelot's ability to transcend territorial boundaries; he is loved by
the people of Logres as well as by those of his own country. The
image of a strong and holy Lancelot which the *Mort Artu* projects is
tantamount to the image of strength and holiness that Capetian kings
sought to create or project as existing in themselves. The *Mort Artu*
stands near the beginning of the thirteenth century and is precisely

contemporaneous with the period which witnessed the endeavors of Philip Augustus to forge his own identity as *rex christianissimus* as a means to transcend his limited identity as a feudal monarch. Like Lancelot, Philip experienced setbacks on the road to his transformation. The sobriquet *christianissimus* was disassociated from his name during the time when he abandoned his wife in order to live with his mistress.[17] However, his reconciliation with his wife and his victory at Bouvines made it possible for Philip's moral lapses to be overlooked.[18] Once again he was the holy king. Soon after his death in 1223, miraculous signs attesting to the king's sanctity were reported,[19] and in an obituary that enumerates Philip's many virtues and links his victories in battle to St. Denis, he is also labeled "defensor maximus et protector" of the Church.[20] Such groundwork laid for Philip's sanctity prepared the way for the popular and canonical sanctity of Philip's grandson, Saint Louis. By the end of the thirteenth century, "the king of France had become the object of intense devotion on the part of his subjects."[21] With his ability to obtain a spontaneous outpouring of devotion from the people of different domains, the *Mort Artu*'s Lancelot can be situated within that development; unmatched by other men, he is like the sun, as Bors tells Guenevere, while others are like stars (*Mort* 59. 77).

On the whole, the experience of English monarchs with saints and their cults differed markedly from the experience of the thirteenth-century kings of France. Although English kings also attempted to ally themselves with saints as the French had done, more often than not English monarchs had to fend off the activities of popular saints; they frequently found themselves in the annoying position of having to suppress cults of popular saints—taking up a sort of antisaint stand that no king would willingly seek for himself. One of the reasons for this unfortunate state of affairs, at least from a king's point of view, was that antiroyalists also figured out the advantages of manipulating cultic piety.[22] Whereas the cult of St. Denis in France was used successfully to unite the kingdom of France, cults in England created political dissension. By the fifteenth century in England, the political use of popular cults was, as J. W. McKenna has observed, "a recognized instrument of political factionalism, a double-edged sword of royal and anti-royal policy."[23] In English history, antiroyalists proved to be very effective in deploying popular religiosity to undermine the authority of the reigning monarch.[24] Kings who had ascended the throne by deposing their predecessor were especially vulnerable to this form of antiroyalist agitation. Henry IV and Edward IV are two fifteenth-century examples.

In 1405, Archbishop Richard Scrope took part in a rebellion against Henry IV. The archbishop was caught and summarily executed for treason. Although Henry IV ridded himself of a traitor, the execution of a prelate proved to be a political liability. Scrope was styled as a Christian martyr and became the object of "widespread veneration."[25] *Annales Henrici Quarti* record that the field where the archbishop was beheaded "redderet fructum eo anno quantum antea non reddiderat in multis annis"[26] ("kept producing a great quantity of fruit that year, much greater than in previous years"), with one stalk producing seven different spices, all perfectly formed. Even more damaging to Henry IV were the tales that the sainted Scrope had caused him to be afflicted with leprosy. The connection between Henry IV's reputed disease and the death of the archbishop is recorded in political poems and chronicles of the fifteenth century. *An English Chronicle*, for example, renders the following account:

> Thanne were the archebishoppe of York and the lord Mowbray dampned unto deth . . . And whenne the archebisshoppe sholde die, he said, "Lo!" I shalle die for the lawes and good rewle of Engelond." And he saide unto thayme that sholde die with him, "Lat us suffre deth mekely, for we shul this nyghte, be Goddis grace, be in paradis." Thanne saide tharchbishop to him that sholde smyte of his hed, "For His loue that suffried v wondes for alle mankynde, yeue me v strokes, and I foryeve the my dethe." And so he dede: and thus they deide.
>
> And anon aftir, as it was said, the king was smyte withe a lepir: for the whiche archebisshoppe, Almyghti God sone aftirwarde wroughte meny grete miracles.[27]

As can be seen from this account, the archbishop is cast as the defender of both the law of God and the law of England. Conversely, Henry IV occupies a position outside both spiritual and temporal law, and he is punished by God with leprosy for such lawlessness. Henry IV retaliated against such stories by forbidding the veneration of Scrope and by arresting vagabonds who sought news of his health.[28]

The account of Scrope's death and Henry IV's disease proved to have a resilient vitality. Attempts to have the archbishop canonized were still occurring as late as the middle of the century. Additionally, Scrope's execution and God's disfavor with Henry IV proved a handy tool for Yorkist opposition to Lancastrian rule. In his work dedicated to Edward IV, the Yorkist who deposed Henry VI, the chronicler John Capgrave tells the story of Scrope's death and Henry IV's leprosy and claims that Henry IV was so afflicted by the disease that the king "lost the beute of his face . . . [and he grew] ever fowlere and fowlere. For in his deth, as thei recorded that sey him, he was so contracte, that his body was scarse a cubit of length."[29] Accounts such as these portrayed the Yorkist opposition to the Lancastrian kings as righteous, an enactment of divine justice against a dynastic family, the Lancastrians, who ruled by sin rather than by right.[30]

But the deposition of the Lancastrian Henry VI and the accession of Edward of York did not ensure that right had triumphed. Henry VI's deposition and his death gave birth to another political cult: that of Henry VI, the deposed king. Pilgrims journeyed to his tomb, miracles were performed—once again divine displeasure with the reigning monarch was shown, and Edward IV found it necessary to ban the popular veneration of Henry VI. It is important to remember that even as Scrope and Henry VI were venerated as saints, they were at the same time traitors who had borne the legal consequences of treason. Scrope was summarily executed and Henry VI attainted for treason. With such a jumble of saints and traitors in the historico-political background of the *Morte Darthur*, it is perhaps politically as well as morally significant that Malory has Lancelot lie prostrate with grief at Arthur's tomb rather than at the altar of Christ. In light of its historical context, this scene in Malory suggests the possibility that a secular form of retaliation and punishment for the crime of treason exists alongside Lancelot's elevation to sanctity.

We may recoil at the idea of retaliation against Lancelot, since his death attests to the special favor God has bestowed upon him. However, at one time in the history of the Church, saints could be punished for having failed to protect those devoted to them.[31] Performed by a religious community, the rite of humiliation against a saint sought to recall the hallowed one to his duties. This rite entailed the removal of the relics of the derelict saint from an elevated place of honor to a place of dishonor, the floor, for example. A clamor was then raised against the saint for leaving the community unprotected. Once the threat to the community had passed, the relics were restored once again to their privileged place. Officially the rite was instituted for the use of monastic communities, but the practice had a life beyond the cloister. At times, lay people took it upon themselves to wake up the saint. For example, there is the tale of a woman who, having been robbed by a well-known malefactor, rushed to church to accuse St. Benedict. Striking the altar, she cried, "Benedict, you sluggard, you sloth, what are you doing? Why do you sleep?"[32] By worshipping their patron saints, people earned the right to be protected by them. The complaints people made against their saints are not unlike Arthur's complaint against Lancelot. Responding to the reasons Lancelot gives for abducting the queen and killing so many of the king's knights, Arthur declares: "Well, well, sir Launcelot . . . I have gyvyn you no cause to do to me as ye have done, for I have worshipt you and youres more than ony othir knyghtes" (Malory 1197). Arthur, like the worshippers of the patron saints, does not deserve such treatment.

Such abuse of the saints eventually led the Church to look at the practice with disfavor, and in 1274 humiliation was condemned.[33] However, the concept lying behind the rite of humiliation shares certain traits with Malory's representation of treason and sanctity. By the practice of humiliation, an inversion of hierarchical order occured: the human order for a time exercised control over the divine.[34] Put another way, the secular world sat in judgment over the spiritual, a type of inversion that was prophetic of evolving church-state relations in England in the late Middle Ages. Such a context along with a law that declares adultery with the king's wife as high treason allows us to re-examine Malory's representation of Lancelot as an object worthy of devotion.

Malory's text makes many departures from the *Mort Artu*, but one of the most significant for this line of inquiry is that Lancelot's stature as a type of patron saint is grounded in deeds, not in formulations which construct his virtue as self-evident, as in the *Mort Artu*. When Agravain, in the *Morte Darthur*, threatens to tell Arthur of Lancelot's liaison with the queen, Gawain defends Lancelot by pointing to his deeds. You must remember, Gawain tells Agravain, that many times "Launcelot hath rescowed the kynge and the quene; and the beste of us all had bene full colde at the harte-roote had nat sir Launcelot bene bettir than we, and that hathe he preved hymselff full ofte" (Malory 1162). Not only has Lancelot saved the king and queen many times over, but he also has rescued many others from imprisonment and death. Gawain reasons that "suche noble dedis and kyndnes shulde be remembirde" (Malory 1162). At the end of his life, Gawain returns to his defense of Lancelot, telling Arthur that Lancelot held the king's "cankryde enemyes in subjeccion and daungere" (Malory 1230). These statements offer solid evidence that Lancelot has been no sluggard in fulfilling his duties. By banishing Lancelot from the realm, Arthur, in a sense, destroys his realm since it will no longer have Lancelot's protection.

But while Arthur banishes Lancelot for treason, the *Morte Darthur* surreptitiously punishes Lancelot in its own way, as if the text itself were performing its own act of treason against the one called the most noble knight of the world by refusing to allow the issue of treason to recede to the background. Lancelot's alleged treason is kept alive by

Arthur when he informs his barons "how sir Launcelot had beraffte hym hys quene" (Malory 1186); and at Joyous Guard, Arthur makes the accusation once again, but to Lancelot at this time:

> . . . for wyte thou well and truste hit, I am thy mortall foo and ever woll to my deth-day; for thou haste slayne my good knyghtes and full noble men of my blood, that shall I never recover agayne. Also thou haste layne be my quene and holdyn her many wynters, and sytthyn, lyke a traytoure, taken her away fro me by fors.

> (Malory 1187)

Gawain and others then follow suit, calling out over and over again to Lancelot that he is a "false recreayed knyght" (Malory 1189–1201). The same sort of chant arises when Lancelot is confronted by Arthur and Gawain at Benoic. Lancelot is surrounded by the noise of treason.

The insistence of these allegations has little to do with what is true or false, since Malory has made sure that no one knows with certainty if Lancelot and the queen were "abed other at other maner of disportis" (Malory 1165) or if Lancelot knowingly killed Gawain's two unarmed brothers in his rescue of the queen. Rather, the allegations take on a life of their own, forcing Lancelot to link his own name with that of traitor and determining the actions that he takes to clear himself. In Malory's hands, the accusation of treason itself engenders a form of punishment that restricts Lancelot's activities in such a way as to render him virtually incapacitated. By curtailing the opportunities for Lancelot to perform the deeds which constitute his renown and his image as a patron saint, Malory's text can be seen to inaugurate and complete a disabling process against Lancelot and thus to commit its own act of treason against its most noble knight.

The *Morte Darthur* begins to restrict Lancelot's activities once he is accused of treason. Such circumscription can be seen in the speech Lancelot makes to his knights, after Agravain and his men have tried to trap Lancelot with the queen. This speech is Malory's invention, and in it Lancelot asks his friends to direct his course. They advise him to rescue the queen, and then Lancelot wonders: "And if so be that I may wynne the quene away, where shall I kepe her?" (Malory 1172). He is told to take her to Joyous Guard. Given direction by others here, Lancelot later in the text is prodded into battle against Arthur at Joyous Guard and Benoic. When Lancelot is called traitor by both the king and Gawain, his knights urge him to defend himself. Thus, as Lancelot explains to Arthur, he is "conjured and requyred" to defend himself against the charge of treason; he has no choice. The promptings of Lancelot's knights do illustrate his reluctance to enter upon manifest treason, open warfare against the king, but they also offer an implicit challenge to Lancelot's status as a knight and as a lord over his people. His courtesy, as Bademagus points out to him, "hath waked all thys sorow" (Malory 1211) and will shame them all for they were "never wonte to coure in castels nother in noble townys" (Malory 1212). While Lancelot keeps to his castle for weeks, Arthur lays waste to the people and lands around Joyous Guard and Benoic. Not only, then, does Lancelot's hesitancy threaten his knights with dishonor, but it also brings destruction and death to the people who depend on him for their protection. In the face of such dereliction, Lancelot's companions recall him to his duties: "Now thynke what ye ar and what men we ar. . . . deffende you lyke a knyght" (Malory 1214–1215).

By having Lancelot's acts determined by others, Malory takes initiative from him, restricting his capacity to act on his own behalf. By way of contrast, in the *Mort Artu*, Lancelot himself makes the decision to rescue the queen. And rather than being a virtual prisoner in a castle for fifteen weeks while Arthur lays waste to the countryside, the Lancelot of the *Mort Artu* plans an immediate engagement with Arthur's troops and carries it out. Such activities register a capacity to act in accordance with his status as a knight. In the French text, Lancelot is not disabled in any way by the accusation of treason. Unlike the criticism which Lancelot's inactivity provokes in the *Morte Darthur*, the actions taken by Lancelot in the *Mort Artu* do not warrant such an attack on his knighthood.

Lancelot's abdication of the responsibility to make decisions and take action is not voluntary. No decision that Lancelot could make at this point, whether to fight or not, could restore him to his former capacity. We can see Lancelot, here, as a victim of the dilemma brought about by the accusation of treason. He is, in fact, incapacitated by his association with this crime. Such an inability, as Lancelot exhibits, to function, to act on his own behalf, as befitting a knight, can be related to acts of attainder legislated against traitors in the fifteenth century. In addition to legalizing forfeiture of a traitor's land, acts of attainder could also include a provision that disabled the traitor at law. Through disablement at law, acts of attainder deprived persons of their civil rights. They were, for example, effectively barred from entering into any legal contracts. Although physically alive, traitors suffered civil death.[35] Thus, no longer capable of acting in their former capacities, traitors were deprived of their former identities, rendered disfunctional in the civil life of the realm.

Attainders of the rebel Jack Cade, the duke of York, and the earl of Northumberland during Henry VI's reign offer examples of this type of punishment. In the case of Cade, parliamentary rolls record the forfeiture of goods, lands, and income and the stipulation that he and his blood be "disabled for ever."[36] Likewise, attainders of York and his allies required that they be "disabled for ever to have or enjoye any enheritaunce in any wise hereafter . . . and in lyke wise their heires."[37] A record of a petition made by Henry Percy to reverse the attainder of his father, the earl of Northumberland, describes the severity of such a penalty by reciting its consequences:

> Howabeit that by force of an Acte made ayenst his said Fader . . . the same late Erle, among other persons, was unabled to have, hold, enherite or joie, any name of dignitie, estate or preeminence, within this Reame . . . and the heires of the same late Erle, were unable to clayme or have by the same late Erle, any suche name estate or preminence . . . [38]

Deprived of civil rights, attainted traitors were tantamount to social outcasts.

Even though attainders could be reversed, the reversals were, in many cases, posthumous or a piecemeal process. If a traitor succeeded in obtaining a pardon, for example, a person could be "abled unto [the King's] Lawes" but not given back his property or income.[39] Moreover, evidence suggests that even when restoration was complete, the stigma of attainder remained. The experience of Thomas Tresham, the speaker of parliament during the proscription of the Yorkists in 1459, bears out the longevity of attainder. Tresham was attainted and subsequently pardoned by Edward IV. Having incurred debts to "dyvers frendes," Tresham was unable to repay them since he could "make noo chevysaunce of his Lyvelode, in asmuche as noe persone wolle take it for any suerte of their payment, nor bargeyn, nor marye with his sonne and heire, because of the seid Acte."[40] Thus in addition to the forfeiture of a person's property and income by an act of attainder, the force of such an act, even after a reversal, could literally restrict the activities of the traitor such that he was unable to act in his former capacity.

Like an act of attainder legislated against traitors in the fifteenth century, the *Morte Darthur* imposes a similar punishment on Lancelot by restricting his movements once he has been accused of treason.[41] Directed by others at significant moments, Lancelot, in Malory's hands, becomes a passive subject. It is this passivity, linked to the crime of treason, that is comparable to the disabling brought about by an act of attainder, and the *Morte Darthur* continues to enact such a process. Unlike Lancelot in the *Mort Artu*, who returns to England on his own accord once he hears the news of Arthur's troubles with Mordred, Malory's Lancelot is summoned to England by Gawain's letter; but upon receiving the letter, Lancelot does not make the decision to return to England. Instead he utters a lengthy lament blaming the day that he was born and regretting the circumstances that prevent him from killing Mordred. It is Bors who sets the agenda, and in doing so he draws critical attention to Lancelot's prolixity: "Now leve youre complayntes . . . and firste revenge you of the dethe of sir Gawayne . . . and . . . revenge my lorde Arthur and my lady quene Gwenyver" (Malory 1249–1250). Bors's remark registers an exchange of words for deeds; that is, Lancelot's words have supplanted his deeds of prowess.

Indeed, once Lancelot returns to England, Malory gives him no opportunity to display his prowess. He is not given a chance to act "lyke a knyght." There are no battles for him to fight. Even though Mordred and Arthur are dead by the time Lancelot returns to England in the *Mort Artu*, it is Lancelot who engages Mordred's sons in battle and destroys them. Malory's Lancelot, however, must tell his knights: "My fayre lordis, I thanke you all of youre comynge into thys contrey with me. But wyte you well all, we ar com to late" (Malory 1251). In Malory's text, it is Arthur who is given the honor of destroying Mordred's forces. Having denied Lancelot opportunities for deeds of prowess, the *Morte Darthur* relentlessly pursues its disabling process further by having Guenevere reject Lancelot as a lover. In effect, Malory's text severs Lancelot from the world he has known: his capacity to act as a knight of worship is taken from him. Thus the *Morte Darthur* subjects Lancelot to a type of punishment, a process of involuntary disablement, akin to the penalty of civil death or disablement that constituted many acts of attainder in the fifteenth century.

As we have seen, Malory's text institutes this disablement process long before Lancelot enters upon a religious vocation, a profession emblematic of civil death or death to the world.[42] Rather than inaugurating a change in Lancelot's circumstances, Lancelot's monasticism in the *Morte Darthur* paradigmatically formalizes and completes a civil death procedure. During Lancelot's sojourn as a hermit and priest, Malory effectively erases all traces of his knighthood. In fact, the acts of penance which Lancelot performs cause his appearance to alter so much that he, much like Capgrave's Henry IV, begins to shrink:

. . . syr Launcelot never after ete but lytel mete, nor dranke, tyl he was dede, for than he seekened more and more and dryed and dwyned awaye . . . [such] that he was waxen by a kybbet shorter than he was, that the peple coude not knowe hym.

(Malory 1257)

The image Malory paints, in this passage, accords with ascetism; however, a shriveled and emaciated Lancelot does not accord with knighthood, especially with a knight who, when he chose to do his "utterance," was matched only by Tristram and Lamorak. Not only, then, does Malory curtail Lancelot's opportunities for prowess, but through the vehicle of monasticism, he also renders Lancelot physically incapable of the deeds that constitute his role as a type of cultic object in the *Morte Darthur*. From the perspective of disablement and civil death, we can see, then, that the text institutes a comparable procedure against Lancelot. Moreover, Malory's text ultimately inscribes such a penalty on Lancelot's body, rendering it aberrant and debilitated. Under such strictures, it is not surprising that the most renowned knight of the world can no longer be recognized; with Lancelot's former identity thoroughly effaced, "the peple," Malory writes, "coude not knowe hym."

If we allow that Lancelot is a type of patron saint, then his groveling at Arthur's tomb can be seen as humiliation, a sign of wrongdoing. As graphically as the relics of derelict saints were taken from their elevated place of honor and moved to a place of dishonor, Lancelot's exalted status is taken from him as he lies prostrate at Arthur's tomb. And this move has a secular cast to it. By having Lancelot prostrate himself at the king's tomb rather than at the altar of Christ, Malory subjects Lancelot to the law of the Round Table. According to the oath Lancelot has sworn, he cannot commit treason without forfeiting the worship of his king. With an emaciated Lancelot lying as a supplicant before Arthur's tomb, the secular realm, then, exacts its retribution from him.

Enveloping Lancelot's death in sanctity can almost be seen as a cruel gesture, akin to reversals of attainder granted to traitors after they were dead. But the signs of sanctity are there in Lancelot's death (he does die a holy death as Merlin prophesized), and the signs of sanctity are there in the deeds he performs for Arthur and his realm before he is accused of treason. The particular strain of political sanctity in fifteenth-century England helped to produce such a narrative as Malory's. Depending on the teller, royalist or antiroyalist, cultic activity could be seen as evidence of treason or as evidence of holiness. That dual functionality of political sanctity brought about by opposing interpretive pressures yielded the possibility for a different type of narrative: a narrative that could conflate the secular and the sacred in such a way that it could both substantiate the holiness and the criminal guilt of a cultic object. Malory's retelling of the *Mort Artu* forms just this type of narrative. Depending on his fluctuating relation to the king and the throne, Lancelot is both traitor and saint.

Notes

1. Peter F. Dembowski, "Literary Problems of Hagiography in Old French," *Medievalia et Humanistica* 7 (1976): 119.

2. Thomas Malory, *The Works of Sir Thomas Malory*, edited by Eugene Vinaver, revised by P. J. C. Field (Oxford, 1990). All further quotations are from this edition, by page number. I refer to Malory's text as the *Morte Darthur*, Caxton's title.

3. Jean Frappier, ed., *La Mort le roi Artu* (Geneva: Droz; Paris: Minard, 1964). All references are to this edition. Translations are my own.

4. *The Statutes of the Realm*, 25 Edward III, stat. 5, chap. 2 (London: Dawsons, 1963) 1: 319–320.

5. Alexandre Micha, *Essais sur le cycle du Lancelot-Graal* (Geneva: Droz, 1987): 292.

6. Patrick Geary, "Humiliation of Saints," in *Saints and Their Cults: Studies in Religious Sociology, Folklore and History*, edited by Stephen Wilson (London: Cambridge University Press, 1983): 123.

7. See the *Oxford English Dictionary* and also Georges Duby, *The Knight, the Lady, and the Priest: The Making of Modern Marriage in Medieval France*, translated by Barbara Bray (New York: Pantheon, 1983): 291 n. 14.

8. Gabrielle M. Spiegel, "The Cult of St. Denis and Capetian Kingship" in *Saints and Their Cults*, p. 158 n. 6.

9. Ibid.

10. For a description of the relationship between English kings and their subjects from the perspective of medieval French romance see P. Rickard, *Britain in Medieval French Literature (1100–1500)* (Cambridge: Cambridge University Press, 1956): 189.

11. By way of contrast, Lancelot in the *Morte Darthur* calls a parliament for the crowning of his relatives (Malory 1204).

12. Spiegel, "Cult of St. Denis," 157 and 167 n. 87 and n. 88. See also John W. Baldwin, *The Government of Philip Augustus, Foundations of French Royal Power in the Middle Ages* (Berkeley: University of California Press, 1986), particularly pp. 355–393. For Philip's promotion of the cult of Charlemagne for purposes of conquest, see Spiegel, "The Reditus Regni ad Stirpen Karoli Magni: A New Look," *French Historical Studies* 7 (1971): 145–174.

13. See Colette Beaune, *The Birth of an Idealogy: Myths and Symbols of Nation in Late-Medieval France* (Berkeley: University of California Press, 1991): 8.

14. For an illustration of this difference between the king of France and other kings, see the characterization of King John and the Emperor Otto in *Oeuvres de Rigord et de Guillaume le Breton*, edited by H. Francis Delaborde (Paris: Société de l'Histoire de France, 1882–1885) 1: 244, 273. See Baldwin, *Philip Augustus*, 386–387.

15. Charles T. Wood, *Joan of Arc and Richard III: Sex, Saints, and Government in the Middle Ages* (New York: Oxford University Press, 1988): 21; Ernst H. Kantorowicz, *The King's Two Bodies: A Study in Mediaeval Political Theology* (Princeton, N.J.: Princeton University Press, 1957): 252–253. See Joseph R. Strayer, "France: the Holy Land, the Chosen People and the Most Christian King" in *Action and Conviction in Early Modern Europe: Essays in Memory of E. H. Harbison*, edited by Theodore K. Rabb and Jerrold E. Siegel (Princeton, N.J.: Princeton University Press, 1969): 3–16.

16. Spiegel, "Cult of St. Denis," 159.

17. Baldwin, *Philip Augustus*, 380.

18. Ibid., 380–381.

19. Delaborde, *Oeuvres*, 2: 369–371. See Baldwin, *Philip Augustus*, 391.

20. Delaborde, *Oeuvres*, 1: 323. See Baldwin, *Philip Augustus*, 378.

21. Spiegel, "Cult of St. Denis," 160.

22. For an excellent discussion of political saints and Angevin kings, see Josiah Cox Russell, "The Canonization of Opposition to the King in Angevin England" in *Anniversary Essays in Medieval History by Students of Charles Homer Haskins*, edited by C. H. Taylor and J. L. Monte (Boston: Houghton Mifflin, 1929): 279–290.

23. J. W. McKenna, "Popular Canonization as Political Propaganda: The Cult of Archbishop Scrope," *Speculum* 45 (1970): 611. For a general discussion of the differences between medieval French and English monarchs see Wood, *Joan of Arc and Richard III*, 3–47.

24. McKenna, "Popular Canonization," 622–623.

25. Ibid., 611.

26. *Chronica et Annales, Regnantibus Henrico Tertio, Edwardo Primo, Edwardo Secundo, Ricardo Secundo et Henrico Quarto*, edited by Henry Thomas Riley, *Rolls Series* 28, pt. 4 (1886): 410. See McKenna, "Popular Canonization," 611 n. 13.

27. *An English Chronicle of the Reigns of Richard II, Henry IV, Henry V, and Henry VI*, edited by John S. Davies, Camden Society, 64 (1855–1856): 33. See also *Chronica et Annales*, 409–410; John Capgrave, *The Chronicle of England*, edited by Francis Charles Hingeston, *Rolls Series* (1858): 291, 302; McKenna, "Popular Canonization," 612; and *Historical Poems of the XIVth and XVth Centuries*, edited by R. H. Robbins (New York: Columbia University Press, 1959): 222, 295.

28. McKenna, "Popular Canonization," 612, 614.

29. Capgrave, *Chronicle of England*, 291. See McKenna, "Popular Canonization," 613.

30. McKenna, "Popular Canonization," 619–620. See also McKenna, "Piety and Propaganda: The Cult of King Henry VI," in *Chaucer and Middle English Studies in Honour of Rossell Hope Robbins*, edited by Beryl Rowland (London: George Allen and Unwin Ltd., 1974): 72–88; and "Henry VI of England and the Dual Monarchy: Aspects of Royal Political Propaganda, 1422–1432," *Journal of the Warburg and Courtauld Institute* 28 (1965): 145–162.

31. My discussion of saints and their worshippers relies on Geary, "Humiliation of Saints."

32. E. de Certain, ed., *Les Miracles de Saint Benoît*, (Paris: Société de l'Histoire de France, 1858): 282–283, quoted in Geary, "Humiliation of Saints," 135.

33. Geary, "Humiliation of Saints," 137.

34. Ibid., 128.

35. J. R. Lander, "Attainder and Forfeiture, 1453 to 1509," *The Historical Journal* 4 (1961): 123–124. See also Kim L. Scheppele, "Facing Facts in Legal Interpretation," *Representations* 30 (1990): 50–51; John G. Bellamy, *The Law of Treason in England in the Later Middle Ages* (Cambridge: Cambridge University Press, 1970): 177–205; Michael Hicks, "Attainder, Resumption and Coercion 1461–1529," *Parliamentary History* 3 (1984): 15–31; Margaret Kekewich, "The Attainder of the Yorkists in 1459: Two Contemporary Accounts," *Bulletin of the Institute of Historical Research* 55 (1982): 25–34; Ann Crawford, "Victims of Attainder: The Howard and de Vere Women in the Late Fifteenth Century," *Reading Medieval Studies* 15 (1989): 59–74; and Joel T. Rosenthal, *Patriarchy and Families of Privilege in Fifteenth-Century England* (Philadelphia: University of Pennsylvania Press, 1991): 55–57.

36. *Rotuli Parliamentorum: ut et petitiones, et placita in parliamento*, edited by J. Strachey, et al. (London, 1767–1777) 5: 224.

37. Ibid., 349.

38. Ibid., 389.

39. Ibid., 6: 230–231, 616–617. See Lander, "Attainder," 139–140 n. 91.

40. *Rotuli*, 6: 616–617.

41. Although I have confined the discussion of attainder to treason against the king, ordinary citizens sought, in the fifteenth century, to adopt the procedure for use in minor cases. Bellamy notes the unusual direction of this adoption: "Far from being a punishment reserved to deal with exceptional dangers to the king, attainder could be observed in everyday use against relatively trivial offences, so lightly were held the sanctions of state in the last years of the Lancastrian dynasty. In terms of law a real novelty had been created. The law of parliament in the shape of attainder was being incorporated within the common law, the reverse of the fate of notoriety and appeal in the century before" (Bellamy, *The Law of Treason*, 191). Although Bellamy observes that this "everyday use" of attainder indicates a trivialization of the process, attainder was an effective means for the crown to check the power of ambitious magnates and control the size of the nobility. Rather than necessarily indicating a trivialization of the process, the appropriation of attainder by ordinary citizens could attest just as well to its effectiveness. We would

not expect such appropriation if the punishment were without consequence. Given this broad dissemination of the principles of attainder policy, it is not unusual to see its features at work implicitly in the *Morte Darthur*.

42. For a discussion of the privileged place of secular interests over spiritual in Middle English romances, see Susan Crane, *Insular Romance: Politics, Faith, and Culture in Anglo-Norman and Middle English Literature* (Berkeley: University of California Press, 1986): 12, 92–133.

Index of Passages Cited
from the Lancelot-Grail Cycle

Index of Names and Themes

Lightning Source UK Ltd.
Milton Keynes UK
UKHW020442291022
411179UK00021B/458